Using Psychology in the Classroom

Education at SAGE

SAGE is a leading international publisher of journals, books, and electronic media for academic, educational, and professional markets.

Our education publishing includes:

- accessible and comprehensive texts for aspiring education professionals and practitioners looking to further their careers through continuing professional development

- inspirational advice and guidance for the classroom

- authoritative state of the art reference from the leading authors in the field

Find out more at: **www.sagepub.co.uk/education**

Using Psychology in the Classroom

Stephen
James
Minton

SAGE

Los Angeles | London | New Delhi
Singapore | Washington DC

SAGE Publications Ltd
1 Oliver's Yard
55 City Road
London EC1Y 1SP

SAGE Publications Inc.
2455 Teller Road
Thousand Oaks, California 91320

SAGE Publications India Pvt Ltd
B 1/I 1 Mohan Cooperative Industrial Area
Mathura Road
New Delhi 110 044

SAGE Publications Asia-Pacific Pte Ltd
3 Church Street
#10-04 Samsung Hub
Singapore 049483

Library of Congress Control Number: 2011933714

British Library Cataloguing in Publication data
A catalogue record for this book is available from the British Library

ISBN 978-1-4462-0165-7
ISBN 978-1-4462-0166-4 (pbk)

Typeset by Kestrel Data, Exeter, Devon
Printed in Great Britain by MPG Books Group, Bodmin, Cornwall
Printed on paper from sustainable resources

Contents

List of figures   ix
About the author   xi
Acknowledgements   xiii

1   Introducing psychology in the classroom   1
    • What is psychology?   1
    • A very brief history of psychology   7
    • The psychology of education and about this book   11

2   An overview of child and adolescent psychological development   14
    • Theories of cognitive development   14
    • Issues in socioemotional development   20
    • Systemic and contextual models of development   26
    • Implications for educators   28

3   The self, self-esteem, and self-esteem enhancement through
    educational practice   31
    • The self and society   31
    • Psychological models of selfhood   32
    • Defining and towards a working model of self-esteem   33
    • An existential-analytic model of selfhood and self-esteem   34
    • Developmental aspects of selfhood and self-esteem   37
    • Family and peer influences on the development of self-esteem   39
    • Self-esteem and educational attainment   41
    • Self-esteem enhancement through teaching and educational practice   42
    • Implications for educators   44

4   Intelligence, learning styles and educational attainment   47
    •   Traditional views of intelligence   47
    •   Intelligence testing   48
    •   Is intelligence 'in the genes'? The 'nature versus nurture' debate   49
    •   Multiple intelligences   52
    •   Intelligence and educational attainment   54
    •   Emotional intelligence   56
    •   A model of learning styles   57
    •   Implications for educators   60

5   Positive discipline, conflict resolution and co-operative learning
     in schools   64
    •   What is meant by positive discipline?   64
    •   Conflict resolution and conflict management   66
    •   Understanding social groups   69
    •   Co-operative learning   75
    •   Implications for educators   79

6   Thinking about special educational needs   81
    •   General and specific learning difficulties   82
    •   Autistic spectrum disorders   87
    •   Attention deficit hyperactivity disorder   91
    •   Implications for educators   95

7   Preventing and countering bullying behaviour and cyber-bullying
     in schools   98
    •   What is school bullying?   98
    •   Types of bullying behaviour   100
    •   Bullying behaviour and cyber-bullying in schools: the evidence   102
    •   Key issues for schools and school staff   104
    •   Practical ideas for anti-bullying work in schools   106
    •   Implications for educators   113

8   Dealing with prejudice – racism, homophobia and alterophobia
     in schools   116
    •   Racism, ethnic bias and schools   117
    •   The psychology of prejudice and attitude formation   122
    •   Homophobia and schools   124
    •   Alterophobia and schools   128
    •   Implications for educators   130

9   Stress and stress management for teachers and educators   132

- The physiology of stress   132
- Understanding the psychology of stress   133
- Psychological and physical ways of coping with stress   139
- Stress and the teaching profession: avoiding burnout   142
- Implications for educators   146

10   Conclusions   148

References   151
Index   167

List of Figures

3.1 Schematic model of Lawrence's description of self-concept   33

3.2 Schematic model of Heidegger's description of *Dasein*   35

3.3 A proposed working model of self-esteem   36

About the Author

Dr Stephen James Minton is a chartered psychologist and a full-time lecturer in the psychology of education at the School of Education, Trinity College Dublin, and a graduate of the University of Glasgow and Trinity College Dublin. He is the co-author of *Dealing with Bullying in Schools: A Training Manual for Teachers, Parents and Other Professionals* (SAGE, 2004), and has authored and co-authored numerous scholarly articles on the psychology of education, particularly on the subject of school bullying and violence. Dr Minton is regularly called upon to provide training to various groups within schools and the broader community in Ireland and beyond.

Dr Stephen James Minton CPsychol
School of Education
Trinity College Dublin
Ireland

Tel: +353 1 896 2216
E-mail: mintonst@tcd.ie

Acknowledgements

Personally, I would like to thank the following family members for their help, support and inspiration over the years: my wife, Patricia Minton; my mother, Rosemary Elizabeth Fox; my sister, Sarah Minton; my daughter, Anna Rebecca Minton; and my son, Conor James Minton.

On a professional level, I would like to thank Jude Bowen and her colleagues at Sage for their encouragement, interest and help in producing this book. I would also like to express my sincere thanks to my colleagues and students, past and present, at the School of Education, Trinity College Dublin, and to all of the students, staff members and parents in school communities all over Ireland with whom I have had the pleasure of working in the past. In this respect, I would particularly like to thank Rose Conway-Walsh and the people of the schools and the broader community of Erris, Co. Mayo. I would also like to thank the organisations who generously financially supported the research of my own that appears in this book – the *Irish Independent* newspaper, the Irish Research Council for the Humanities and Social Sciences, the Irish Youth Foundation, Raidió Teilifís Éireann, and Trinity College Dublin's Arts and Social Sciences Benefactions Fund.

Finally, in ways which I cannot adequately articulate, but nevertheless hold to be true, much of what lies behind what might be called the 'spirit' of this book was inspired by my memory of my late maternal grandfather, James Sneddon (1925–1977), and it is to his memory that I dedicate this book. *In my defens God me defend.*

1

Introducing Psychology in the Classroom

The goals for this introductory chapter are two-fold. Firstly, it is designed to provide the reader with an understanding of the scope of psychology as it applies to educational practice. This is undertaken through examining the question *'What is psychology?'*, before providing *a very brief history of psychology.* The second aim is to inform the reader about *the psychology of education* and *about this book.* This chapter concludes with a selective and annotated list of *further reading* and *useful websites.*

What is Psychology?

Defining Psychology

In the *Penguin Dictionary of Psychology,* under the entry for 'psychology', Arthur S. Reber (1995) asserts that 'psychology cannot be defined; indeed, it cannot even easily be characterised'. He argues that definitions such as '"the science of mental life", "the science of behaviour" . . . reflect the prejudices of the definer more than the actual nature of the field', but does state that 'psychology is what scientists and philosophers of various persuasions have created to try and fulfil the need to understand the minds and behaviours of various organisms from the most primitive to the most complex' (p. 617).

Reber's (1995) assertions are certainly well-made, given the diversity of the field of psychology, its areas of inquiry, and it applications. However, a shorter – and,

I would argue, broadly acceptable – defining statement is that psychology is 'the science of mind and behaviour' (Gross, 2010), which applies to most modern (and especially experimental) psychology. However, even at this early stage we run into problems. The scientific method, to which we shall return below, and again according to Reber (1995), is characterised by: (i) a clearly defined problem being stated in a way that (ii) ties it in with 'existing theory and known empirical fact' (p. 458), (iii) leading to the formulation of a testable hypothesis and (iv) the determination of investigatory procedures, which lead to (v) the collection and analysis of data which, when analysed, in turn lead to (vi) the support or rejection of the hypothesis, and ultimately to (vii) the modification of the existing body of scientific knowledge to accommodate the new findings. With this is mind, one can see how the scientific method may be more easily applied to the study of 'behaviour', which is, after all, external, physical, observable and measurable, than it might be to the study of the 'mind', which is, of course, an internal, metaphysical, non-observable entity with no clear means of direct 'measurement'. Yet Gross's (2010) definition comes at least close to incorporating, in a single sentence, an accurate description of the ways in which modern psychology is, or at least should be, conducted (the 'scientific method'), and the broad areas with which psychologists have concerned themselves. Indeed, the roots of the word 'psychology' come from the Ancient Greek *psyche*, meaning 'the mind' (notice this prefix in many related terms, such as 'psychiatrist' and 'psychoanalyst'), and *-ology*, meaning 'the study of' (again, notice this common suffix in the names of many academic fields, e.g. 'biology' and 'sociology').

A respectable proportion of what trainee teachers learn in both theoretical and methodological modules in their pre-service education is informed by the discipline of psychology. However, psychologists who are proud of their discipline's contribution should be aware that education and teaching are informed by many disciplines, of which psychology is just one (which is one reason why pre-service teacher training can be challenging). In order to see how psychology can be related to other disciplines, we will now turn our attention to the origins of psychology.

The Philosophical Background of Psychology

How can psychology, as a discipline, be framed within the more general field of human inquiry? Indeed, how can the field of human inquiry itself be systematised? In terms of the latter, few have tried; but one attempt is particularly well known. In 1946, the British philosopher Bertrand Russell wrote his *History of Western Philosophy*, based on the series of lectures he had given during the war years in the United States. The book seems to divide commentators: Ray Monk says it 'remains unchallenged as the perfect introduction to its subject' (Russell, 1995); Richard H. Popkin (1999a) describes it as 'most engaging as Russelliana, but hardly as a history of philosophy'. Be that as it may, the book is an attempt to connect western philosophy with 'political and social circumstances from the earliest times to the present day', and is structured into three divisions that, helpfully for this discussion, constitute three major time periods within both western thought and political/social history:

> *Ancient Philosophy* (corresponding to the period of Classical Civilisation) (ca. 500 BC – ca. 400 AD);
> *Catholic Philosophy* (corresponding to the Middle Ages (ca. 400 AD – ca. 1600 AD); and
> *Modern Philosophy* (corresponding to the Modern, post-Renaissance Period (ca. 1600 AD – the present day).

Viewed in this light, some of the problems that western *philosophers* have been engaged with over the last 2,500 years (e.g. the nature and scope of knowledge, questions of belief and of the best way to live, how we perceive and reason, the nature of the mind, the nature and usage of language and so on) are also engaged with today by *psychologists*. The feature that is unique to the discipline of psychology is *how* these problems are engaged with. To my mind, therefore, the chief demarcation point of psychology – at least, as a research discipline – from its parent discipline of philosophy is in the methods of inquiry that it uses. Whereas in philosophy one might use logical analysis, introspection, rational argument and so on, the methods that psychologists use belong to the modern period, and in particular to the methods of *science*.

Important Philosophical Ideas in Psychology

The scientific method, as it applies to psychology, owes a good deal to the philosophy that is known as *British Empiricism*. 'British' here is used in a geographical sense, referring to the British Isles origin of its original proponents, and to the region in which it first attained greatest popularity and influence. In a curious correspondence with many schoolyard jokes, these 'original proponents' were an Englishman, an Irishman and a Scotsman – respectively, John Locke (1632–1704), George Berkeley (1685–1753) and David Hume (1711–1776). All were interested in the nature and limits of human knowledge; all argued that knowledge was dependent on *experience*. This opposed the philosophy of René Descartes (1596–1650), which asserted that 'there were fundamental truths innate in the human mind only awaiting identification by an active intellect' (Rogers, 1999). For example, in book one (*Of Innate Notions*) of his *Essay Concerning Human*

Understanding (1689), Locke argued there was no *a priori* knowledge; the mind, at birth, is a *tabula rasa* ('blank tablet', or 'blank slate'), upon which knowledge, gained solely through life's experiences, may be written. An image for teachers arises here – of an empty blackboard/whiteboard/exercise book, which is filled with (hopefully) useful knowledge as is, as a consequence, the student's mind. One can understand, perhaps, how influential Locke's empiricism has been in informing traditional 'chalk-and-talk' methods of teaching over the past 300 years. As we shall see (below), Locke's arguments were also important for a particular type of psychology known as *behaviourism.*

Berkeley is known for articulating the anti-materialist idea that essence and perception are one and the same; there is no hidden 'real world' behind what we perceive. We can *only* say that we *perceive* chocolate to be brown and sweet; it is an abstraction too far to say that it *is* so. With this principle, he believed he had established a sound basis for the limits of human knowledge (Bracken, 1999). Hume was influenced by Berkeley's writing, and praised his arguments on abstraction; the purpose of his *A Treatise of Human Nature* (1739) was to 'introduce the Newtonian method of reasoning into moral subjects' (Popkin, 1999b). Although Hume expected the book to be a success, it was not well received (Gaarder, 1991); however, he re-worked the material into two more popular presentations, *An Enquiry Concerning the Principles of Human Morals* (1751), and *An Enquiry Concerning Human Understanding* (1777). According to Hume, we can only know, from an inspection of our ideas, things that resemble or contradict each other, and degrees of quantity or number. In Section XII of the latter, Hume asserts:

> If we take into our hand any volume – of divinity or school metaphysics, for instance – let us ask, 'Does it contain any abstract reasoning concerning quantity or number?' No. 'Does it contain any experimental reasoning concerning matter of fact and existence?' No. Consign it then to the flames – for it can contain nothing but sophistry and illusion.

This well-known quote has been interpreted both as a caution against metaphysical enquiry (in both philosophy and psychology) and a limit of what we can be said to know (which is perhaps closer to Hume's original purpose). One such limit is *causality* – according to Hume, we do not perceive that one thing causes another, we perceive only the progression of sense impressions in time (Popkin, 1999b), and learn to expect that this sequence will reoccur in future instances. But because we learn to expect things – our experience of the world effectively becomes ridden with such perceptual habits – it is easy to conclude things prematurely, which is surely a point of some importance and caution in a human science such as psychology. If we are to be genuinely unbiased and scientific in our enquiries, even though we may have seen many and only black crows in our life, for a scientist 'it can be important not to reject the possibility of finding a white crow. You might almost say that hunting for the "white crow" is science's principal task' (Gaarder, 1991, p. 231). This is a point to which we will have occasion to return in a short while.

The skepticism and limits to knowledge and enquiry advanced by the British Empiricists has had considerable influence in the way in which science, and scientific psychology, is undertaken, where Hume's attempt to use the methods of the physical sciences in enquiries into human nature and behaviour remains an ideal. In scientific psychology, as you will see from reading this book, there is a preference for experimental or at least broad-scale survey research methods, and psychological investigations are very carefully designed. 'Evidence' that is gained in other ways – from opinion, literature, introspection, rhetoric and so on – is not, to the scientific psychologist, really evidence at all, and is thus dismissed as 'anecdotal evidence', inadmissible on the grounds of its unreliability, and being impossible to validly generalise from. 'Consign it then to flames', indeed.

Furthermore, in the twentieth century, two well-known philosophers independently turned their attention to science, each highlighting (in different ways) that the neutrality and objectivity which scientists pride themselves on may in fact be compromised. Their names were Karl Popper (1902–1994) and Thomas Kuhn (1922–1996), and what they had to say in this respect carries important implications for the self-monitoring way in which scientific psychology *should* conduct itself. The 'white crow' argument outlined above by Gaarder (1991) to illustrate Hume's arguments also exemplifies what Popper had to say about *falsification* and its position as a standard in science. In *The Logic of Scientific Discovery*, Popper (1959) was critical of a good deal of what passed for human science in the nineteenth and early-twentieth century; in particular, he was dissatisfied with the circularity which abounded in many theoretical positions, such as Marxism (in sociology) and Freudian theory (psychology). With regard to these examples, criticism is difficult to advance to their adherents, as it may be taken to be evidence of 'false' or 'bourgeois consciousness', or 'resistance to uncomfortable truths', respectively. Popper was concerned that any intellectual system which thus defended itself from the testing of its hypotheses necessarily became biased. Falsification is the hallmark of empirical science; as soon as a theory ceases to be falsifiable, it ceases to be scientific – we should always look out for the 'white crow'. Falsification has important implications for the design of psychological investigations, and also for the statistical procedures that psychologists use in the assessment of their data (the latter of which, the non-mathematically-minded reader may be relieved to know, is beyond the scope of this book). Along these lines, the reader of this text is therefore cautioned against accepting dogmatism of any kind, and will be encouraged to think critically about the material that is presented, and how it may be applied in practical situations.

Thomas Kuhn's use of the notion of *paradigms* (in *The Structure of Scientific Revolutions*, 1962) alerted many to the fact that science does not, in fact, operate in a vacuum of unhindered neutrality – instead it is, as Russell (1946) said of philosophy, influenced by the political and social circumstances of the historical period in which it is conducted. As paradigms influence the entire intellectual climate of a period in time, they are often invisible, or apparently non-existent, until they *change*. For example, until the late-nineteenth century, biologists were informed by a creationist paradigm – their work was essentially about uncovering the wonders of God's masterpiece. Since the publication of *On the Origin of Species* (Darwin, 1859), biologists have been operating under an evolutionary paradigm – they assert neutrality, and yet every piece of evidence seems to confirm a Darwinian position. Of course, whether this is because they are now neutrally uncovering the truth, or are unwittingly participating in the sort of circularity that Popper cautioned against, is something that only time (and potential paradigm shifts in the future) will tell!

Finally, in contradiction to the nod that psychology sometimes gives to the influence of Berkeley (see above), psychologists generally do adhere to the philosophical position of *materialism* – that there is a 'real world' structure which lies behind our perceptions and investigations. Generally, the metaphysical entity of the 'mind' is represented in the physical structure of the brain, which psychologists assume to be the physical 'seat' of mental functioning.

Areas of Focus in Psychology

So what do psychologists do? There are many different possible specialisations, of which the 10 divisions and 14 sections of the British Psychological Society (BPS), the representative body for psychologists and psychology in the United Kingdom, gives an idea. The divisions (open to practitioners in a certain field of psychology; only professionally qualified psychologists are entitled to full membership) comprise the Divisions of Child and Educational Psychology, Clinical Psychology, Counselling Psychology, Forensic Psychology, Health Psychology, Occupational Psychology, Neuropsychology, Sport and Exercise Psychology, Teachers and Researchers in Psychology, and the Scottish Division of Educational Psychology. The sections (interest groups open to all BPS members) comprise Cognitive Psychology, Community Psychology, Consciousness and Experiential Psychology, Developmental Psychology, History and Philosophy of Psychology, Mathematical Statistical and Computing, Psychobiology, Psychology of Education, Psychology of Sexualities, Psychology of Women, Psychotherapy, Qualitative Methods in Psychology, Social Psychology, and Transpersonal Psychology (British Psychological Society, 2011).

The psychologists that teachers are most likely to encounter in their professional lives are educational psychologists. Elliott et al. (2000) define educational psychology (in a deliberately broad way) as 'the application of psychology and psychological methods to the study of development, learning, motivation, instruction, assessment, and related issues that influence the interaction of teaching and learning'. They go on to describe the field's key concepts as: understanding what it means to teach; knowledge of students (cognitive, linguistic, psychosocial, moral and atypical development; the impact of culture, class, and gender); understanding the learning processes (theories of learning and motivation); understanding instructional strategies (and their evidence-basis); and understanding assessment strategies (using measurement tools to identify students who need educational or psychological assistance; helping teachers to develop instructional programmes to facilitate all students' functioning). In the United Kingdom, status as a chartered educational psychologist (and eligibility for full membership of the BPS's Division of Child and Educational Psychology) is achieved by completing a BPS-recognised undergraduate degree in psychology (providing the graduate basis for registration with the BPS); having two or three years' experience working with children, young people and their families (previously, training and working for two years as a teacher); and completing a BPS-recognised three-year professional doctoral programme in educational psychology (British Psychological Society, 2011).

A Very Brief History of Psychology

The discipline of scientific psychology has a rather short history compared with that which I have asserted to be its parent discipline, western philosophy: 150 years (British Psychological Society, 2010) and around 2,500 years (Russell, 1946) respectively. Nevertheless, a good deal has occurred since the publication of Gustav Fechner's *Elemente der Psychophysik* [*Elements of Psychophysics*] in 1860, which may be taken to mark the beginnings of *experimental psychology* (British Psychological Society, 2010). With an eye on what is perhaps most interesting for educators, we can take a brief overview of some of these developments.

For 40 years after the publication of Fechner's landmark publication, he and other *psychophysicists* investigated the human sensory, perceptual and memory systems using careful experimentation. By 1875, experimental psychology had become a transatlantic discipline; Wilhelm Wundt, who published *Principles of Physiological Psychology* in 1874, and William James, who published *Principles of Psychology* in 1890, set up the first psychological laboratories, at the Universities of Leipzig and Harvard respectively (British Psychological Society, 2010). Not all of what passed for 'psychology' at that time, or the then fashionable *anthropometrics*, adhered to Fechner et al.'s diligent experimentalism. Spiritualism, mesmerism, hypnosis, conjuring, clairvoyance, fortune-telling and related areas of charlatanry competed for the attention and the wallets of the public at large, as they continue to do so today; however, in the late-nineteenth century, some of these areas achieved varying levels of respectability amongst academic audiences (Szasz, 1978).

One such area was *phrenology*. Phrenologists correctly believed that the mental functions were located in the brain, which as an organ exhibits 'localisation of function' – different parts of the brain are associated with different physical and psychological functions. However, the phrenologists believed – wrongly – that if a psychological characteristic was pronounced in an individual, that a corresponding part of the brain would become enlarged, as would the part of the skull that overlay that brain region. Consequently, phrenologists believed – also wrongly – that it was possible to 'map' these psychological characteristics by examining 'bumps' on people's crania. Hence, they devoted much time to producing schemes through this activity, in the forms of diagrams and busts. No-one seriously believes in phrenology these days (although oddly enough, some psychologists, me included, keep phrenology busts as curios in their offices), and the discipline has been dismissed, at best, as a 'pseudoscience' (van Whye, 2011). One of the few references to phrenology that still exists in everyday life is when a Londoner calls into question someone's sanity by recommending a consultation with a phrenologist – 'You want your bumps feeling, mate!'

Over the first 30 years of the twentieth century, two very different approaches within psychology developed (the *psychodynamic* approach and *behaviourism*), both of which are still influential today (in the psychology of education, chiefly in the areas of understanding motivation and learning respectively). The *psychodynamic* approach began with the astonishingly divisive work of the Viennese neurologist, Sigmund Freud (1856–1939; ever since, people tend to either love or loathe his ideas), who, like those who followed him, was interested chiefly in the workings of the unconscious mind, and conducted most of his enquiries into the human mind via learning from those he treated (as a practitioner of what would become known as 'psychoanalysis', or 'psychoanalytical psychotherapy') and trained. His masterwork, *The Interpretation of Dreams*, was published in 1900. Freud's views on the primacy of the sexual instinct, how children develop, and his views on culture and religion, continue to challenge psychologists and the broader public to the present day (see Freud, 1940, for an overview).

Behaviourism, on the other hand, was an attempt to base psychology strictly on scientific principles; behaviourists had no tolerance of Freudian speculation about unconscious instincts, and, sometimes invoking Locke's *tabula rasa* and Hume's rejection of metaphysical enquiry (see above), preferred to work from the observation of simple processes of learning in non-human species. Their task was to understand what sort of stimuli and factors positively or negatively reinforced learning, and then how this could be generalised to the human experience. An early view was provided by John Watson (1913); in its mature form, B.F. Skinner developed behaviourism from a data-rich discipline (1938), which as well as being massively influential in psychology, was also influential in education (amongst other things, Skinner asserted that positive reinforcement is more effective than punishment (1968)), to a philosophy in itself (1972).

Except from Freud's approach to the subject (1908, 1909), most of the major models of *child development* – the approaches of Jean Piaget, Lev Vygotsky and Erik Erikson – date from the 1920s to the 1950s. Chapter 2 of this book provides a topical overview of this important area of psychology (child and developmental psychology) for teachers. At around this time, the *psychology of individual differences* – first manifested in the testing of intelligence, as we shall see in Chapter 4 of this text – also developed, which would also see the assessment of human personality come under the spotlight (see Phares and Chaplin, 1997). Another influential school of psychological thought that was first developed before the Second World War was *ethology*. Like the behaviourists, ethologists were interested in animal behaviour, but only naturally-occurring animal behaviour, not that which could be created in laboratory experiments. They sought to understand the evolutionary origins and significance of behaviour in non-human animal and human species, and have made significant contributions to our understanding of parenting, attachment, reproductive behaviour, and perhaps most of all, aggression (see Lorenz, 1953, 1966).

After the Second World War, psychodynamic psychology continued in its own right, and predominantly as an influence in the field of psychotherapy, as it does to the present day (Bongar and Beutler, 1995). Behaviourism dominated the world of scientific psychology until the 1950s, when in its radical form – which was preoccupied with learning only, and went as far to deny the existence of mental structures (Skinner, 1972) – gave way to *cognitive psychology*, which inherited the scientific mantle and experimental research methods of the behaviourists, but could focus on the full remit of psychological functions (see Eysenck and Keane, 2010). 'Cognition' refers to the way in which people think; it includes our mental faculties of perception, attention, memory, planning, reasoning, problem solving, knowledge representation and thought (Minton, 2011). From the mid- to late-twentieth century, there was an explosion of interest in psychology, and psychologists involved themselves in the scientific investigation of any number of mental and social phenomena (see Gleitman, 2010) and, in an applied sense, areas such as education, health and industry. Cognitive psychology remains the dominant influence in scientific/theoretical psychology to the present day, but many applied areas of psychology, especially education, are equally influenced by another approach towards understanding learning and motivation: *humanism*.

In the post-Second World War years, *humanism* (also known as 'phenomenological psychology') became known as the 'third force' in psychology. The first 'force', historically speaking, was reckoned to be psychoanalysis, which critics from a humanistic standpoint felt placed too much focus on the unconscious aspects of the mind, particularly our supposedly 'animalistic' drives. The second 'force' was behaviourism, which humanists have seen as being too reductionistic, placing too much emphasis on animal learning, and attempting – inaccurately – to generalise to human experience from such perspectives (Minton, 2011). What was needed, argued one of the greatest of all the humanistic psychologists, Abraham Maslow, was a new approach – a genuine psychology of human beings (Maslow, 1954). Humanists feel that it is necessary to view the whole human and his or her existence, and focuses on areas such as the construction of identity and personal meaning, and human growth and potential. It is deeply and unapologetically subjective; its main figures, Carl Rogers (1951, 1967) and Abraham Maslow (1954, 1968), were involved in the fields of psychotherapy, personality theory and education, and motivation, respectively.

During the 1970s and 1980s, there was a fruitful interplay between the disciplines of cognitive psychology and information technology, and an approach known as *cognitive science* was developed. The mind had long been likened to a machine (this approach ultimately dates back to a line of argument developed in the French philosopher René Descartes' *Meditations on a First Philosophy* (1641)). With the development of computers being envisioned and realised by the brilliant, yet tragic, British mathematician, Alan Turing, in the 1930s and 1940s (see Turing, 1950), and microcomputers being produced as broadly affordable systems from the late 1970s, cognitive scientists from the 1970s onwards began to 'model' human psychological functions in artificial intelligence systems as a method of research (e.g. Johnson-Laird, 1980). Of course, it is possible for the comparability between the very different human and computer intelligence systems to be over-stated. Just because such modelling can be undertaken does not mean that this is how a given function operates in a human system – only that this is what *could* be happening. However, from the late-1980s, brain-imaging techniques became more sophisticated (with the development of magnetic resonance imagery, or MRI) and more affordable, and were increasingly applied within psychological research – in order to track what the human brain was *actually* doing. Hence, in very recent times, 'the methods of experimental psychology are increasingly combined with those of brain imaging, of molecular biology and of pharmacology' (British Psychological Society, 2010). This now cutting-edge combination of the disciplines of cognitive psychology, information technology and neurology is known as *cognitive neuroscience*.

The Psychology of Education and About this Book

This book is about the application of psychology in the classroom by educational professionals. It is *not* a book on either child or developmental psychology (many excellent texts on these colossal areas exist). For purposes of reliability, and out of respect for the integrity of the disciplines of both psychology and education, it is a book that concerns itself with *scientific*, and *not* popular or 'self-help' psychology; it is grounded within the discipline of the *psychology of education*, rather than *educational psychology*. Woolfolk et al. (2008) differentiate these similar-sounding terms in the following way: educational psychology (as we have already seen, above)

> can refer to the broad area of training and work of educational psychologists, who apply psychological theories, research and teaching to help children and young people who may be having learning difficulties, emotional or behavioural problems . . . in contrast, the psychology of education, is the study of how psychological theories and research inform and support the work of educational professionals working across the whole range of teaching and learning settings. (p. 4)

At the time of writing, with my primary training being in psychology, I have spent more than a decade working in school and university settings, providing pre- and in-service training to students of education and educational professionals – more often than not, as I think of it, 'teaching teachers the psychology they need to know for the job'. I have had the privilege of doing this in my position as a lecturer in the psychology of education at the School of Education, Trinity College Dublin, at a variety of other settings throughout Ireland, and occasionally internationally. This book, then, is an attempt to communicate this sort of work to a broader audience. So after introducing the scope of the discipline of psychology as it applies in educational practice (a goal for the current chapter), and taking a topical overview of child and adolescent development (Chapter 2), and before drawing conclusions (Chapter 10), Chapters 3 to 9 inclusively are focused upon seven areas of contemporary concern in education, and showing how psychological approaches can help teachers in these key areas of practice. These areas of contemporary concern are ones that have been the focus of my pre- and in-service training work, and have been arrived at by developments in the fields of both psychology and education, and expressions of need by students of education, teachers and members of school communities. They comprise the self, self-esteem and self-esteem enhancement through educational practice (Chapter 3); intelligence, learning styles and educational attainment (Chapter 4); positive discipline, conflict resolution and co-operative learning in schools (Chapter 5); thinking about special educational needs (Chapter 6); preventing and countering bullying behaviour and cyber-bullying in schools (Chapter 7); dealing with prejudice – racism, homophobia and alterophobia in schools (Chapter 8); and stress and stress management for teachers and educators (Chapter 9).

Each of the seven chapters on 'contemporary concern in education' follows a common format. After a statement of *chapter objectives*, the text is interspersed with *activities* for the reader, in which he or she is typically invited to think about the material of the chapter in an applied or critical way (or both), either alone in a reflective exercise or in discussion with colleagues, and occasionally in classroom and school activities with young people. Each chapter also incorporates a *case study* in which good and interesting educational practice, research, legislature or policy is used to illustrate the points that are being made – for the purposes of variety and promoting international comparison, each case study is drawn from a different country. The reflective focus is continued to the conclusion of each chapter in sections on 'implications for educators' *to think about* and final *points for discussion*, prior to the provision of short, annotated lists of *further reading* and sometimes *useful websites*.

My aim in writing this book was to produce a text that would be both of practical use to undergraduate and postgraduate students of education, and of interest to educational professionals in practice. No book can hope to cover everything, but it is hoped that through a focus on areas of contemporary concern in education, and how applied psychology can illuminate these, I will be able to both communicate key ideas to pre-service students and to refresh the knowledge of, and even inspire, teachers engaging in in-service training and advanced study.

Above all, I hoped to produce a hands-on and practical book, whilst being true to the scientific principles of psychology, thus reflecting my own approach to the psychology of education (which, as those who know me can testify, is distinctively *not* one of the so-called 'ivory tower'). Only time (and reviews and sales figures!) will tell how successful I have been in achieving these aims, but suffice it to say, I have done my best, and I hope that you will find the book to be enjoyable, interesting, and above all, useful.

As psychology is likely to feature throughout your studies and practice as an educator, I would recommend that you familiarise yourself with a good reference textbook on either general psychology or child and educational psychology. There are a large number available, and the intense competition that exists in the market for undergraduate psychology texts keeps the general standard high. I advise my own students of education to visit the library, or a bookseller, and leaf through the range of such texts in order to find a text they are comfortable with. I repeat this advice to you, the reader. Some of the more popular choices amongst my students have been:

Gleitman, H. (2010) *Psychology*, 8th edn. London: Norton.
Snowman, J., McCown, R. and Biehler (2009) *Psychology Applied to Teaching*, 12th edn. Boston: Houghton-Mifflin.
Woolfolk, A., Hughes, M. and Walkup, V. (2008) *Psychology in Education*. Harlow: Pearson Education.

The British Psychological Society. Available at www.bps.org.uk (accessed May 2011). The professional body for psychologists in the United Kingdom, and an important repository of resources for anyone with an interest in psychology.

2

An Overview of Child and Adolescent Psychological Development

The primary goal for this chapter is to provide a brief, topical overview of child and adolescent psychological development, in order to provide a context for much of the information that has been included elsewhere in this text. We will first examine *theories of cognitive development*, including those of *Piaget, Vygotsky* and the *information processing theorists*, the latter of which will be reviewed with explicit regard to understanding how *memory* works. We will then attend to some *issues in socioemotional development* during middle childhood and adolescence – the *development of gender role understanding* and the *development of moral reasoning* – before progressing on to considering two contemporary systemic and contextual models of psychological development – *Bronfenbrenner's ecological model* and the *Bildung-Psychology approach*. This chapter concludes with a reflective examination of some *implications for educators*, *points for discussion*, and a selective and annotated list of *further reading* and a *useful website*.

Theories of Cognitive Development

When developmental psychologists – those who study age-related developments in thought and behaviour – systematise their approach to research and practice, they sometimes make reference to three 'spheres' of development: *physical, cognitive* and *socioemotional development* (Fogel and Melson, 1988). Physical development, although exerting an effect on psychological and social systems, is largely the province of medics and clinicians; psychologists and educators more often focus on cognitive and socioemotional development, to which we will confine our consideration.

Cognition refers to the way in which people *think*; it includes our mental faculties of attention, memory, planning, problem-solving and reasoning. The reader should note that many areas *relating to* cognitive development are mentioned elsewhere throughout this text – in particular, Chapter 4 addresses intelligence, learning styles and educational attainment, and Chapter 6 addresses special educational needs, and hence atypical cognitive development. For now, though, we shall attend to cognitive development *in itself*, and the finding that whilst some classical psychological research indicates that infants, young children, older children, adolescents and adults appear to think in globally different ways (notably, that of Jean Piaget (1896–1980)), other perspectives – notably, the *information processing approach* – examine how individual cognitive faculties develop and improve over time.

Piaget's Model of Cognitive Development

Piaget's model of cognitive development is called a *qualitative* approach because he believed that there are qualitative differences in the orderly progression of the global intellect. Some commentators believe that this 'unfolding-of-characteristics' idea is perhaps traceable to Piaget's own primary scientific training as a biologist, and his interest in embryology (Gleitman, 2010). In Piaget's model, there are four main stages: the *sensory-motor intelligence* (infancy, 0–2 years); the *pre-operational* stage (early childhood, 2–7 years); the *concrete-operational* stage (middle/late childhood, 7–11 years) and the *formal-operational/formal-logical* stage (adolescence on, hence 12 years on).

The three later stages, in which primary and secondary educators will surely have the most interest, are marked by the development towards what Piaget called mental 'operations', which ultimately allow us to manipulate ideas according to sets of rules. However, in the second stage, the *pre-operational stage*, these operations have not yet emerged. One limitation at this stage is *egocentrism* – the child assumes that others literally and physically see the world in exactly the same way as they do (Piaget and Inhelder, 1956). Another limit involves what Piaget called *conservation*. For example (problems with conservation of *mass*), the pre-operational child may be presented with two equally sized balls of clay. He or she is asked, 'Do these balls contain the same amount of clay?', to which he or she will then answer , 'Yes'. One ball is then rolled out into a long thin 'sausage'. The question is repeated. The pre-operational child will indicate that the long, thin 'sausage' contains more clay than the ball does. The failure to conserve is caused by the child's inability to attend simultaneously to all of the dimensions of the objects. Resolving conservation difficulties comes when the transforming action becomes mentally represented as a reversible operation (Piaget, 1953).

The *concrete operational* child is limited neither by egocentrism nor conservation difficulties; he or she can understand the realities of apparently abstract things such as number and quantity. Adolescence is marked by a further advancement: the *formal operational stage*. Adolescents can *logically reason* about *hypothetical situations*, too – they can plan, strategise, and form realistic goals. Fantasy thinking is evident at a much younger age (as evidenced by the play and dreams of very young children); however, only in adolescence (and thereafter) can a person be logical and realistic about her or his dreams and aspirations. Neo-Piagetians Gisela Labouvie-Vief (1982) and William Perry (1981) have pointed out (separately) that adolescents tend to be *literal* and *dualistic* in their logical thinking. In contrast, adult thinking is necessarily *relativistic* – teenage 'black-and-whiteness' gives way to the 'grey area' of multiply-determined adult decision making.

Piaget's observations and theories have not been without criticism. Methodologically, many have commented that much of Piaget's research was conducted on his own children. Furthermore, on subsequent empirical investigation, the pre-operational child does not appear to be quite as limited by conservation failures as Piaget might have expected; conversely, it seems that he might have over-estimated the abilities of adolescents (Gleitman, 2010). Many people have pointed out that some adults are not capable of formal-logical thought, never mind teenagers (Fogel and Melson, 1988). Furthermore, we should not assume (as Piaget did) that these stages are universal. Piaget focussed on mental development along lines of formal logic; some non-western cultures do not develop in this way at all (Santrock, 1996). Finally, especially if one reads Piaget at source, it seems as though he is describing the child's intellectual development as occurring almost spontaneously, in the absence of social relationships: 'as a budding scientist systematically encountering problems in the material world, developing hypotheses and learning by discovery and activity' (Burman, 1994, in Beckett, 2007, p. 84).

Other Models of Cognitive Development
Piaget's account of cognitive development, then, is seen as not fully recognising the role of social interaction and language in child development (Beckett, 2007;

Trawick-Smith, 2010). The Russian psychologist Lev Vygotsky (1896–1934) argued that children solve problems far better when they are assisted by a more competent peer or adult, who thereby provides 'scaffolding' for the child's development of problem-solving abilities. This is, of course, something that parents, family members and teachers naturally do (Trawick-Smith, 2010) – a supportive structure is provided for the child who is learning, but the eventual solution is the child's own. Vygotsky also commented on the private, or 'self-directed' speech that a pre-school typically uses when undertaking a task, originating from instructions that are given to the child by others (e.g. peers, parents, teachers). This self-directed speech, as early-years teachers will recognise, often appears as the 'chattering' of the child when 'busy', does not disappear with age but instead becomes internalised, and develops into 'an interior monologue, which goes on in our head even as adults' (Beckett, 2007, p. 85).

The *information processing approach* is a *quantitative* approach; from this point of view, a child can be seen as a *limited* mental processor – essentially, an adult can process more information, or process information more quickly. In the information processing approach, it is common to focus upon one facet of cognition at a time, rather trying to explain, in a global way, how people think (as Piaget did). To illustrate, we will look at just one area of cognition – *memory*.

Atkinson and Shifrin's (1968) popular *two-process model of memory* holds that information enters the human system (input) through the 'sensory register'. There is, in any given situation, a wide array of stimuli that one could potentially register. For example, if you want to memorise the present text, you must first position it where you can *perceive* (see) it. Next, you must be able to *attend* to it; you will need to selectively *filter out* other stimuli (internal and external). The information first enters the short-term memory (STM), which has a very limited capacity (generally held to be 7 plus-or-minus 2 items) (Atkinson and Shifrin, 1968; Gleitman, 2010). One can make the most of this capacity by a strategy called *chunking* – that is, to *link* bits of information with each other. For example, imagine that you are given a 16-digit number to remember:

1, 9, 1, 4, 1, 9, 1, 8, 1, 9, 3, 9, 1, 9, 4, 5.

Notice how, apparently spontaneously, we 'chunk' this information together. We first notice the repetition of the 19 pattern, and see that it looks as if there are four dates:

1914, 1918, 1939, 1945.

If we remember history, we might recall that these are the starting and end dates of the two world wars:

1914–1918, 1939–1945.

So now we have 'chunked' our way from 16 to just one piece of information to hold in the STM.

In order to retain newly acquired information within the STM, we must keep it 'fresh' by *maintenance rehearsal* – in its simplest form, by repeating the information to ourselves. For example, you may be given an unfamiliar telephone number, but you do not have a pen with which to write it down. You then repeat the number to yourself, either out loud or internally, until you successfully dial it. But notice what happens if this 'maintenance rehearsal pattern' is interrupted – say, someone else asks you a question – you forget the number!

A fruitful approach for teachers has also been developed using the concept of 'working memory', which is 'the ability we have to hold and manipulate information in the mind over short periods of time' (Gathercole and Alloway, 2009, p. 2). Whereas short-term memory usually deals with *verbal* information (e.g. remembering unfamiliar telephone numbers), working memory may deal with *any* sort of information (such as remembering lengthy directions on how to reach somewhere) (Gathercole and Alloway, 2009). Children with poorer working memory can be identified by teachers in a variety of ways; obviously, they score consistently lower on standardised tests of working memory, but they also tend to be reserved in larger group activities in the classroom, rarely volunteering information and becoming withdrawn or distracted. They are also likely to show poorer academic progression, a failure to follow instructions, and attention problems. However, interventions can be put in place, such as (i) a recognition of working memory problems; (ii) monitoring the child for warning signs; (iii) evaluation and reduction (where necessary) of working memory loads in teaching content and classroom instructions; (iv) repetition of key information; (v) use of memory aids (e.g. wall charts, posters, audio-visual recording, computer software); and (vi) the development of the child's own memory strategies (e.g. asking for help, rehearsal, organisational strategies) (Gathercole and Alloway, 2009). As we shall see later (Chapter 6, 'Thinking about Special Educational Needs'), the use of working memory has been applied to areas such as ADHD and autistic spectrum disorders (Alloway, 2011).

Short-term and working memory have limited capacities, so information that we wish to retain is typically transferred to the long-term memory (LTM), or risks being lost from the system via *decay* (i.e. forgotten). Various explanations exist as to how the LTM is organised (see Gleitman, 2010, for review). Gathercole and Alloway (2009) discuss four types of long-term memory: episodic, autobiographical, semantic and procedural. All of these types can last a lifetime; episodic memory, and to a lesser extent autobiographical memory, is accessed almost as a (not perfect!) recording (audio or visual) of an event – when we recall these experiences, we literally 're-view' them. Of these two 'iconic' forms of memory, episodic memory is usually quite fleeting, whereas autobiographical memories tend to be more long-lasting – many of us remember our first day at school as a series of visual images with accompanying emotional content, and may remember other significant life events in a similar way. Semantic memory is our memory for facts, including personal facts ('knowing-that') and procedural memory is our memory for how to do things which become 'automatic' activities ('knowing-how'). To illustrate with the clichéd example of 'you never forget how to ride a bike' (procedural memory) – you may also remember seeing a cyclist on your way to work this morning (episodic memory); you may remember getting a bicycle as a birthday or Christmas present as a child (autobiographical memory); and, if you are a sports fan, you may be able to recall the last five winners of the Tour de France, or if you are a parent of young children, the prices of bicycles in different shops in your nearest town (semantic memory).

From an information processing viewpoint, the reason why children's memories are generally not as good as those of healthy adults is because they are for some reason poorer in the use of memory strategies (either they have not learnt them, or they apply them ineffectively or inconsistently) and that their long-term memories are less well organised. Things will, and indeed do, improve over time, and in most standardised tests of memory (those not involving tests of specific material), those in the late-teenage years perform about as well as do adults (Gathercole and Alloway, 2009).

Flashbulb Memories

A peculiar yet familiar feature of long-term memory is the existence of so-called 'flashbulb memories' (Brown and Kulik, 1977, in Gleitman, 2010) – vivid memories of particular (usually dramatic) events that all people of a certain age within a society will share. Not only is the event recalled in considerable detail, but so is our experience of hearing the news – where we were, whom we were with, how we felt about it and so on. The event is of such power that a mental 'flashbulb' is set off, preserving not only our visual memory of the event, but also relatively trivial personal details connected with our experience of that scene. The interesting thing is that everyone else of approximately the same age range and culture has a similar type of memory for the event as well. Flashbulb memories are, therefore, a specific form of shared autobiographical memories.

The following are some world events that have been reported as having elicited 'flashbulb' memories. If you are old enough for it to be possible, see if you share any of these:

> John F. Kennedy shot dead in Dallas in 1963
> The death of Diana, Princess of Wales in 1997
> The attack on the World Trade Centre in 2001

Few 'flashbulb' memories are universal because so few events affect or are equally vivid to all people worldwide. Most are, of course, localised, that is, specific to a country. For example, immediately before writing up this activity for this text, I discussed this point with colleagues in Macedonia. For Macedonian people over the age of 55, the 1963 earthquake that killed over 1,000 people and destroyed 80 per cent of the city of Skopje (now the country's capital and extensively re-built) is a flashbulb memory, yet is (shamefully) an event almost unheard of outside the Balkans.

Now, think about the country where you live, and what the flashbulb memories are likely to be for people there. If you have the opportunity to discuss flashbulb memories with people from other countries, please do so.

Issues in Socioemotional Development

First, it is again suggested that the reader notes that many other issues in socioemotional development are mentioned elsewhere throughout this text. Chapter 3 addresses the development of the self and self-esteem; and Chapters 7 and 8 examine peer relationships, through their focus on bullying and prejudice. For the purposes of illustration in this chapter, then, we shall confine ourselves to two examples – the *development of gender role understanding* and the *development of moral reasoning* – which are to be seen in the upper primary and secondary school years.

The Development of Gender Role Understanding

The term *sex* refers to the 'biological dimension of being either male or female'; that is to say, being in the possession of the physical characteristics of the male or female type. The related term *gender* is far more complex, referring to the 'sociocultural dimension of being male or female', with the frequently used term *gender role* referring to 'a set of expectations that prescribes how males and females should think, act and feel' (Santrock, 1996, p. 353).

To what extent are the notions of sex and gender linked? Early in the twentieth century, the argument that 'anatomy is destiny' still persisted unchallenged. And yet, gender itself is undeniably mediated by an array of other factors. Social scientists have shown that parents, peers, schools and the mass media all have important influence on the development of gender, as does culture in general (Santrock, 1996). Hence, gender may be seen as being *socially constructed*; we bring up boys and girls in different ways, according to our expectations of how men and women will think, act, feel and behave in the family and in society. Traditionally, the developmental period of adolescence is seen as *the* critical stage in gender development; the physical maturation stage of puberty being psychologically adapted to by something called *gender intensification*. The gender intensification hypothesis states that:

> psychological and behavioural differences between boys and girls become greater during early adolescence because of increased socialisation pressures to conform to traditional masculine and feminine gender roles. (Hill and Lynch, 1983, Lynch, 1991, in Santrock, 1996)

This being said, it has become incredibly important to note how, across many of the world's developed countries, the twentieth century brought massive changes in how society at large has defined the gender roles of women. In *The Second Sex* (1949), Simone de Beauvoir asserted that the social prejudice and persecution that exists towards women in many societies results from and perpetuates women being positioned as 'Other', before mounting a comprehensive critique of the 'anatomy is destiny' standpoint, demolishing many fallacious arguments that had been used to define what women's roles 'should' be. An excellent contemporary take on the positions of women can be found in Carol Tavris's *The Mismeasure of Woman* (1992). Politically, the women's movement in general has been important in the partial redressing of the balance of power and influence that exists between men and women in society, although there is clearly some distance to go.

The role of men is changing too, and whilst the women's movement is over 60 years old, the focus on men's gender issues is much more recent. Herbert Goldberg (1980) advocates that men need to become more attuned to their inner selves and emotional makeup and work on developing positive close relationships. Robert Bly, another key player in the fledgling men's movement, believes that men too have been short-changed by patriarchy. He argues that men have not had their fathers around since the Industrial Revolution, which prompted the system of long, physical working hours away from the home for men, and women attempting the impossible task of being both mother and father to their sons. Bly advocates that men need to get in touch with a deep, ancient masculine identity, which for Bly is about spontaneity, risk-taking, leadership, sexuality, action-taking, preserving the Earth and nurturing children (Bly, 1999).

Men have perhaps yet to realise constructive ways to work with the construct of masculinity. One such attempt has been piloted within the Irish education system. *Exploring Masculinities* was a school curriculum-based 'programme in personal and social development for boys and young men', designed to address the 'lagging behind' of traditional attitudes apparent in Irish society, despite the wide-ranging social changes apparent over the previous 25 years (Department of Education and Science, 2000, p. 1). The programme's ethos closely followed the United Nations' Declaration of Universal Human Rights. However, *Exploring Masculinities* did not meet with universal approval. It was described by one journalist, who called for its immediate withdrawal, as a 'flabby, intellectually dishonest vehicle for the implanting of a stealth of feminist ideologies in the heads of teenage boys' (Waters, 2000). Waters was correct in raising the question as to how effective the programme would be, but he was surely wide of the mark in suggesting that as far as suicide rates amongst young males go, 'there is every risk that this programme . . . will make this situation far worse'. However, Waters got his wish; *Exploring Masculinities* was never mainstreamed.

Moral Development

The story goes that observing boys playing marbles prompted Jean Piaget's first reflections on how children develop in a moral sense. In learning the rules of the game, Piaget reasoned, the boys were also learning about rules in general (Fogel and Melson, 1988). According to Piaget, the first form of moral reasoning we learn is that of *moral realism* (also referred to as the phase of *autonomous morality*). Here, children treat rules as inviolable, unchangeable, and as if handed down by some ultimate external authority. Piaget referred to this style of thinking as the *morality of constraint*; it dominates the reasoning of children from about 8 to 10 years of age (before 8, Piaget considered children to be pre-moral). Later on, at 11 years or older, children engage in a form of moral reasoning known as *moral relativism*. They realise that it is people themselves who make rules, via consent around the common good. This is also known as *heteronomous morality*, or the *morality of co-operation*. In order to distinguish the two, we can examine a test used by Piaget himself – a pair of stories, which he would ask children of different ages to discuss (Piaget, 1932/1965, p. 122):

A: There was a little boy called Julian. His father had gone out and Julian thought it would be fun to play with his father's ink-pot. First he played with the pen, and then he made a little blot on the table.

B: A little boy who was called Augustus once noticed that his father's ink-pot was empty. One day when his father was away he thought of filling his ink-pot so as to help his father, and so that he should find it full when he came home. But while he was opening the ink-bottle, he made a big blot on the tablecloth.

Are these children equally guilty? Which of the two is the naughtiest, and why?

In interpreting the stories, younger children would invariably see Augustus as the naughtiest, as he had made the bigger ink-blot. Older children would see Julian as the naughtiest, as Augustus had after all been trying to help his father – they would take into account the *intent* of the two boys in the stories, unlike the younger children.

Piaget's ideas were developed and expanded by Lawrence Kohlberg over the 1950s and 1960s. Methodologically, Kohlberg used a similar method to that of Piaget; he would construct stories containing hypothetical moral dilemmas, and ask people how they reasoned about and solved them. Kohlberg's method of 'scoring' was complex, and beyond the bounds of this text; however, it will be useful to look at a typical 'story', and to review some summaries of the stage model that resulted from Kohlberg's research:

> In Europe a woman was near death from cancer. One drug might save her, a form of radium that a druggist in the same town had recently discovered. The druggist was charging $2,000, ten times what the drug cost him to make. The sick woman's husband, Heinz, went to everyone he knew to borrow the money, but he could only get together about half of what it cost. He told the druggist that his wife was dying and asked him to sell it cheaper or let him pay later, but the druggist said 'No'. The husband got desperate and broke into the man's store to steal the drug for his wife. Should the husband have done that? Why? (Kohlberg, 1969, p. 376)

In Kohlberg's approach, there are three 'levels', each of which is divided into two 'stages' (hence, six stages in all). *Level One* ('pre-conventional morality') is so-called because at this point, children do not understand the 'conventions' or rules of society; it is most typical of those aged under 9 years. In *Stage One* ('punishment and obedience orientation'), we obey authority in order to avoid the punishment, the physical consequences of which determine what we see as 'good' or 'bad'. In *Stage Two* ('instrumental relativist orientation'), what is 'good' is what satisfies our own needs, or at least involves what we might call a 'fair trade'; if we keep to the rules, we expect to be rewarded. *Level Two* ('conventional morality') is so-called because at this point, most 9 to 20-year-olds (of whom this level is typical) conform to the conventions of society. In *Stage Three* ('good boy/nice girl orientation'), we judge actions as being 'right' if they would be likely to please others; by *Stage Four* ('law-and-order orientation'), we have an internalised understanding of the need to respect authority, and that rules are necessary to maintain social order for the common good. *Level Three* ('post-conventional morality') is ordinarily reached only after the age of 20 years, and then by only a small proportion of the population; it is so-called because it is then that we understand the moral principles that *underlie* the rules of society. In *Stage Five*, ('social contract orientation') we understand that obeying rules should not be based on blind obedience to authority, but rather on the basis of mutual agreement; rules are needed, but individual rights must be protected. In *Stage Six* ('universal ethical principal orientation'), it is understood that moral decisions should be made according to self-chosen principles, which should in turn be applied in consistent ways (Snowman et al., 2009).

Working with Kohlberg's Model of Moral Development

1 Before reading the key text below, consider the story of Heinz's druggist dilemma (above). How would you solve it yourself, and how did you come to your conclusions? Note: it is more important to record how you came to your conclusions, rather than the conclusion in itself.

2 Try this out on yourself, your colleagues, friends and family members – and potentially, even your students – and remember to openly debate the issues. Now, read the key text below.

Key Text: Santrock (1996, p. 424) suggests the following might be typical of how people at different stages of moral development solve the Heinz dilemma. In Stage One, reasoning that might support Heinz's theft of the drug might be, 'Heinz should not let his wife die; if he does, he will be in big trouble'; reasoning 'against' might be, 'Heinz might get caught and sent to jail'. In Stage Two, reasoning 'for' might be 'If Heinz gets caught, he could give the drug back and maybe they would not give him a long jail sentence'; reasoning 'against' might be, 'The druggist is a businessman and needs to make money'. In Stage Three, reasoning 'for' might be, 'Heinz was only doing something that a good husband would do; it shows how much he loves his wife'; reasoning 'against' might be, 'If the wife dies, he can't be blamed for it; it is the druggist's fault. He is the selfish one'. In Stage Four, reasoning 'for' might be, 'If you did nothing, you would be letting your wife die; it is your responsibility if she dies. You have to steal it with the idea of paying back the druggist later'; reasoning 'against' might be, 'It is always wrong to steal; Heinz will always feel guilty if he steals the drug'. In Stage Five, reasoning 'for' might be, 'The law was not set up for these circumstances; taking the drug is not really right, but Heinz is justified in doing it'; reasoning 'against' might be 'You can't really blame someone for stealing, but extreme circumstances don't really justify taking the law into your own hands. You might lose respect for yourself if you let your emotions take over; you have to think about the long term'. In Stage Six, reasoning 'for' might be, 'By stealing the drug, you would have lived up to society's rules, but you would have let down your own conscience'; reasoning 'against' might be 'Heinz is faced with the decision of whether to consider other people who need the drug as badly as his wife. He needs to act by considering the value of all the lives involved'.

3 Now consider where you, your colleagues, friends, family members and students fit in. Please note that all of this will be indicative only – Kohlberg found that several dozen meticulously-scored scenarios were needed in order to be accurate.
4 Try to make your own hypothetical 'moral dilemmas', suitable for working with the students that you teach. It would also be possible to engage older secondary school students in such a task, after explaining the material of this section of this chapter to them.

Both Kohlberg's and Piaget's approaches have been criticised on the basis that they focus too much on moral *thought*, and not enough on moral *behaviour*. It is important to recognise that there may be many factors that exist between *knowing* the correct thing to do and actually *doing* it. Additionally, moral reasoning and behaviour is apparently more culturally-specific than Kohlberg appeared to recognise. For example, the present (14th) Dalai Lama of Tibet, Tenzin Gyatso, described a conversation he had had with a brother monk, who had spent 20 years in captivity under the Chinese, where he had been physically tortured daily – the monk had lost an eye, and his bones had been broken many times. When the Dalai Lama asked the monk what had been the worst thing about captivity, the monk replied that the worst thing was that he had nearly lost his compassion for his torturers (Gyatso, 1990). Undoubtedly, this universal compassion for all living beings that is emphasised so strongly in Tibetan Buddhism is moral reasoning of the highest order. In fact, this is an example of moral behaviour that is almost incomprehensible to the western mind; it must also have been particularly striking even in a Tibetan monk, otherwise the Dalai Lama might not have mentioned it. Significantly, it is also moral reasoning that would not be explicitly credited in Kohlberg's model.

Systemic and Contextual Models of Development

As we have seen above, Piaget has been criticised as having ignored the social context of child development. The following examples can be considered as models in which the context of development is strongly emphasised.

Bronfenbrenner's Ecological Model

Bronfenbrenner (1979) describes the child developing at the centre of a multi-layered set of interconnected environmental systems – the *micro-, meso-, exo-, macro-* and *chrono-systems*. The *micro-system* comprises those who are physically and emotionally closest to the child – usually, the family of origin. The *meso-system* includes socialising influences such as the neighbourhood, the school and the child's other peers. The *exo-system* comprises influences in which the child is not directly involved, but nevertheless have an effect, for example the parents' places of work and governmental agencies. Broader still is the *macro-system*, which includes regional, international or global changes, that is the cultural, ideological and organisational patterns within which the meso- and exo-systems are set. In 1989, Bronfenbrenner added the *chrono-system*, the 'temporal component' in which the ecosystem is immersed. Although the macro- and chrono-system may seem far removed, it is to be acknowledged that there is a world of difference between (say) growing up in London and sub-Saharan Africa in the 2010s, or indeed growing up in the London of the 1940s and the London of the 2010s.

The 'Linkedness' Model: An Ecological Approach to Child Development in Action (Belgium)

Since the late 1990s, an approach that is simultaneously a conceptual position and a practical method of working with whole-school communities on the issues of non-respectful behaviour and school violence has emerged in Flanders (Deklerck et al., 2003). This approach is known as *verbondenheid*, a Dutch/Flemish word that is rendered 'linkedness' in English. The conceptual position holds that so-called 'delinquency' and non-respectful behaviour at school are non-accidental, and 'in broad terms, involve the interaction between person-related factors (both endogenous and exogenous) on the one hand, and context-related factors on the other'. The consequent ecological approach to such problems takes into account five levels: the personal, the interaction, the material, the broad social environment and the 'natural living' environment levels (Deboutte et al., 2006). The argument is that 'de-linq-ency' is in general 'always the expression of the lack of a link between the offender and (one or more dimensions of) the victimised environment' (Deklerck et al., 2003, p. 321) and 'consequently, re-linking is the logical answer' (Deboutte et al., 2006, p. 11).

The 'linkedness' concept has been applied in whole-school programmes undertaken in Flanders and beyond. In such programmes, the goals of applying the 'linkedness' concept have been the creation of a positive school ethos and environment, and the reduction of non-respectful and violent behaviour in schools, through co-operative endeavours involving the entire school team (Deboutte et al., 2006). Through the VISTA (Violence in Schools Training Action) project (Cowie et al., 2006), 'linkedness' resources are available in Bulgarian, Dutch, English, German and Spanish.

The Bildung-Psychology Approach

In recent years, the Bildung-Psychology approach, described as having 'a strong focus on life-long learning', has been proposed as a framework that would 'allow for systematic representations of activities [in] fields that exist on the interface between development and education in general, and in educational psychology in particular' (Spiel et al., 2008, p. 154). Bildung-Psychology is derived from the German language term *Bildung* which, as Spiel et al. (2008, p. 154) note, has 'no precise equivalent in English'. It may be seen as a 'German conception of self-formation or self-cultivation', and defined on the formative level 'as a product (desirable personal characteristics from the standpoint of social norms) as well as a process (how those characteristics are developed)', and on the substantive level, as dealing with 'the question of which products (individual character traits) are really desirable' (2008, p. 154).

Spiel et al. (2008) present a three-dimensional model in which (i) longitudinally, a person's 'Bildung-career', given by age-specific educational phases of the entire lifespan (infancy and early childhood, pre-school, primary school, secondary school, tertiary school, middle adulthood and advanced adulthood) is plotted against; (ii) horizontally, a variety of functional areas, which may be the subject of enquiry or action (research, counselling, prevention, intervention and controlling); and (iii) vertically, different levels of abstraction and activity (the micro-, meso- and macro- levels), bringing to mind Bronfenbrenners' ecosystemic approach.

Spiel et al. (2008) have outlined the potential for Bildung-Psychology, as an emerging discipline, to be applied within life-long learning (in the contexts of how multinational bodies such as the European Commission and UNESCO conceptualise and use the term), the development of school-based social competence-building programs, and co-operative initiatives with other scientific disciplines.

Implications for Educators

In the course of this chapter we have examined contrasting approaches to cognitive development, two issues within socioemotional development, and two systemic and contextual models of psychological development, as well as seeing an example – through the case study provided – of how systemic developmental thinking can be applied to addressing the problem of non-respectful and violent behaviour in schools. Cognitive development is of importance to educators for a number of reasons. First of all, much of that which is taught in schools relates to the transmission of facts and information, so the way in which children and adolescents become progressively more adept and efficient as thinkers is of interest to educators. Second, it is important to recognise the reality of cognitive limitations in approaching the education of young people – whether one subscribes to a Piagetian-style stage theory or views the child as a limited information processor, the fact remains that what is taught must be at least near age-appropriate in content and methodology if it is to be successfully transmitted. Cognitive psychologists have also taught us about the importance of individual cognitive functions: attention, memory, reasoning, knowledge representation, problem solving and so on. Any one of these could have been selected to exemplify the information processing approach, but memory was chosen as an understanding of how information is encoded, retained and retrieved is of obvious importance when one considers how educational attainment of any kind is generally assessed.

Socioemotional development is a feature of children's and adolescent's lives to which psychologists and educators alike have keenly attended, and indeed, various aspects of it are featured throughout this text, as was acknowledged above. The development of gender role and moral understanding were chosen as illustrations as they are generally held to be developed during middle childhood and adolescence – age groups which members of the intended readership for this text are likely to work with. How students think about these issues, plus the other areas related to socioemotional development discussed elsewhere in the text – selfhood, self-esteem, bullying, prejudice, stress and so on – is of real and obvious importance to any educator with a pastoral element to his or her occupational role. We have brought such considerations into context via the contextual and systemic models of development that have been concluded towards the end of this chapter, which incorporate the multiplicity of factors that can determine a person's educational and overall development. This is something that Piaget failed to consider, but is, of course, of relevance to today's educator.

Please think about, write short notes on, but above all, take the opportunity to discuss with colleagues the following pair of questions:

1 Throughout this chapter, we have examined five different approaches to understanding child development: (a) Jean Piaget's account; (b) the approach of Lev Vygotsky; (c) information processing theory; (d) Bronfenbrenner's ecological model; and (e) the Bildung-Psychology approach. If psychology is strictly a science, as it was argued that it aims to be in Chapter 1, why should a multiplicity of models exist? Why are 'older' models, such as those of Piaget and Vygotsky, considered 'classics' and not merely replaced by newer perspectives, as is usually the case in the physical sciences? Finally, which of the approaches do you find to be most and least: (i) appealing; (ii) convincing; (iii) instructive; and (iv) given your choice of profession, of practical use – what strengths and weaknesses does each of the approaches have?

2 Consider what was said in this chapter regarding the development of gender role understanding. From your general reading, understanding and experience, what do you consider the arguments for gender being biologically determined to be? And what do you consider the arguments for gender being socially determined to be? Which side of this 'nature–nurture' debate would you align yourself more closely to? And what implications exist regarding your choice of 'side' for individuals who are transgendered and inter-gendered? Finally, with your profession of choice in mind, are these important questions? If so, why? If not, why not?

Bee, H. and Boyd, D. (2010) *The Developing Child*, 12th edn. London: Pearson. Many excellent textbooks have been written on child and adolescent development, and I think that such a large resource text is invaluable to teachers both in training and in practice; my pre-service student teachers of child and educational psychology over the last decade have consistently preferred this one.

Gathercole, S.E. and Alloway, T.P. (2009) *Working Memory and Learning: A Practical Guide for Teachers*. London: Sage. A well-written, contemporary evidence-based, yet very practical book for teachers, which amongst other things documents how to identify and support students with poorer working memory.

VISTA (Violence in Schools Training Action) Available at www.vista-europe.org (accessed May 2011). An integrated, systemic online repository of resources, produced by a multi-national team, for 'practitioners and policy-makers and all those working with children and young people affected by violence'. Amongst much else, contains resources relating to the case study referred to in this chapter.

The Self, Self-esteem and Self-esteem Enhancement through Educational Practice

The primary goal for this chapter is to provide the reader with an introduction to the concepts of selfhood and self-esteem, and a working knowledge of how student self-esteem may be enhanced through educational practice. We will examine *the self, psychological models of selfhood*, and how an interested teacher can prepare for *self-esteem work in the school and the classroom*. We will then attend to *defining* and progressing *towards a working model of self-esteem, developmental aspects of self-esteem, family and peer influences on the development of self-esteem, expectancy effects in education, self-esteem and educational attainment* and the 'whole school' approach in *self-esteem enhancement through teaching and educational practice*. This chapter concludes with a reflective examination of some *implications for educators, points for discussion*, a selective and annotated list of *further reading* and a *useful website*.

The Self and Society

In Western society, human beings have a strong sense of themselves as unique, individual entities – separate from other living and non-living things, and separate from their environment. Heavy emphasis is placed on individual achievement; public awareness has always been captured by prominent *individuals* (from the ancient cult of saints, to the elevation of 'great men' of science, art, literature, exploration and the military, to today's media obsession with celebrities). Note that this is *not* the case in many non-western societies. In some tribal societies, the primary unit of survival may be the extended family/kinship group. Systems of belief amongst tribal peoples may stress the interdependence of all (living and sometimes non-living) things, rather than seeing human beings as being the created rulers of other living beings or as the pinnacle of the evolutionary process. However, *all* human beings, regardless of culture, are ultimately social animals – consider how deep our need for social contact is. One of the more fiendish forms of punitive practise is solitary confinement; by extension, life as a hermit would scarcely be a psychologically healthy alternative for most of us. So although we in the West may see ourselves as 'unique, individual entities', and many psychologists have investigated our behaviour and inferred our inner motivations based on such assumptions, we must never lose sight of the fact that there is a strong 'relating-to' aspect to selfhood.

Psychological Models of Selfhood

In the earliest general text on psychology, *Principles of Psychology* (1890), William James posited the idea that self-concept, essentially an 'inner witness', fulfilled the human quality of introspection. In other words, unlike non-human species, human beings can retrospectively examine their past actions, and hypothesise and plan their future actions, and therefore can experience regret, guilt, shame, anticipation and other complex emotions. Throughout the early-twentieth century, 'depth' psychologists such as C.G. Jung (1921) credited the 'self' with an organising or developmental purpose. In these 'depth' approaches, all other structures within the psyche (mind) are at some level connected to the 'self', which facilitates the overall psychological growth of the individual. From the 1930s onwards, many academic psychologists focussed less on describing the 'self' (or indeed, the overall structure of the mind), and more upon the assessment of *personality*. However, from the 1940s and 1950s, there was a resurgence of interest in selfhood from quite a different set of thinkers within psychology – the humanistic school, who often emphasised the *potential* aspects of the self. From this approach, people are motivated in their thinking and behaviour not by what they *are*, but what they *could* (or should) *be*. Human beings are, at base, essentially good; we may be frustrated by other people's expectations of us, our place in the world and so on, but our most basic motivation is that of self-actualisation – becoming everything that one might be (Maslow, 1954, 1968).

Defining and Towards a Working Model of Self-esteem

Arthur S. Reber (1995) defines self-esteem very simply as 'the degree to which one values oneself'. This definition, although appealingly short, does not tell us a great deal about what self-esteem is like. However, before expanding on precisely that over the course of the rest of this chapter, it is of some importance to note in the first place that the study of self-esteem is a new area within both education and the social sciences. Furedi (2004) contends that until recently,

> not only was a lack of self-esteem not perceived as a problem, the term itself had no therapeutic connotations. In the seventeenth century it referred to a sense of independence, self-judgement or self-will. In the eighteenth and nineteenth century its meaning was modified to the act of self-knowledge. Indeed, as late as 1989, the *Oxford English Dictionary* defines it as 'favourable appreciation or opinion of oneself', and makes no link with problems of the emotions. (pp. 2–3)

A Factiva search of 300 British newspapers in 1980 did not find a single reference to the term 'self-esteem', and only three references in 1986. The number of references grew exponentially over the 1990s, being 103 and 3,328 in 1990 and 2000 respectively (Furedi, 2004). Although only recently identified, many psychologists, educators and members of the general public alike these days seem convinced of its importance. Perhaps predictably, a bewildering variety of models of self-esteem have been developed, although none has yet gained universal acceptance. Denis Lawrence (2006), for example, in his excellent *Self-Esteem Enhancement in the Classroom*, gives an umbrella construct of *self-concept*, which in my understanding constitutes our thoughts, ideas and feelings about ourselves (see Figure 3.1).

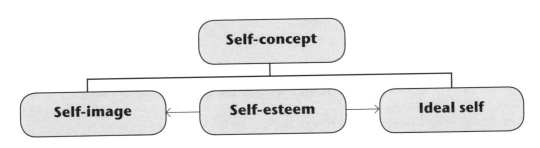

Figure 3.1   Schematic model of Lawrence's (2006) description of self-concept

In this understanding, self-concept is divided into our *self-image* (what we believe ourselves *to* be) and *ideal self* (what we believe – prompted by the ideas, and our internalisation of the ideas, of others – that we *should* be). The gap between the self-image and self-concept equates to *self-esteem*, with the size of that gap being inversely proportional to the 'size' of our self-esteem. In other words, the closer we feel ourselves to be to our own ideal self, the better we will feel about ourselves.

I have found this to be an excellent model, one with which adults (say, in teacher training) can grasp hold of the idea of what self-esteem is for themselves. However, I have found that the notion of the ideal self is not that easily (and is certainly not spontaneously) understood by children and adolescents. I have found that in adolescents, an 'ideal self' is almost invariably projected onto fantasy figures. Even after explaining the terms involved in this model to 12 to 13-year-olds in schools in Ireland, when I have subsequently asked of the students, 'So, what would your own ideal self be like?', I have received the names of soccer players and recording artists many more times than I have heard a reflection on one's own positive attributes and how they may be realistically extended.

This is by no means meant as a criticism of Lawrence; after all, the problem I have been faced with could be due to *my* lack of ability in communicating a proper understanding of his model to young people. The point I would like to make is that it is the understanding of self-esteem that we have as educators that is important to us in our work with young students, and that this understanding can come from *thinking about the matter for ourselves* with regard to what will work at a *practical level* with young people. As we have seen, self-esteem is a new area within both psychology and education; what I have proposed to my education students over the years, and now propose to the reader, is that if there is no universally accepted 'best model', we as educators can at least learn from the indications in constructing our own working models.

An Existential-Analytic Model of Selfhood and Self-esteem

The model of self-esteem I describe in the section below is of my own construction. It stems from a philosophical/psychological area (existential analysis) that I find to be personally satisfying, but *more importantly*, has been extremely helpful *to me* in planning and implementing self-esteem enhancement sessions and programmes with young people in schools, and in my awareness and skills training of others in the general area of self-esteem.

In 1927, a German philosopher by the name of Martin Heidegger published a book entitled *Being and Time*, in which he attempted to describe accurately what a specific type of being, human existence (which he called *Dasein*), was like – literally, what it meant to be human. *Dasein*, according to Heidegger, exists within three dimensions (*Umwelt*, *Mitwelt*, and *Eigenwelt*); as humans, we 'inhabit' three 'worlds' simultaneously. A fourth world, *Überwelt*, has been added by thinkers within this tradition (van Deurzen-Smith, 1988). *Umwelt* is the physical world of being (hence the meaning of this word in modern German, 'environment'). *Mitwelt* (literally, 'with-world'), is the world of everyday social relationships, although not those relationships which convey a deeper sense of personal meaning or identity – these belong to *Eigenwelt*, which corresponds to one's relationship to oneself. *Eigenwelt* comprises our very deepest sense of who and what we are, which lies at the core of our individuality. *Überwelt* (literally, 'above-world'), is composed of our relationship to the Ultimate or Absolute – for believers, our relationship to God(s), or our idea of Him/Her/them, and for atheists, to whatever power we owe to be higher than that of human beings – 'fate', 'destiny' or the scientific laws of our existence.

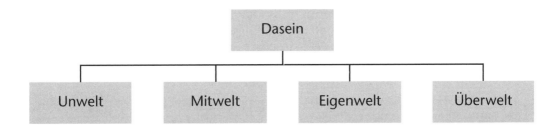

Figure 3.2 Schematic model of Heidegger's (1927) description of *Dasein*

My approach has been to relate the model in Figure 3.2 – based on *Dasein* – to the construct of selfhood, and to our own evaluations of selfhood – self-esteem. Hence, *Dasein* becomes 'self-esteem', with its four 'worlds' (or dimensions) of physical selfhood/self-esteem (equating to *Umwelt*), social selfhood/self-esteem (equating to *Mitwelt*), personal/individual/core selfhood/self-esteem (equating to *Eigenwelt*), and transpersonal/spiritual selfhood/self-esteem (equating to *Überwelt*). This model, though perhaps a little complex in its conception, offers two advantages. In the first place, it provides a loose framework that is helpful in planning the key areas that might be included in (say) a self-esteem enhancement intervention programme.

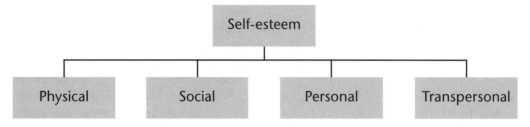

Figure 3.3   A proposed working model of self-esteem (Minton, 2011)

In the second place – and this is a factor that might also be important in planning interventions – it is quite possible that different areas of selfhood and self-esteem are given more or less importance at different points in the lifespan (see Figure 3.3). It is quite likely that in the adolescent phase, physical and social aspects of existence are important in terms of self-esteem. Equally, developmental psychologists (e.g. Erikson, 1963) often hold that late adulthood is a time of concern with one's own personal integrity and mortality (personal selfhood/self-esteem) and that spiritual concerns are more likely to be emphasised (transpersonal selfhood/self-esteem). Individual identity (personal selfhood/self-esteem) is likely to be an issue at both adolescence and mid-life – hence the conflict that sometimes ensues in a household that combines teenagers with their parents at mid-life.

Preparing for Self-Esteem Work in Schools and the Classroom

In many countries, there are curriculum-based ways of working with student self-esteem, but what about the teacher who wishes to work constructively with student self-esteem outside of those curriculum-based subjects – for example, within his or her role as a class/form tutor, year head, guidance counsellor, pastoral care role, or simply through his or her usual subject teaching? Because self-esteem has been such a recent focus in education, one cannot assume at the outset that self-esteem has been focussed upon in every teacher's pre-service training. You could try answering the following question either as a thought exercise or, better still, by discussing it with your colleagues:

1   Think about the teaching colleagues you have at present, or have had in the past. From your conversations with them, would you say that all teachers have equal knowledge of, and place equal value on, holistic/socioemotional aspects of

education in general, and on self-esteem enhancement through teaching practice in particular? Why do you think this is? This question is important, because if you want to work constructively and consistently in your school (in whatever capacity), as with any whole-school issue, it will be immeasurably easier if all staff members are on at least a partially even footing. Now, try the following exercise (again, as a thought exercise, or better still, as a discussion):

2   Imagine you were a teacher who was trying to convince his or her colleagues about the benefits of working constructively with self-esteem in schools. Work out ways in which you could brief your peers on:

- What self-esteem is, and why it is important.
- How a teacher could become aware of a student with low self-esteem.
- Provide a rationale for this sort of work to be done in schools.

What sort of arguments might you expect from an unconvinced audience, and what sort of counter-arguments might you make? Please make a note of these.

Developmental Aspects of Selfhood and Self-Esteem

Let us now return to *selfhood* for a moment, and ask ourselves at what point, *developmentally*, do human beings become self-aware – that is, when our sense of self or self-concept forms. One simple and replicable laboratory test indicates that this occurs in human infants at around 15 months old. What is involved is the reaction of infants to their own reflections in a mirror. Younger infants apparently see 'a baby-in-the-mirror', whereas older infants see themselves. In order to demonstrate this, a baby is first placed in front of the mirror, where he or she will show interest in the mirror image of himself or herself. Then, a change is made to the baby's appearance – in the classic set-up, a spot of rouge or lipstick is applied to the baby's forehead. Lewis and Brooks-Gunn (1979, in Fogel and Melson, 1988) reported that babies under 15 months touch the spot on their *mirror image*, whereas babies of 15 months and older touch their *own foreheads*. So it can be said that human beings typically recognise themselves as unique physical entities in infancy.

However, recognising oneself is only the beginning of self-concept formation. Some research has focussed around *self-descriptions* – very simply, a person is asked to describe himself or herself. What one notices is that in the early years, children describe themselves in physical ways, and that their descriptions are brief. Adults describe themselves in terms of psychological characteristics, career or social role, and interpersonal relationships. Our social world expands as we get older, and this, combined with our increased understanding of ourselves and others, leads to an increasingly sophisticated and broadened self-concept over time; this in turn is reflected in how we describe ourselves (Fogel and Melson, 1988).

Selfhood and Self-Esteem in Childhood and Adolescence

Please try the following as a group discussion exercise with your colleagues – it is easy and fun to do. If you don't have the opportunity to do this, it will also work as a thought exercise.

First of all, group members should mentally take themselves back to early childhood (2–6 years), and then ask themselves:

- Where did you live, and who did you live with?
- Who were the people in your first school class? Who were your friends amongst them? How did you become friends with them? Where are they now?

Write a self-description in the way you would have done at 5 years old.

Then, go back to middle childhood (6–12 years):

- Who were your friends? How did you become friends with them? What sort of things did you do with your friends?
- Did your parents/guardians like your friends, and why?

Write a self-description in the way you would have done at 10 years old.

Then, back to mid-adolescence (15–16 years):

- Write down a typical day in your life.
- What were your hobbies and interests? What type of clothes did you like to wear? What was your favourite music?
- What sort of things did you do with your friends?
- Who influenced you most – your friends, or your parents? Why?
- Did your parents/guardians like your friends, and why?

Write a self-description in the way you would have done at 15 years old.

Group members should discuss their answers, and the relative influence and importance of friends/peers and parents/family members, at the three pre-adult phases outlined above. Did any common themes emerge? Please keep these in mind as you read the text below.

Family and Peer Influences on the Development of Self-esteem

Self-esteem is built in people from *early childhood*, and is associated with what is called 'positive parenting' (Canadian Mental Health Association, 2011). Positive (or self-esteem-building) parenting includes *showing love and respect* for the young person through verbal and non-verbal demonstrations of appropriate *affection and encouragement*, and ensuring that a *sense of security* for the young person is provided in the home, and that he or she is not subjected to neglect nor any form of abuse. It also involves setting *firm boundaries and rules* for the young person. These limits should be negotiable within the limits of what is in the young person's own best interests, rather than what the young person decides he or she feels like doing at any given time. The young person should *be involved in day-to-day decisions*, but *not overloaded* with responsibility inappropriate to either his or her age or family role, and *realistic expectations* should be set. A young person should be *praised* when he or she does something well; however, that praise should be genuine, and appropriate to the amount of effort the young person has made, and never 'over-the-top' or effusive.

Empirical evidence exists to point to the fact that these specific types of parenting are associated with positive self-esteem. In an extensive study, Stanley Coopersmith (1967) measured boys' self-esteem, and interviewed their mothers about their family relationships. Essentially, the following attributes were associated with the boys' high self-esteem: expression of affection; concern about the boys' problems; harmony in the home; participation in joint family activities; availability to give competent, organised help to the boys when they needed it; setting clear and fair rules, and abiding by them; and allowing the boys freedom within well-prescribed limits (Coopersmith, 1967, in Santrock, 1996).

As children become older, and enter the developmental period of *adolescence*, the influence of peer relationships becomes more apparent. Indeed, although parenting support was the most important factor in children and early adolescents, Susan Harter (1987) found that in late adolescence, peer support was more important in terms of self-esteem than was parental support; furthermore, general popularity, or 'classmate support', was more important than was 'close friend support'. Santrock (1996) interprets this finding thus: 'as close friends provide considerable support, it may be that their regard is not perceived as [self-esteem] enhancing; rather, the adolescent may need to turn to somewhat more objective sources of support in order to validate his or her self-esteem' (p. 328). One's perception of one's physical appearance also seems to be an important factor – recent studies in the United States and Australia indicates that satisfaction with one's body or otherwise is closely related to adolescent self-esteem, in boys and girls of all ethnic and socioeconomic backgrounds (Mellor et al., 2010; van den Berg et al., 2010). Furthermore, appearance appraisal was the chief predictor of self-esteem in a sample of 656 elementary and middle school girls in the United States (Kutob et al., 2010). Additionally, low self-esteem individuals tend to underestimate their acceptance by potential romantic partners (Cameron et al., 2010).

So as we have seen, selfhood and self-esteem have a large 'relating-to' or social component – in other words, what others think about us, and how they interact with, relate to and treat us, has large influence on how we come to see and feel about ourselves. Other people's pre-judgements of what we, or 'people like us' might be like or do, depending on the social power and position of the other, potentially influences our self-perceptions. Social scientists call these *expectancy effects*. Human beings have tendency to *label* others, and what sometimes results from labelling is a *self-fulfilling prophecy*; essentially, a person fulfils the behaviour we expect them to exhibit. If this behaviour is desirable, we call this a positive expectancy effect; if the behaviour is undesirable, then it is a negative expectancy effect.

A famous demonstration of a positive expectancy effect (called *Pygmalion in the Classroom*) occurred when teachers at an elementary school in California were told that a named 20 per cent of the children within their classes could be expected to show rapid intellectual growth (Rosenthal and Jacobsen, 1968). IQ tests before and after the school year showed that this intellectual growth did in fact occur. However, this was a study that involved the deception of the teachers; the students who were named as being likely to show rapid intellectual growth had in fact been selected at random. Although the experimenters did not observe what happened in the classroom, they speculated that the teachers' manner, facial expressions, posture, degree of friendliness and encouragement (Haralambos, 1989) communicated a belief that these students would do well, and a self-fulfilling prophecy was thereby set up. They therefore concluded that teachers' expectations can significantly affect their students' performance.

Expectancy Effects in Education

Of course, the existence of expectancy effects in education can also be grasped experientially. Try thinking about the following:

- As a child at school yourself, were you subject to any expectancy effects? If so, what do you think these were based upon? Your social background? Physical aspects of yourself? Your siblings or family?
- As an educator, have you ever found yourself to be operating under expectancy effects?
- Think about the case of a child whose older sibling has attended a school before him or her. Is such a child sometimes expected to have similar characteristics to his or her sibling? Has the first exhibition of disruptive behaviour by a younger brother ever been met by his teacher with the thought, 'Oh, he's probably going to be as difficult as his brother was last year'?

Please note that expectancy effects, whilst they are undesirable and should be countered in a mindful teacher, are quite natural!

Self-esteem and Educational Attainment

It has been suggested that the self-image that a child develops will influence his or her investment of time and effort; consequently, those who see themselves as bad students are less likely to focus on their school work (Darling-Hammond and Bransford, 2005). However, empirical research into this area is by no means conclusive. Wang et al. (1999), in a study of 1,927 respondents, found that self-esteem and a range of other measures (parental education level, parental occupation and locus of control) significantly affect educational and occupational attainments. However, an early study by Bachman and O'Malley (1977) provided an analysis of the relationships between self-esteem, educational attainment and occupational status in a longitudinal study of more than 1,600 American young men. It was found that self-esteem during high school has little influence on later educational and occupational attainment, and that self-esteem and attainment are correlated primarily because of shared prior causes, including family background, ability and scholastic performance.

A more recent longitudinal study undertaken in Britain (Flouri, 2006), involving a sample of 1,737 men and 2,033 women born in 1970, showed that whilst internal locus of control and mother's interest in education were significantly related to educational attainment in both men and women at age 26 years, self-esteem (measured at age 10 years) was not. It has also been suggested (e.g. Baumeister et al., 2003) that the relationship involving self-esteem and educational attainment may be one of achieving high self-esteem through educational attainment, rather than the other way around.

This being said, it should of course be recalled that although an important focus, promoting scholastic attainment is just one of the functions of a modern school, and that student self-esteem has an important influence on other issues in school life – for example, involvement in bullying behaviour (Gendron et al., 2011; O'Moore and Kirkham, 2001; see also this book, Chapter 7). O'Moore and Kirkham (2001) recommended that priority should be given by parents and teachers to preventing and reducing feelings of poor self-worth among children and adolescents; Ruth (2006) argued that this could be achieved by teachers showing encouragement, respect, support, empathy, and through their having high expectations of their students. With the increasing emphasis being placed on holistic education, teacher attention to self-esteem looks set to maintain its value.

Self-esteem Enhancement through Teaching and Educational Practice

In day-to-day subject teaching, teaching styles that promote the enhancement of self-esteem include motivating student through the use of appropriate rules and choices, and realistic goal-setting, task-analysis and evaluation (Irish National Teachers' Organisation, 1995). As educators, we have many opportunities to work constructively with student self-esteem within our roles. However, if we are to be effective in this, we must first start with ourselves – to think about our own training, and what it has equipped us with (i.e. knowledge and skills) regarding pastoral care work. What are the boundaries of that training? Which issues would we be comfortable in discussing with young people? Then, we can think about the group of students we would like to work with, its age and gender composition, and the context within which we see this group. This will determine how much time can be devoted to self-esteem enhancement tasks, and influences what can be accomplished. We can then assess what we perceive the specific needs of this group to be, and specify some areas of focus and methodologies. I have found that a combination of creative and discursive activities is best. We must be reasonable about what can be achieved, considering also literacy, motivation and the social skills of the group members.

I would contend that the most effective framework in which to ground one's efforts to raise the self-esteem of students within the classroom is the 'whole-school' approach. In a nutshell, this approach involves conducting needs assessments and designing, implementing and evaluating consequent intervention strategies with all interest groups (or at all 'levels') within the school community. At its most simple, one works simultaneously with (i) the school management representatives (usually on matters of policy); (ii) all teaching and non-teaching staff (usually on matters of day-to-day practise); (iii) parents (usually as a consultative and interest group); and (iv) students (usually within the classroom context, but students' councils and extra-curricular activities which represent students' interests are also extremely valuable opportunities to shape attitudes and even behaviour). There is certainly a common-sense appeal to the rationale for such a manner of working; for example, there would be little point in (say) one teacher in a secondary school exploring issues of personal development in an affirming way with his or her students, if the next class the students walked into was being held by a teacher who relied heavily on negativistic and punitive discipline in the classroom.

Likewise, even if all the teachers in a school were equally committed to and active in self-esteem enhancement classroom work, such combined efforts might have a more limited effect if the school management did not support the teachers' efforts (perhaps through under-resourcing, or management policy and teacher practice being at odds) or if the parents of the students were either unaware or disapproving of self-esteem enhancement work being undertaken in the school. We can see how such a 'whole school' measure was achieved in the case study that follows immediately below.

The 'Pathways through Education' Project (Republic of Ireland)

The 'Pathways through Education' project (1998 to 2010) was a programme that ran under the Community Links division of Dublin Institute of Technology, under the direction of Dr Tommy Cooke. Its principal aim was to reduce early school leaving, via enhancing the self-esteem, confidence and motivation of students in at first three (1998–2000), and then later two (2000–2010) inner-city schools (Coyle, 2000; Craig, 2000; Minton, 2001; Uhleman, 2000). The core issues of concern for the programme included the development of a whole-school approach towards these aims, the retention of students in secondary education, and utilising a range of interventions (psychologically-based, and preventative in nature) including classroom interventions, work with staff and work with parents (Uhleman, 2000). For its first two years of operation, 'Pathways through Education' was funded by the European Union Youthstart initiative, a requirement of which was that 'Pathways' developed and maintained transnational partnerships with programmes with similar aims in other countries (in this case, in Finland, Sweden and the UK) (Uhleman, 2000). A further requirement for 'Youthstart' funding was that of an external assessment of the programme, using quantitative indicators. Participation in 'Pathways' was associated with greater than average attendance and a lower than average number of discipline offences (Craig, 2000). Qualitative measures, taken over the duration of the project (e.g. Craig, 2000; Minton, 2001), indicated an extremely favourable response from participating students towards the project; this was also reflected in teachers', principals' and parents' evaluations (Craig, 2000; Minton, 2001). From 2000 until 2010, a direct contribution to the funding of the project was made by the participating schools themselves.

As well as work with students (which always included a double-period each week with first-year students, and a variety of contact types with other school years), work with school management staff on school policy, teachers and parents was undertaken. The work with first-year students involved class-specific whole class sessions, facilitated by intervention teams comprising project psychologists and class teachers. The project also facilitated magazine and film production and various other events, as well as work with mentoring and perfecting programmes. Teachers could attend a 10-week training programme, for which ECTS credits were awarded. Project teams also facilitated in-service training sessions for school staff and evening presentations and meetings for parents. Thus, a 'whole-school' programme design and implementation strategy was consistently maintained – it was deemed extremely important to give students a consistent message regarding self-esteem, confidence and motivation, and to embed such ideals within an overall improvement of school ethos (Charles and McHugh, 2000).

Implications for Educators

As we have seen in this chapter, although the 'self' has been studied and conceptualised by psychologists in a variety of ways for over 100 years, the concept of self-esteem, although these days frequently used in both psychological and educational circles, has a much shorter history. An artefact of this short history, of course, is that there are, as yet, no widely-accepted best models of nor universal definitions of self-esteem. Nor has there been time for an extensive empirically-based research literature to be developed on self-esteem in either the educational or psychological literature. Whereas resources abound in the field, few of these draw on a reliable evidence basis, but more on the experience and intuition of their practitioner-authors. As this book seeks to demonstrate to the reader the use of *scientific* psychology in the classroom – which, unlike *popular* psychology, draws its models from an evidence basis – such resources have been omitted from this chapter. The reader has been asked to think through and to develop and improve his or her own practice from first principles and the resources that have been provided here.

I believe that the 'thinking-through' focus I have taken here is important, because although the literature shows that although the link between self-esteem and educational attainment is unclear (as we have seen, some studies show high student self-esteem predicting success, others that the two are not linked, and others that the causal relationship may be the reverse), it is no accident that student self-esteem has arisen as a prominent issue in education at this point in time. As we have seen, student self-esteem is seen in self-development, parenting and family relationships, the examination of expectancy effects, involvement in bullying behaviour – all of which have long (or reasonably lengthy) research histories in both the psychological and educational literature, and all of which are important issues for schools with a holistic, 'whole-child' or 'whole-school'/'school community' ethos. As teachers and schools move from the inward-looking, authoritarian and now-outmoded 'purely instructional' ethos common to some education systems in the past, self-esteem provides a handy focus in working with the healthy psychoeducational development of young people in society. It is necessary for us *all* to 'think through' such positions, given that their importance is such that 'short-cuts' through this process are undesirable.

Please think about, write short notes on, but above all, take the opportunity to discuss with colleagues the following pair of questions:

1   Reflect on the answer you gave to the question in the 'To Think About' activity above concerning whether all teachers have equal knowledge of and place equal value on holistic/socioemotional aspects of education in general, and why. What did you find? Were the differences down to age? Any other demographic factors? Experience? Personality? The point in time at which one conducted one's pre-service education? One's subsequent investment in in-service education? School culture? For whatever you have found, try to construct explanations. Think out also the implications for this regarding school planning in general.

2 In this chapter, we have focussed entirely on student self-esteem, rather than teacher self-esteem (which shall be incorporated into subsequent chapters, especially Chapter 9). For now, though, what do you think the relationships between teacher self-esteem and student self-esteem/student educational attainment are likely to be?

Furedi, F. (2004) *Therapy Culture: Cultivating Vulnerability in an Uncertain Age.* London: Routledge. A critical look at the impact of our growing awareness of self-esteem and related issues through the recent development of 'therapy culture'.

Lawrence, D. (2006) *Enhancing Self-Esteem in the Classroom,* 3rd edn. London: Sage. A clearly-written guide for the teacher on how to enhance self-esteem through classroom and school practice, including lesson plans and other practical tips.

Reber, A.S., Allen, R. and Reber, E.S. (2009) *The Penguin Dictionary of Psychology,* 4th revised edn. Harmondsworth: Penguin. A great jargon-busting tool for anyone who finds the technical language used by many psychologists to be a challenge.

Community Links Programme. Dublin Institute of Technology. Available at http://communitylinks.ie (accessed February 2011). For anyone who wishes to read more about the section, and ethos, that developed the 'Pathways through Education' programme referred to in the case study in this chapter.

4

Intelligence, Learning Styles and Educational Attainment

The primary goal for this chapter is to provide the reader with an introduction to, and an applied psychological knowledge of, the inter-connected areas of intelligence, learning styles and educational attainment. We will examine *traditional views of intelligence*, *intelligence testing*, and the debate as to whether intelligence (as measured by IQ tests) is more influenced by biological/genetic factors or learning/environmental factors – the so-called *nature versus nurture debate*, which has been a controversial and often bitter argument in psychology and in education. We will also examine the idea of *multiple intelligences*, the relationship between *intelligence and educational attainment*, emotional *intelligence*, and one of a number of possible models of *learning styles* – all in order to underline the fact that we do not, despite what many systems of education/instruction assume, all learn in the same way. This chapter concludes with a reflective examination of some *implications for educators*, *questions for discussion*, and a selective and annotated list of *further reading*.

Traditional Views of Intelligence

So what does it mean, to be 'intelligent'? Emotionally speaking, it seems to mean a great deal. Consider, for example, that many mental characteristics are, according to at least some psychologists, measurable – everything from short-term memory capacity, to aspects of personality and, of course, intelligence. Following participation in psychological research, if I found that I had scored within the 'below average' range for the general population in terms of my short-term memory capacity, I would not be overly disturbed; likewise, if I scored 'below average' on a personality measure such as (say) impulsiveness, I would not lose a great deal of sleep. But what if I scored 'below average' on an intelligence test? Well, that would seem to be a different matter entirely!

Although there has never been a universally-accepted definition of intelligence, the study of intelligence, and the development of intelligence testing, has a relatively lengthy history within the disciplines of psychology and education. The first person to study human abilities in a systematic way was Francis Galton (1822–1911), an Englishman and a half-cousin of Charles Darwin, who wrote a book called *Hereditary Genius* (1869), in which he traced the genealogy of eminent men in a number of different fields. Galton argued that 'genius' did indeed seem to run in families. Galton is also well-known as being the first to coin the phrase *eugenics*; his argument, in his 1883 *Inquiries into Human Faculty and its Development*, was that at the time, individuals in many so-called 'high-ranking' families married late, and consequently had fewer children than did so-called 'low-ranking' individuals. He went on to advocate that incentives should exist for eminent people who were willing to curb this trend; his own marriage, however, produced no children (Bulmer, 2003; Forrest, 1974). There are, of course, profound social implications that emerge from the application of eugenic thinking to human populations. Although our everyday experience as people, and professional experience as educators, teaches us that people have strengths and weaknesses in different academic areas, Galton's picture of 'genius' or 'intelligence' being a single, all-round, hereditary ability remained mostly unchallenged for around 100 years.

Intelligence Testing

Galton was himself a capable statistician and an enthusiastic tester of human abilities, and combined the two in the development of the first mental tests (Bulmer, 2003; Forrest, 1974). But the physical design of modern-day intelligence tests was influenced rather more by another pioneer in the field – a Frenchman, Alfred Binet (1857–1911), who, along with a medical student collaborator named Theodore Simon, developed tests of intelligence between 1908 and 1911. Like many intelligence tests in use today, Binet and Simon's tests consisted of written assessments based on lists of progressively more difficult tasks of mental reasoning. In 1916, Lewis Therman, of Stanford University in California, took up Binet's tests and advocated that an individual's score be given as his or her 'intelligence quotient' (IQ). This is why ever since written IQ tests based on verbal items have been known as Stanford-Binet tests (Gould, 1997; Jensen, 1980).

Generations of psychologists and statisticians have been involved in the development and standardisation of intelligence tests (see Herrnstein and Murray, 1996). The range of IQ scores in the general population follows what is known as a 'normal distribution', with the average IQ being 100 points, and most people (around 68 per cent) falling within one standard deviation of either side of the mean (i.e. 85–115 points) (Gleitman, 2010). Mensa, the high-IQ society, requires of its members that they achieve an IQ score at or above the 98th percentile on a standard test of intelligence test (Mensa International, 2010). This is around 132 points or higher on most Stanford-Binet tests.

Is Intelligence 'in the Genes'? The 'Nature versus Nurture' Debate

A further point of controversy (in a field that has always been controversial – see, for example, Steven Jay Gould's *The Mismeasure of Man* (1997)) came about during the late 1960s, when the American researcher Arthur Robert Jensen (born 1923) published data indicating that the mean IQ amongst the African-American population was one standard deviation (in this case, 15 IQ points) lower than that which existed amongst the white American population (Biesheuvel, 2002; see also Jensen, 1969, 1980). Furthermore, Jensen (1969) advised that funding for summer educational programmes for African-American children (e.g. Project 'Head Start') should be withdrawn (see also Gould, 1997; Montagu, 2002), an argument based on what Galton (1883) had referred to as 'statistical regression towards the mean'. Essentially, this holds that as intelligence is genetically determined, the effects of environmental influences (such as additional education) are minimal, and therefore things like IQ cannot be boosted. And all of this during the period when African-Americans were lobbying for their civil rights (including the desegregation of schooling).

Jensen's critics, of whom there have been many, have often accused him of advancing a biologically-deterministic racist attitude – that is, claiming that African-Americans were *genetically* inferior in terms of intelligence. This is something that Jensen (1981) has denied himself:

Nowhere have I 'claimed' an 'innate deficiency' of intelligence in blacks. My position on this question is clearly spelled out in my most recent book: 'The plain fact is that at present there exists no scientifically satisfactory explanation for the differences between the IQ distributions in the black and white populations. The only genuine consensus among well-informed scientists on this topic is that the cause of the difference remains an open question'. (p. 213)

However, for the record, despite his work being subjected to sustained academic and sociopolitical scrutiny (see Eysenck and Kamin, 1981; Gould, 1997; Montagu, 2002), Jensen has never changed his mind about either racial differences in intelligence or the heritability of intelligence (see Jensen, 1980, 1981, 1998, and especially Rushton and Jensen, 2005). Jensen's critics have argued that the score one attains on an IQ test is directly related to what sort of *environment* a person grows up and lives in. Gould (1997) asserted that Jensen undertook at least some of his initial testing in areas of the country where racially segregated schools were still the norm. In such situations, on just about any educational or social measure one cares to name, African-Americans were severely disadvantaged compared to whites. Furthermore, Gould (1997) argued that African-Americans tested in racially-integrated schools then, and since, generally show similar mean IQs to whites; thus, what Jensen's findings actually supported was the effects of institutionalised racism (see also Biesheuvel, 2002).

Partly as a result of the wealth of 'environmentally' or 'nuture'-based responses to what is perceived as Jensen's (and others') genetically-deterministic position (Gould, 1997; Montagu, 2002), the *balance* of research conducted on intelligence to date seems to point to a *diathetic* position – where a genetic propensity towards intelligence may or may not be brought out by a person's learning environment. Of course, exactly how much genetics contributes to one's intelligence, and how much is contributed by one's environment – the so-called 'nature-nurture' balance – is still unresolved, and, it seems, despite the heated arguments in the past (see Eysenck and Kamin, 1981), likely to remain so. It is to be recalled that, in assessing this debate, the greater the contribution that 'nurture' – or the 'environment' – can be said to make towards intelligence, the greater is the influence that teachers and educations systems can exert on developing young people's mental abilities.

The Nature of Intelligence

1 Think about your own school attainment as a student, and in particular, your preparation for the end-of-school examinations, the results of which may have determined your career entry or university entrance.

- Were there subjects in which you excelled – did this determine your subject option choices? Please write down these, your intellectual 'strong' subjects.
- Were there subjects in which you were weaker – did you manage to avoid these in your subject option choices, or were these the examinations that you dreaded if you were waiting for an aggregate set of grades? Please write down these, your intellectual 'weak' subjects.
- Have any of these 'strong' and 'weak' subjects changed in your adult life, through different levels of motivation and learning/occupational experiences you may have had after your school days? Please make a note of any changes you have observed.
- Why should any of this be true if intelligence really is a single, all-round hereditary ability?

2 Galton's version of eugenics has since become known, rather charitably, as 'positive eugenics' – the 'breeding' *for* 'desirable' characteristics. However, it was only a matter of time before 'negative eugenics' – the breeding *out* of 'undesirable' characteristics – was developed and applied to human populations with obvious and dreadful consequences. This idea perhaps reached its extreme in the race laws and concentration camps of the Third Reich.

- Think of other examples of where negative eugenics has been applied in human history. Think about, and discuss with others if you can, what these 'obvious and dreadful consequences' were.
- Is the social practice of negative eugenics really the result of a scientific idea, or does it reveal something deeper and darker about human nature, which perhaps clothes itself in supposedly 'scientific' justifications? Again, think about, and discuss with others if you can, any other examples you can find of the social consequences of the abuse of scientific and pseudo-scientific theories.

Readers in Great Britain, and those in Northern Ireland, may be interested to read about the case of Sir Cyril Burt (1883–1971), a former President of the British Psychological Society, honorary President of Mensa, and the first British psychologist to be knighted (1946). Like Galton, Burt was both a keen proponent of the 'genetic', or 'nature', position in the intelligence debate (see, for example, Burt, 1945, 1958) and a eugenicist (Mackintosh, 1995). From the 1930s to the1950s, he was also one of Britain's foremost educational psychologists, and acted as a consultant to the committees that developed the Eleven Plus examinations (Burt, 1959). In the United Kingdom, from 1944, the Eleven Plus examination, which was taken in the final year of one's primary education, determined one's entry (or, for around 80 per cent of people, otherwise) to grammar schools (which prepared one for university entrance, and therefore access to the professions). After Burt's death, it became evident that some of the twin studies data that he had published was fraudulent, and there remain questions concerning the very existence of two of his named research assistants. With the development of comprehensive schools in Great Britain, the Eleven Plus examination was phased out in most areas from the early 1970s; however, the system was retained in Northern Ireland. The abolition of the Eleven Plus examination there continues to face opposition from certain politicians, parents and grammar schools. The discontinuation of transfer to secondary schools on the basis of academic selection in Northern Ireland was originally planned for 2008; 2013 is now the intended date (BBC News, 2008). The 'Burt affair' is reported in Gould (1997), and at greater length, following a more extensive period of debate, in Mackintosh (1995).

Multiple Intelligences

The idea that there might be more than one type of intelligence actually made an early, but not a massively influential appearance in the psychological literature. As early as the 1930s, an eminent American psychologist and psychometrician named Louis Leon Thurstone (1887–1955) argued that general intelligence comprised seven sub-components, which he called 'primary mental abilities' (Thurstone, 1938). From the 1940s onwards, under the influence of the Romanian-born American, David Wechsler (1896–1981), who developed intelligence tests for both children and adults (see Frank, 1983; Wechsler, 1939), intelligence came to be split into two broad factors: verbal and 'performance' (non-verbal) intelligence. The Wechsler Adult Intelligence Scale (WAIS) (Wechsler, 1939) is the most commonly used psychological test today (Kaplan and Sacuzzo, 2008). Another dichotomy that was suggested in the 1960s by the British psychologist and psychometrician Raymond Cattell (1905–1908) was the difference between 'fluid' (the ability to grasp and acquire new ideas) and 'crystallised' (knowledge, and the ability to access this) intelligence (Horn and Cattell, 1966). However, at the practical level, these sub-components were summed at the end of tests to give a general intelligence score.

A very different approach came to light in the mid-1980s, when Howard Gardner published work on *multiple intelligences* (see Gardner, 1999, 2011). Gardner describes no fewer than eight intelligences, of which, as Davis (2000) notes, only the first two are focussed upon in many education systems:

> *Verbal-linguistic* (sounds, rhythms and word meanings)
> *Logical-mathematical* (logical or numerical patterns and chains of reasoning)
> *Musical* (rhythm, pitch, timbre and musical expressiveness)
> *Bodily-kinaesthetic* (the control of body movements and the skilful handling of objects)
> *Spatial* (to accurately perceive and represent the spatial world)
> *Naturalistic* (to recognise living things and to make distinctions about the natural world)
> *Interpersonal* (to discern and respond accurately to the feelings and motivations of other people)
> *Intrapersonal* (to be aware of, and to be able to access one's own feelings, and to use them to guide behaviour)

Considerable attention (at least, in the United States) has been given to the idea of multiple intelligences, particularly by educationalists who would more or less accept Gardner's and Davis' concerns that the existent system only teaches and rewards the first two intelligences (verbal-linguistic and logical-mathematical). The process of translating these ideas into practical classroom use is perhaps less developed in Europe (although see Department for Education and Skills, 2010; Hyland, 2000), but is very actively pursued in certain parts of the United States (see Davis, 2000; Gardner, 1999, 2011; Lazear, 2005).

Implications of Multiple Intelligences

Consider the eight different multiple intelligences outlined above. For as many of them as you can, think of a) a well-known individual, b) a culture, and c) an individual known to you personally in which that particular intelligence would seem to be well-developed. Try to do this for as many of the intelligences as you can – this is an excellent exercise to undertake as a discussion, so please try this if you have an opportunity to do so.

Finally, spend some time thinking about, and discussing if you have the opportunity to do so, the implications of multiple intelligences for the way in which we, as individuals and a society, educate young people.

Intelligence and Educational Attainment

So after all of this, is intelligence (and IQ) a *meaningful* construct? The short answer is that IQ does indeed seem to predict, or at least be positively correlated with, educational attainment. Deary (2004) reports on a study of 20,000 students in British secondary schools, who were tested for IQ at 11 years of age, which was correlated with their educational attainment (measured by their GCSE results) at 16 years of age. The correlation was positive, giving a co-efficient of 0.74. Lynn and Mikk (2007) cite Luo et al.'s (2003) account of there being three theories to explain the association between intelligence and educational attainment. These are (i) a 'nature'-based argument, that general intelligence 'appears to be more biologically rooted than school achievement' (Jensen, 1998, p.68); (ii) a 'nurture'-based argument, that intellectual abilities are partly a product of education; and (iii) their own position, that intelligence and school performance are both partly determined by 'basic cognitive processes, which are measured using tasks such as simple reaction time, inspection time, and memory recall and recognition tasks' (Luo et al., 2003, p. 67). Whatever the underlying causes, the association between intelligence and educational attainment does seem to be consistent – the study reported by Deary (2004) above is the largest of nine similar cross-national studies cited by Lynn and Mikk (2007), in which it was found that intelligence is associated with educational attainment at a correlation of between 0.45 and 0.74.

However, it should be noted that this correlation is strong, but not perfect. Why is this? Well, scholastic attainment is about much more than native 'brightness'; it is also about *motivation, aptitude* and the *economic and social circumstances* one is born into and lives within. Einstein, the prototypical genius, had an estimated IQ within the 160s (Sears, 1986). However, surely the sheer hard work he put in (his background was certainly not one of privilege) had an influence in his production of the three papers in 1905 that changed the world of theoretical physics forever. It is also worth remembering that Einstein's physics has all but replaced Newtonian physics, the work of a man whose IQ has been estimated to be 30 points higher (Sears, 1986) than Einstein's. Hence, IQ may well exert an influence upon educational attainment, but so too do individual psychological factors such as motivation, self-belief, working hard towards personal goals and (as we have seen in Chapter 3) possibly self-esteem. In terms of the latter, Carol Dweck (1999) notes that as well as resulting in healthier relationships with peers, children with high self-esteem are also better equipped to cope with mistakes and disappointments; therefore, they are more likely to continue with challenging tasks and to complete learning activities.

IQ and Success (United States and the World)

In one of the most famous case studies in the history of child psychology, Virginia M. Axline (1964) described her treatment of a 5-year-old boy called 'Dibs', who was so emotionally withdrawn that no-one knew whether he was mentally ill, brain-damaged or had what might now be referred to as severe learning difficulties. Dibs rarely spoke; he isolated himself, and he routinely exhibited abnormal and aggressive social behaviour. Dibs came from a materially very well-off, but seemingly emotionally impoverished family background. Dibs' parents (his father was a scientist and his mother had been a surgeon) thought him to be 'mentally defective'; his case was a 'tragedy' they had accepted, and they allowed Axline to treat Dibs not in the expectation of success, but in order to facilitate her 'advancing the understanding of human behaviour'. The book, *Dibs: In Search of Self*, documents Axline's treatment (largely by 'play therapy', of which she was an early pioneer (Axline, 1947)); how Dibs tentatively built a warm relationship with Axline, and came to express himself; how Dibs' personality came to unfold during the sessions, and how his behaviour became more expressive and normalised.

A week after the play therapy sessions ended, a Stanford-Binet intelligence test undertaken by Dibs' revealed an IQ score of 168. Dibs' reading scores at this point were well beyond his age level. In Axline's words, he had 'learned how to be himself, to believe in himself, to free himself. Now he was relaxed and happy. He was able to be a child' (p. 214); he was 'an exceptionally gifted child who was using his intellectual capacities effectively' (p. 219). We last hear of Dibs at the age of 15, defending the honour of his co-student at a school for gifted children who had been unfairly accused of cheating, and described by one of his teachers as 'a brilliant boy. Full of ideas. Concerned about everybody and everything . . . A real leader' (p. 218). Many people (including the present author!) are curious as to what happened to Dibs in later life; however, in the following years, Axline herself lost touch with Dibs' family, and died in 1988.

There are number of sites on the Internet which document the IQ scores (actual, or sometimes estimated) of famous people (one of these is referred to in the section on 'Useful Websites', below). For a bit of fun, you might like to try compiling lists of famous people and their IQs from these sites, and then have your friends, colleagues or even your students (if they are old enough to understand the exercise) match names to IQ scores. Those 'guessing' should be reminded that an average IQ is 100 points; that most people fall between 85 and 115; that 'superior' is from 115 to 130, and 'very superior' is above 130; and that the two per cent of people who are eligible for membership of Mensa, the high-IQ society, have IQ scores of 132 points and above. Once they have finished this exercise, they should take some time to think and reflect. How accurate were they? Were you or they surprised by the results? Taking these individuals in mind, does IQ seem to predict success or not? Also, think – are appearances ever deceptive? Think back to what was said in the previous chapter about expectancy effects and labelling theory.

Emotional Intelligence

Since the mid-1990s, American psychologist Daniel Goleman has been working with the concept of emotional intelligence (Goleman, 1998). As he conceives of it, emotional intelligence is a set of abilities, or skills/competencies that influence the performance of leaders (hence, the model is widely applied in business). The model specifies four main constructs, which are not innate, but must be learnt and consciously developed (Goleman, 1998):

> *Self-awareness* (the ability to read *one's own* emotions and to recognise their impact)
> *Self-management* (controlling one's emotions and impulses, and adapting them in accordance with different situations)
> *Social awareness* (the ability to sense, understand, and react to *others'* emotions, whilst understanding group and social dynamics)
> *Relationship management* (the ability to inspire, influence and develop others, whilst managing conflict)

Goleman (1998) asserts that 'the most effective leaders are alike in one crucial way: they all have a high degree of what has come to be known as emotional intelligence.'

As well as its applications in business, Goleman's work on emotional intelligence, alongside that of Gardner's work on multiple intelligences, has been very influential in informing the development of SEAL (Social and Emotional Aspects of Learning) activities in the UK schools context (Department for Education and Skills, 2010). Some have dismissed Goleman's model as being mere 'popular psychology', and others (e.g. Brody, 2004; Eysenck, 1998; Locke, 2005; Roberts et al., 2001; Schulte et al., 2004) would argue that emotional intelligence is not, in fact, a type of intelligence, at least in as far as the concept of intelligence has traditionally been understood. As Eysenck, in his characteristically strongly-worded style, put it:

[Goleman] exemplifies more clearly than most the fundamental absurdity of the tendency to class almost any type of behaviour as an 'intelligence' . . . [if these] abilities 'define' 'emotional intelligence', we would expect some evidence that they are highly correlated; Goleman admits that they might be quite uncorrelated, and in any case if we cannot measure them, how do we know they are related? So the whole theory is built on quicksand: there is no sound scientific basis. (2000, pp. 109–110)

An alternative and more methodologically rigorous approach to this subject has been provided by K.V. Petrides and his colleagues (Petrides and Furnham, 2001; Petrides et al., 2007), who see emotional intelligence as a trait rather than a set of competencies; that is to say, as a stable, innate characteristic. Emotional intelligence is conceived of as a constellation of personality traits concerning people's perceptions of their emotional abilities; people differ widely on this (Petrides et al., 2007). In this model, emotional intelligence is positioned outside of cognitive ability, and it is argued that it should, therefore, be investigated as an aspect of personality via various self-report tests that have already been developed (Petrides et al., 2007). However, it could be argued that deliberately placing a construct outside the range of cognitive abilities somewhat limits the validity of referring to it as a form of intelligence. Nevertheless, Petrides et al.'s (2007) academically rigorous attempts to demonstrate how trait emotional intelligence predicts life satisfaction, coping strategies and rumination looks set to continue, and seem rather less susceptible to accusations of being mere 'pop psychology' than Goleman's 'abilities' approach.

A Model of Learning Styles

Having reviewed the classic and contemporary approached to intelligence, an important question to ask ourselves at this point is, do we all learn in the same way, as the systems of education in many countries seem to assume? Unfortunately, the answer seems to be 'No'. A key criticism of the 'traditional' or 'chalk-and-talk' method of classroom learning is that the learners' role is essentially a *passive* one (i.e. the recipient of the teacher's knowledge). In such a situation, the material that the learner receives will most often be *verbal*; it will be delivered in a *written* form; and, it will be concerned with *facts* to be committed to *memory*. Although prevalent in the 'traditional' classroom (and in large lecture theatres in universities today), this is only one of a myriad of ways in which it is possible to teach and learn; and different people do learn in different ways.

For example, one set of skills that people today have often learnt in their adult life is the use of computers. Let's consider the possible ways in which this can be learnt. Some people will join a *university programme* and be taught by lecturers. Here, they will be passive learners; the material they learn will be factually based and will be in an oral format. Some people will join an *evening course*, taught by a facilitator. They will be more active in their learning; the material they will learn is more skills-based and will be in oral format. Some people will learn *at home, using a manual, or figuring it out for themselves*. These learners are the most active of all; the material they learn is skills-based, and is in the form of written feedback from the manual or the computer's software.

There are pros and cons to all of these methods. The person on a university course is likely to have the broadest and the most theoretically-driven knowledge of information technology. However, the process of acquiring this knowledge is lengthy. The novice who figures it out for herself or himself is most likely to have quite a narrow knowledge base (at least to begin with), but can acquire the skills she or he needs quite quickly – and yet the possibility of making mistakes is quite high in the beginning. The key point is that for the adult learner trying to develop a grasp of IT, there is no right or wrong way. Everything will depend on *the extent and type of knowledge/skills the person wishes to acquire*, and *how the person learns best* (in other words, her or his *learning style*).

Felder and Soloman (2000) present one of a number of possible schemes of learning styles in terms of four bipolar constructs:

> Active and Reflective Learners
> Sensing and Intuitive Learners
> Visual and Verbal Learners
> Sequential and Global Learners

Felder and Soloman (2000) assert that those we may consider to be *active* learners learn best by their discussing new information, applying that new information to other situations, or by explaining new material to others. In this sense, one would expect to find a high proportion of active learners amongst a population of teachers and other educations. *Passive* learners, on the other hand, prefer to think quietly about new information at first, and are characterised as preferring to work alone. The bipolar construct of sensing versus intuitive learners – which seems to be borrowed from C.G. Jung's description of psychological types (1921), particularly where he referred to how new information enters the conscious part of the mind – can be distinguished on whether the person prefers to learn facts in isolation (sensing) or in context (intuitive). The *intuitive* learner prefers to discover relationships between facts, and responds well to innovative teaching methods. The *sensing* learner prefers established methods of teaching, and is held to dislike surprises in the learning process. The distinction between visual and verbal learners is a simple one, referring to what sort of sensory input in teaching methods these learners respond best to, or remember best: essentially, *visual* learners learn best from what they can see (pictures, films, diagrams, demonstrations), whereas *verbal* learners learn best from linguistic input (the spoken and the written word). Finally, *sequential* learners employ what cognitive psychologists sometimes call 'algorithmic' reasoning styles – they follow logical steps in finding solutions to problems. *Global* learners employ what is sometimes referred to as a 'heuristic' reasoning style – relying on mental shortcuts, rules of thumb and 'Eureka' moments of insight, they may be able to solve complicated problems in a creative way, but equally may have difficulty in explaining to others how they solved those problems. (This seems to me to be a style better suited to, say, a researcher rather than a teacher, and why it takes more than eminence in one's chosen subject to be an effective teacher.) Consequently, when they approach the learning of new information, sequential learners prefer to gain understanding in small, logical steps (and so respond well to very programmed learning and highly structured texts), whereas the global learner tends to learn in large jumps, with things suddenly 'clicking' into place following inspirational material.

In general, one advantage of being able to recognise one's own learning style is that what is missing in the learning environment one can make up for in one's private study. (For instance, imagine a reflective, global adult trying to learn IT skills in an active evening class geared around step-by-step demonstrations. Her or his home study should involve solo trial-and-error investigative learning using her or his own computer.) In the classroom, it is advantageous for a teacher to be able to recognise both her or his own learning style and the learning styles of her or his students. In the case of the former, one's learning style is likely to affect how one teaches, and this could disadvantage a learner who had a very different learning style to that of her or his teacher; in terms of the latter, one could plan one's lessons accordingly to the students' learning styles. For example, a predominance of visual, active, global, intuitive learners in a history class might suggest that the viewing and discussion of a period film might be a more effective way to deliver the material than a set of written exercises.

Naturally, Felder and Solomon's (2000) approach, outlined above, is just one of many such schemes that has been developed, and this lack of consensus is one reason that has led to the concept of learning styles being heavily criticised. Howard-Jones (2011; also Howard-Jones et al., 2009) describes the existence of learning styles as a 'myth': although 82 per cent of their sample of 158 graduate trainees about to enter secondary teaching in the UK believed that teaching children in their preferred learning styles would improve learning outcomes, Howard-Jones (2010, 2011) argues that neurological evidence does not support the existence of learning styles, and in this he joins Geake (2005), who also described learning styles as a 'neuromyth'. It is to be acknowledged that early attempts to ground learning styles in neural terms made reference to outmoded notions such as hemispheric dominance (e.g. Dunn et al., 1989). However, it is also to be noted that the neural basis of many of the so-called 'higher' psychological functions is still not fully understood, including those with currency in educational settings – such as self-esteem and intelligence. Hence, I would argue that the usefulness of the *concept* of learning styles in helping us think about students as individual learners is not diminished by the fact that its neural basis has not been sufficiently ascertained.

Some Practical Applications of Learning Styles in Education

1   Consider the learning styles outlined above, then answer the following questions:
   - Where do you fit in yourself?
   - What does this depend on? The type of material to be learnt? Your pre-existing expertise in a field? Your social situation at the point of learning? Any other factors?
   - Please make the appropriate notes in order to define your own leaning style(s) as closely as you can.

2   If you are a teacher (of any sort), think about the students in your class/classes with respect to the learning styles mentioned above. Then attempt the following:
   - Can you think what individual students' learning styles might be?
   - Can you think of at least one individual student to exemplify each learning style?
   - In the class or the classes that you teach, is there a predominance of any single learning style? If so, has an intuitive sense of this on your own part affected the way in which you have planned teaching methodologies in the past? Or has an ignorance of student's learning styles (say, when the class was 'new' to you) ever meant that certain methodologies/class plans have 'fallen flat'?
   - Knowing what you now do about learning styles, is the way in which you plan classes/teaching methodologies likely to change for certain students or classes? If so, how? It may help to make a list.

Implications for Educators

As we have seen, the ways in which psychologists and educators have approached the measurement of mental abilities have profound implications for educators today. We have seen (see the section above on 'Traditional Views of Intelligence') that for around the first *century* of the testing of mental abilities it was assumed that intelligence was a single, all-round, heritable ability. We can see this assumption echoed today in many systems of education both in the existence of mixed-ability, single-teacher primary school classes and in the use of an aggregate score-based examination system that determines university entrance. The pros and cons of these systems could certainly be considered. For example, are they pedagogically justified or not? To what extent are they an artefact of the way in which mental abilities have been studied and tested? To what extent do they arise out of convenience? Is it possible to re-imagine the way in which the education of primary-aged children and assessment regarding university entrance could be undertaken?

More recently, of course, we have seen the old assumption that intelligence is *entirely* 'in the genes' break down. This has been through the vigorous debate of whether racial differences exist regarding IQ, and if they do, what underlies them – the assumed biologically-based intellectual inferiority of certain races, or the existence of profound social inequalities between people of different races within the same societies. Many have found rather newer approaches presented in this chapter, such as the multiplicity of intelligences, the concept of emotional intelligence, and the increased attention being paid to learning styles to have a greater intuitive appeal than what seems to be the dogmatic approaches of the early researchers in the field.

We have also seen that intelligence (as measured by IQ) seems to predict, or at least is strongly associated with, educational attainment. However, we have reflected upon the fact that other factors are also likely to be associated with educational attainment – social, economic, historical and cultural factors, and also individual factors such as motivation and (as we have seen in the previous chapter) possibly self-esteem. These days, the avowed ethos of most educational establishments goes beyond merely the development of the intellect; indeed, the focus on the 'whole child', or indeed, in schools with a religious ethos, spiritual aspects of child adolescent development, is commonplace. Properly considered, then, from both a psychological and educational point of view, mental ability is one aspect to be developed in the school years – an important aspect, yes, but after all, just one aspect.

Please think about, write short notes on, but above all take the opportunity to discuss with colleagues the following pair of questions:

1 Does it make a difference, practically speaking, if a psychological feature such as intelligence (or, for that matter, something else, such as aggression) is 'in the genes' or determined by a students' environment? What implications would this have (say) for a government minister? A teacher? A parent? The student himself or herself? If the implications differ according to the person involved or the psychological feature under consideration, why is this?
2 Which would you say is more important to you and your work – the gathering of data based on test scores by external agencies, or promoting teachers' own understanding of their students' learning styles? How much time is spent in your school on each, and why do you think this is?

Axline, V.M. (1964) *Dibs: In Search of Self.* Boston, MA: Houghton-Mifflin. This is the classic case study that is mentioned above; it is an instructive read, and generally held to be exceptionally beautifully written.

Gardner, H. (2011) *Frames of Mind: The Theory of Multiple Intelligences*, 3rd edn. London: Heinemann. Offers an overview of this interesting development in how intelligence and attainment amongst children in schools may be approached.

Lazear, D. (2005) *Higher-Order Thinking the Multiple Intelligences Way.* Bethel, CT: Crown House. Practical applications of the multiple intelligences approach in schools and classrooms.

Montagu, A. (ed.) (2002) *Race and IQ.* Expanded edn. Oxford: Oxford University Press. A very readable collection of essays that catalogue some of the ways in which tests of mental ability have been used, and often, as the authors argue, abused.

Aceviper.net. *Famous People IQs.* Available at http://aceviper.net/estimated_iq_of_famous_people.phpo (accessed January 2011). Just for fun – this site comprises a list of famous people through the ages and their estimated IQ scores.

Felder, R.M. and Soloman, B.A. *Learning Styles and Strategies.* Available at www.ncsu.edu/unity/lockers/users/f/felder/public/ILSdir/styles.htm (accessed June 2011). Provides an overview of Felder and Soloman's learning styles scheme, links to learning styles and questionnaires and keys to their use.

5

Positive Discipline, Conflict Resolution and Co-operative Learning in Schools

The primary goal for this chapter is to provide the reader with an introduction to, and an applied psychological knowledge of, the interconnected areas of positive discipline, conflict resolution and co-operative learning in schools. After considering *what is meant by positive discipline*, the chapter proceeds by introducing the area of and examining skills in *conflict resolution and conflict management*. We then turn our attention towards *understanding social groups*, at first in general, and then with a focus on child and adolescent groups, before addressing the area of *co-operative learning*. This chapter concludes with an examination of some *implications for educators*, *points for discussion*, and a selective and annotated list of *further reading* and *useful websites*.

What is Meant by Positive Discipline?

The well-known educational consultant Bill Rogers (2007) notes that, to many, 'positive discipline' sounds like a contradiction in terms; this is because 'discipline is still seen by some teachers (and parents) in punitive terms – and correction and consequences in discipline are clearly necessary' (p. 51). However, he goes on to assert that:

> Discipline is [primarily] concerned with guidance and instruction; it is the way we teach and enhance a social order where rights and responsibilities are balanced . . . Teachers should, and most do, make every effort to plan for a positive working environment, cater for mixed abilities and have thoughtful routines for the smooth day-to-day running of the class . . . we will need to correct student behaviour [but] it is still more positive if consideration is given to our language and manner . . . The mark of an effective discipline plan includes a balance of prevention and correction; short- and long-term discipline; correction and encouragement; and, repairing and rebuilding strained relationships between teacher and student, student and student. (2007, p. 51, p. 53)

Rogers' emphasis on 'language and manner' (p. 51) includes the 'planning the language of correction' (p. 54). This in turn includes skills and strategies such as being brief, especially when giving directions; becoming aware of, limiting and rephrasing negatives, including our over-use of the word 'Don't'; focusing on behaviour, particularly that which is desired, rather than attacking the student; calming oneself before calming the student; balancing correction with encouragement; using students' names, reminders, privately understood signals, tactical pauses and tactical ignoring, and relocation in the room; avoiding hostile gestures and put-downs; and, emphasising the concepts of choice and consequences in discipline contexts (Rogers, 2007).

Becoming Aware of Teachers' Methods of Problem-Solving through Role-Play

The following exercise has been designed to raise awareness of the communication and strategies that teachers use in their attempts to help students with their school-related difficulties – in Rogers' (2007) words (see above), 'language and manner'. This exercise is one that requires three participants in each working group, and as trust needs to exist between members of the group, the reader should attempt this with close colleagues only.

One person is allocated to the role of the 'student', and thinks of a hypothetical but realistic, exclusively school-related, everyday problem with which a student might approach a teacher. Another person is allocated to the role of the 'teacher', who performs the act of talking with the 'student' and deciding upon a course of action regarding the 'problem' – in other words, he or she plays how a teacher might 'deal with it'. The third person is allocated the 'observer' role. His or her task is to make notes (mental or written) on the verbal and non-verbal communication of the 'student' and the 'teacher', and the strategies that the 'teacher' employs in talking with the 'student' regarding the 'problem'. After the 'student' and the 'teacher' have played out the scenario, the 'observer's' task is to feed back to the 'teacher' and the 'student' his or her observations.

It should be recalled that those playing the role of 'teacher' are the most emotionally vulnerable of those playing the three possible roles – after all, little 'acting' is involved in the 'teacher' role when participants in this activity are teachers in real-life, and we all have an emotional investment in our positive professional practice. Therefore, the feedback provided by the 'observer' should focus primarily on the positive aspects of the 'teacher's' performance, and if criticism is offered it should be constructive, focussing on how positive aspects of communication styles and strategies can be built upon.

The 'teacher' then offers his or her response to the 'observer's' feedback; the 'observer's' comments are checked against the 'student's' experiences of the scenario. The 'student' may also offer his or her feedback to the 'teacher' concerning the 'teacher's' communication styles and strategies.

After the scenario, the roles then rotate between the members of the working group; each member has a turn in each of the roles. After this has been accomplished, a general discussion can be conducted concerning communication styles and strategies that teachers may employ in real-life situations of helping students with their school-related difficulties.

Conflict Resolution and Conflict Management

O'Moore and Minton (2004) outline five stages in a typical model of problem-solving/conflict resolution:

> *Identification* of the person(s) who is/are a cause for concern, i.e. WHO.
> *Assessment* of the problem, i.e. WHAT it is.
> *Formulation* of the causes of the problem, i.e. WHY it occurs.
> *Intervention* finding ways to deal with the problem, i.e. HOW.
> *Evaluation* of the intervention, i.e. SO WHAT?

This model can be applied to the results of the task of the previous group activity (see above), which is one that I have adopted from a method that is commonly used in the training of counsellors and psychotherapists in basic counselling skills; in 'triad' exercises in counsellor-training situations, the process is more or less the same, but uses the roles of 'therapist', 'client' and 'observer' (rather than 'teacher', 'student' and 'observer'). I have had extensive personal experience of using this method in the training of both teachers and counsellors, and an interesting difference (to me) invariably appears; if one sets no time limit for the exercise, trainee counsellors take very much longer over the 'dialogue' phase than do trainee teachers. There are undoubtedly many reasons for this, but if we apply the five-stage model (above) to understanding this difference, it seems that trainee teachers pass from the 'identification' stage to the 'intervention' stage very quickly – as is the nature of their professional role. Teachers have to find solutions very quickly, because rarely are they faced with a single problem at a time (as any teacher of younger primary school students who has conducted yard or playground duty recently can tell you).

Naturally, each phase is important: to find the best possible intervention, it is important to be able to understand what the problem is and why it occurs. I would also argue that the 'evaluation' phase is one which can, unfortunately, be overlooked (again, due to the pressure of time and having to deal with multiple problems). Even an informal 'follow-up' conversation with a student can help a teacher ascertain whether his or her advice to a student or intervention was indeed helpful, or whether the problem or conflict was merely pushed out of the teacher's or school's 'sight'.

The psychotherapist and conflict resolution expert Arnold Mindell (1995) has argued that resolving conflict isn't easy, and that it takes courage to get involved in conflict resolution (he calls this 'sitting in the fire', in the attempt to facilitate the reconstructive/creative aspects of conflict rather than the destructive aspects). O'Moore and Minton (2004) point out that 'finding a genuine *solution* depends on *compromise*; if compromise is not possible, or forthcoming, [then] the conflict can be *managed* . . . this depends on all parties voluntarily agreeing to be bound by a new set of rules . . . the conflict is not resolved – but setting rules acts a basis for effective conflict management' (p. 92, italics in the original). It may be that two students have such disparate characters that 'making up' (conflict resolution) after a series of serious confrontations is impossible; but, on a teacher's helping them to recognise individually that their behaviour is causing problems for themselves, they might be able to agree to disagree, or even stay out of each other's way for at least a prescribed period of time (conflict management) until their angry feelings subside.

O'Moore and Minton (2004) argue that the key 'skill' in resolving and managing conflict is *objectivity*; therefore, parties involved in a situation of conflict resolution will need to know *at the outset* that, as an intermediary or facilitator,

> 'You will hear everyone's perspective, to which you will give equal and fair consideration.'
> 'You will not make a decision or take action until you have heard everyone's perspective.'
> 'When action is taken, it will be fair and just, and a direct consequence of the choices made by the person or people in the situation of conflict, and her or his subsequent behaviour.'

Setting up ground rules can be helpful, particularly when working with young people; for example, only one person speaking at a time (everyone shall get her or his turn, so there is no need for interruptions). Obviously, everyone must agree to these ground rules at the start, and if you want to make a fair decision, and be perceived to be doing so, get all of the facts (O'Moore and Minton, 2004).

It is also important to *engage at a feeling level* when dealing with matters of conflict. People rarely argue about events in themselves; they argue about how they *feel* about events. Years ago, I separated two boys, engaged in what might be referred to as 'full conflict' mode; they were equally enthusiastic about soccer, but supporters of rival teams. The flashpoint comment had been when one (a Liverpool supporter) had said about Manchester United that 'They may have won the triple, but they're still sh**'. Rationally, this makes no sense at all (a, shall we say, 'poor' team does not win three trophies in a single season), but due to supporter rivalry, emotionally speaking it is important to a 12-year-old Liverpool fan that Manchester United must always be criticised as strongly and as publically as is possible (and I would say, vice versa). This example goes to show what was said far more succinctly over 2,000 years ago by the philosopher Epictetus: 'Man is not disturbed by events, but only by his interpretation of events' (see Ellis, 1962). Hence, in order to resolve the deeper roots of conflict, one must facilitate the expression of feelings: to attend to the person's/people's safety needs; to use active listening and open-ended and feeling-level questions; and to take an empathic standpoint (O'Moore and Minton, 2004).

As well as resolving conflict between students, educators can be the subject of conflict themselves. Because it is necessary, as an educator, to model non-aggressive behaviour (especially regarding young people and their long-documented capacity to learn aggression from observing adult behaviour (Bandura et al., 1961)), it is important to take charge of negative emotions. As Mindell (1995) points out, for most people, when conflict arises, our emotional response is immediately negative: we feel angry or frustrated (or both) when our antagonist is seeking power or revenge, and our negative feelings are indeed part of the pay-off. If we take charge of our emotions and act reasonably, we simultaneously counter the antagonist's strategy and communicate that we are not willing to play the conflict 'game'. It is suggested that the following strategies can be helpful:

> *Release the pent-up emotions through sport, activity or fantasy*: Many of us in occupations of high stress need this 'cathartic' release (I recall a teacher who took up training for and running marathons as a constructive response to the stress of his inner-city post).
> *Opt to talk about emotive issues later*: The teacher's time-honoured instruction 'Come and talk to me after class' is effective, as it essentially allows a 'cooling-off' for both the teacher and the student.
> *Allow people to save face*: An under-the-breath comment to his or her friends after being disciplined by a teacher may be an embarrassed student's attempt to recover social self-esteem, rather than a re-challenge to the teacher, so providing it is not too out of line, one might consider if it always needs to be countered there and then.
> *Remember, you are the author of your own emotional responses and behavioural choices!*

Individual versus Group Behaviour

Before reading the rest of this chapter, why do you think that young people are more likely to behave in anti-social ways when in groups than they are when alone? Take the opportunity to discuss this with colleagues if you can.

Understanding Social Groups

Amongst social scientists, it is arguable that it is the sociologists who have, by the nature of their discipline (which is defined as 'the study of the bases of social membership' or 'the analysis of the structure of social relationships as constituted by social interaction' (Abercrombie et al., 2000, p. 333), contributed the most to our understanding of social groups. Most introductory courses and even introductory texts on sociology (e.g. Haralambos, 1989) make reference early on to the *norms* and *roles* that exist within social groupings. *Norms* are 'rules' that apply to all members of a social group, or 'expectations about appropriate conduct which serve as common guidelines for social action . . . not necessarily actual behaviour [but] expectations about "correct" or "proper" behaviour . . . deviation from norms is punished by sanctions, norms are acquired by internalisation and socialisation' (Abercrombie et al., 2000, p. 243). The concept of *roles*, which are positions in a group that are governed by rules and expectations, assumes that

> when people occupy social positions, their behaviour is determined mainly by what is expected of that position rather than by their own individual characteristics . . . for example, an individual schoolteacher performs the role of 'teacher', which carries with it certain expected behaviours irrespective of his or her personal feelings at any one time, and therefore it is possible to generalise about the professional role behaviour of teachers regardless of the individual characteristics of the people who occupy these positions. (Abercrombie et al., 2000, p. 301)

Psychologists, as we have seen, concern themselves far more with these 'individual characteristics', and therefore pay rather less attention to social processes than do sociologists. However, despite the occasional misgivings of our sociological colleagues, it is true that psychologists have been examining social processes for many years past. It is towards this *social psychology* that we shall now turn.

Anti-social Group Behaviour

Social psychology is the study of human social behaviour: how human beings behave in groups. The 1950s and 1960s saw a series of controversial experimental demonstrations of the mechanisms believed, by social psychologists, to underlie most of what we might define as anti-social behaviour: Solomon Asch's work on *conformity* (Asch, 1956); Stanley Milgram's study in *obedience* (Milgram, 1965, 1974) and Bibb Latané and John Darley's investigations of *bystander apathy* (see Latané, 1981, for review; also this text Chapter 8); and Philip Zimbardo and his colleagues' infamous *Stanford Prison Experiment* (Haney and Zimbardo, 1977). With the retrospective standpoint that four to five decades provides, the lasting 'fame' of these studies seems due to the lasting importance of the phenomena that these studies successfully demonstrated, rather than to the ethical controversy that some of these studies produced (see below).

Asch was interested in how people will *conform* to the ideas of a group. His set-up was simple, and relied on the use of experimental 'stooges' – persons whom, to the experimental participants, appear to be their fellows but are actually assistants of the experimenter (and hence are 'in' on the *deception* involved in the experiment). Participants were asked to examine sets of lines, projected on a screen, and to say which one (usually, of three) was the longest. Tested alone, participants would estimate this accurately; but if placed with 'stooges' who would deliberately (and often emphatically) provide an incorrect answer, genuine participants would alter their choices – thus conforming to the group, but thereby giving a response that was incorrect. When debriefed, participants sometimes said that they knew that their response was wrong, but had doubted themselves under group pressure – or even, in some cases, doubted their own eyesight (Asch, 1956).

Philip Zimbardo and his colleagues were interested in what factors underpin prison violence. Two 'folk' theories existed at the time: either it was down to the criminal nature of the prisoners, or the assumed authoritarian (or even sadistic) personalities of the prison staff (or possibly a combination of the two). The 'Stanford Prison Experiment' (Haney and Zimbardo, 1977) showed that there was another alternative: that there is something about the environment of prisons themselves that produce such power dynamics and subsequent reactions to those dynamics. So they endeavoured to create a prison environment, but without real-life prisoners or prison guards. Student volunteers from Stanford University in California were assigned (randomly) either a 'guard' or 'prisoner' role in the experiment. Realism was striven for: the basement of the Psychology Department at Stanford was turned into a (fairly realistic) 'prison'; 'guards' wore uniforms and sunglasses with reflective lenses; 'prisoners' wore 'caps' (to imitate shorn hair) and uniforms. The experiment was originally scheduled to run for two weeks, and both 'prisoners' and 'guards' were to keep diaries. The experiment had to be abandoned after just six days due to extremely negative reactions on the part of the 'prisoners' and the increasing sadism of the 'guards'' thinking and behaviour. It should be noted that such experiments have often been criticised from an ethical standpoint, largely due to the fact that participation in these studies caused considerable emotional distress to the people involved (this was the case in the Stanford Prison Experiment) and, in Asch's case, the deceptive nature of the experimental set-up runs entirely contrary to the ethical notion of informed voluntary consent. These factors mean that such experiments could not be accorded ethical approval to be undertaken today.

The 'Prisoner's Dilemma'

The 'Prisoner's Dilemma' is derived from 'gaming theory', and has also been applied in understanding group behaviour. In the classic scenario (as described by Gleitman, 2010), two suspects have been caught at the scene of a crime and are interviewed separately. They are told that if they confess, they will face a lesser charge, but if they don't confess, then they will face a serious charge. There is enough circumstantial evidence to convict them both, so non-confession is seen as non-repentance and there is a possibility to turn State's evidence (against the accomplice) on confession. Hence, there are four possible outcome options:

1 *A confesses, B confesses*: A and B receive sentences of three years each (both are seen as repentant, and charged with a lesser offence).
2 *A confesses, B does not confess*: A goes free (turns State evidence), B receives a sentence of 10 years (is seen as unrepentant, and charged with the serious offence).
3 *A does not confess, B confesses*: The reverse of option 2. A receives a sentence of 10 years (is seen as unrepentant, and charged with the serious offence), B goes free (turns State evidence).
4 *A does not confess, B does not confess*: Both are seen as unrepentant, and charged (on the basis of circumstantial evidence) with the serious offence; each receives a sentence of 8 years.

Which is the most likely outcome? The most likely outcome is option 4. Most of the time people will not confess, as in an ambiguous situation we cannot predict what other people will do.

The Prisoner's Dilemma Experiment has been used to explain anti-social group behaviour, including mob behaviour and also the 'panicky crowd'. Gleitman (2010) asks us to imagine the situation of there being a fire in a public building. For each individual in that building, if he or she rushes to the door, he or she may escape, but others will not. If he or she walks to the door, he or she will probably sustain only minor injuries. The possible outcome options are:

1 *A walks, B walks*: Both A and B escape (each suffers minor injuries).
2 *A rushes, B walks*: A escapes, B suffers major injuries.
3 *A walks, B rushes*: A suffers major injuries, B escapes.
4 *A rushes, B rushes*: Neither A nor B escape.

Once again, the most likely outcome is option 4. Most of the time, people would rush to the door, as they cannot predict whether the other people will walk or rush. Hence, in these types of situations, major injuries are usually sustained by all; psychologically 'panicky' crowds make physically *dangerous* situations *lethal*. A more innocuous situation that teachers may be aware of is when (especially young) students fail to follow a teachers' instruction to exit a class, or to get on a bus, in an orderly fashion – a child cannot predict whether the rest of his or her peers will walk or run, so most of the time everyone ends up running and a 'crush' in the doorway results.

Understanding Child and Adolescent Groups

Aside from these general observations about groups, what have social psychologists had to say about child and adolescent groups in particular? A famous study was undertaken over half a century ago by Muzafer Sherif and colleagues; it is known as the *Robber's Cave Experiment* as it was undertaken at a summer camp in Robbers Cave State Park in Oklahoma, USA. In-group formation and competition between two groups of 12 12-year-old boys, hitherto unknown to one another, was created by bussing them to two separate locations, keeping the groups unknown to one another for the first few days and then subsequently bringing the two groups together into a single camp. Almost as soon as the groups became aware of one another, 'in-groupness' appeared in the boys' language (Sherif had disguised himself as the camp janitor in order to be able to observe such behaviours). Members of the self-named 'Eagles' and the 'Rattlers' groups were openly hostile to one another, and the competitive activities that had been organised for the 'single group' phase of the study could not safely continue. It was not easy to bring the two groups together; this was achieved only by organising activities where the boys had to work co-operatively (physically moving a 'broken-down' camp truck, building a raft to cross a river and so on) (Sherif et al., 1954; in Sherif, 1967). The reader may recognise features of this and similar experiments in the set-up of some recent 'reality television' programmes.

So what functions do childhood and adolescent groups serve? James Vander Zanden (1989) notes that whilst young children, when asked, will often cite non-intimate reasons for choosing one's friends (e.g. living nearby), from 6 to 14 years of age there is an increasing emphasis on reciprocity, intimacy and mutual understanding; in middle childhood, a focus on similarities in preferences (e.g. games, activities and people); and in adolescence, a focus on similarities in internal feelings and personality traits. Young people are simultaneously involved in a number of peer groups, and these can range from reflecting adult values precisely (e.g. scout groups, religious youth groups) to being in open conflict with adult values (e.g. delinquent gangs). Vander Zanden argues that peers are as necessary to children's development as adults are, and notes that peer groups:

> provide an arena in which children can exercise independence from adult controls
> give experience in relationships in which [children] are on an equal footing with others
> [are] the only social institution in which the position of children is not marginal
> [act as] agencies for the transmission of informal knowledge, superstitions, folklore, fads, jokes, riddles, games, and secret modes of gratification. (1989, p.361)

Aside from peer groups, the first social group we are a member of is the one we are born into – our family of origin. The lasting influence of early family relationships, in terms of birth order, has been asserted for many decades. The Viennese physician and psychotherapist Alfred Adler (1870–1937) argued that being born further down the birth order can be a contributory factor to feelings of inferiority that many of us struggle with all our lives (see Adler, 1956). Subsequently, insights into the effects of birth order on psychological development, from the field of systemic family theory and therapy (see Dallos and Draper, 2010), have revealed that the situation may not be as simple and deterministic as Adler described it. The popular psychology author John Bradshaw (1991, 1995) and the psychotherapist Virginia Satir (1983) have argued that different roles and expectations are placed upon children according to their birth order position. For example, the role of the 'hero' can be devolved upon the first (or, in patriarchal societies, first male) child (high expectations, high levels of family authority); the role of the 'baby' can devolve on the youngest (low expectations, low levels of family authority); and a child in the middle of the birth order can become either a 'lost child' or a skilled negotiator and so on. Furthermore, we tend to maintain these roles within the family of origin all our lives, and to re-create these roles for ourselves in situation outside the family of origin (this is referred to as 'primary recapitulation') (Bradshaw, 1991, 1995; Satir, 1983), regardless of how much conscious *sense* this may actually make. For example, it may be obvious for the busy parent to send the 'family hero' child (aged 10 years old) to the local shop, as he or she is more able to accomplish this task than his or her 7- and 5-year-old siblings. What is interesting is the case when we move this hypothetical situation on five decades in time – say, when funeral arrangements have to be made for the recently-deceased parent – the 60-year old 'hero' may still be expected to take the lead, and invariably and unthinkingly fulfils those expectations, even if his or her now 57- and 55-year-old siblings happen to live more locally. Due to the phenomenon of primary recapitulation, it is also quite likely that this 'hero', in the intervening five decades, has maintained a role of high expectancies and authority within the variety of systems in which he or she has been involved.

Incidentally, empirical evidence shows that first and subsequent children tend to have different sets of advantages. Parents may have greater expectations of first-borns, and as they are inexperienced, tend to be both more punitive and more affectionate with them; with subsequent children, they are more realistic and less punitive. First-borns are more likely to have higher IQs and to go to college; however, subsequent children are more popular with peers and more innovative (Baskett, 1985, Eaton et al., 1989, in Vander Zanden, 1989); however, the differences are not great, and do of course vary considerably between individuals and families.

Co-operative Learning

Since the mid-1970s, brothers David and Roger Johnson have been building on earlier insights into the potential benefits of co-operative over individualistic efforts (e.g. May and Doob, 1937) in order to develop a theory of co-operative learning (Johnson and Johnson, 1975, 1989, 1994; Johnson et al., 1988). Co-operative learning approaches are those in which classroom activities are organized into academic and social learning experiences, with the emphasis on the *collective* accomplishment of a learning goal via requesting, utilising and evaluating each other's skills and resources (Chiu, 2000, 2008). The process has five essential elements (Brown and Ciuffetelli, 2009):

> *Positive interdependence* – each group member has a task, and is therefore responsible for their own learning and that of their group, hence must participate fully.
> *Face-to-face promotive interaction* – members assist each other's understanding and success by explaining what they have learnt or are learning.
> *Individual accountability* – as each group member is accountable, 'social loafing' is minimized.
> *Social skills* – leadership, decision-making, trust-building, communication and conflict-management skills must be taught.
> *Group-processing* – groups periodically evaluate their interactions and effectiveness in order to make improvements.

Co-operative learning strategies were the main working mode used in the 'Pathways Through Education' project referred to in the case study of Chapter 3 of this text. As this project started in the late 1990s, such an approach was quite new to teachers and students alike, so there was a need to focus on the practical skills that teachers can use in co-operative approaches (Charles and McHugh, 2000; Minton, 2001). In traditional 'chalk and talk' teaching scenarios, the interpersonal learning dynamic is of 'one-on-many'; that is, one teacher, standing at the front of the classroom, dispenses the information to the many students, who engage passively with the learning content. In co-operative approaches, teachers are positioned as 'facilitators' of a group-based process that involves the active engagement of students with the learning content (Charles and McHugh, 2000; Minton, 2001). This sort of group work presented challenges by its 'newness' for students, too; indeed, the most viable means of setting up and managing groups within a co-operative learning approach proved to be the organisation and implementation of class charters – students were assisted in coming up with their own rules, in order to meet safety needs of individuals and groups (Minton, 2001). From this point on, it was quite possible and extremely productive to work in 'circle time' (Mosley, 1999) and co-operative learning (Johnson and Johnson, 1994) scenarios, including as much discursive and creative activity as was desirable in order to accomplish the programme's learning goals (Charles and McHugh, 2000; Minton, 2001).

A Critical Look at Teamwork (Finland)

Group work is often posited as a helpful and creative classroom teaching methodology, particularly when aspects such as co-operative learning are concerned. Teamwork strategies have also been advocated in certain work environments. Of course, not everyone is convinced of the benefits of teamwork: for example, Pasi Ristelä (2003) cites Finnish Internet entrepreneur Alex Nieminen:

> Teamwork is one of the most horrible plagues in modern world. Just put some people together and hope that some kind of result that satisfies the majority will be achieved. If there is some guy with a great idea in Sweden and he is put into a team, soon nothing will be achieved but pure rubbish.

Ristelä's (2003) study addressed whether teamwork, in the classroom context, is an 'effective activity, or just having a nice time together?' and involved 150 students (in grades three to six inclusively, aged between 9 and 13 years) in three elementary schools in Finland. Students were given experiences of learning curricular content via teamwork-based teaching methodologies. Subsequently, they were asked what they thought they had learned; what might be the benefits and disadvantages of working in a group; and which method (at school) they considered to be the most beneficial/pleasant. Their answers were analysed according to the relative frequencies of comments directed towards the 'task problem level' (or TPL – the actual, normative primary task) and the 'process problem level' (PPL – their readiness to act as part of a group, and assessments of other group members' abilities). The students' class teachers were also questioned as to their own actual use of teamwork as a teaching strategy, and their concerns about the use of teamwork.

Subsequent to the learning tasks, when students were asked 'What do you think that you have learned during the period of teamwork?', 95 of the answers that were received referred to the TPL, and 82 to the PPL (the 150 students could, theoretically, give answers that referred to both, as some clearly did in this case). TPL-related comments commonly referred to new information and skills (e.g. 'I learned new information about the pietists') or new ways of finding information that had been learned (e.g. 'I learned how to look for information in the Internet'). PPL-related comments commonly referred to the development of co-operative skills, learning to work in a group, understanding other people, and getting along with new friends (e.g. 'One learns to work with others than just one's best friend').

When asked what might be the benefits of working in a group, 111 of the answers referred to the PPL (the teamwork itself); improving co-operative skills (e.g. 'I learned to co-operate with the others'); developing communication skills (e.g. 'One learns to listen to the others, too'); the enjoyment of being together with friends (e.g. 'One doesn't have to be alone'). Just 35 of the comments referred to the TPL (e.g. 'Now I know what pietism means'). For both of these questions, the proportion of PPL-related comments increased distinctly within the older age groups. When students were asked 'What might be the disadvantages of working in a group?', only one comment referred directly to a TPL-factor. PPL-related observations concerned conflict and discrepancies between members of the group (mentioned 42 times; e.g. scapegoating – one person being blamed for 'causing trouble', and this reason being given as to why the group was not able to work together properly); inconvenient working environment, e.g. restless and noisy classrooms (mentioned 28 times); and the fairness of the division of labour (e.g. 'Some may just watch, when others do all the work!'). When asked about which teaching method (at school) they considered to be the most beneficial and which to be the most pleasant, the 'social' (teamwork) methods were generally considered be more pleasant (101 mentions) than 'individual' (non-teamwork) ones (28 mentions), and the 'individual' methods (80 mentions) were considered to be more beneficial than the 'social' ones (68 mentions). The proportion of students who considered 'social' methods to be more beneficial increased in the higher age groups.

When the students' class teachers' perspectives were investigated, when asked about their actual use of teamwork as a teaching strategy most reported that they tended to use teamwork at beginning of courses, or at the end (for revision purposes), that is, before or after the bulk of the course material has been delivered. Hence, the academic goal when teamwork is employed was often blurred or non-existent, as the teachers did not rely on teamwork as a method of delivering course content, but only one of introducing or revising it. Teachers concerns about teamwork as a teaching strategy – in other words, the reasons for its non-use – included reports of fears of 'losing control' of the class, or 'losing the grip' on one's course material, as well as creating noise in one's own classroom, thus disturbing the teaching going on in one's colleagues' classrooms.

So can teamwork be both pleasant *and* useful? It seems from this study that teamwork in schools is exposed to ambiguous thinking. On the one hand, working in group is considered important for the growth of an individual and for developing social skills. However, its adoption as a relied-upon teaching methodology for delivering subject content seems limited – traditions stand fast. As we have seen, Ristelä argued that there are attitudes both for teamwork and against it, and that this ambiguity is reflected in the students' and teachers' responses in this study. This being said, he argued that his study shows that teamwork can be both pleasant and profitable, as soon as we are able to look at its profitability on an adequate scale (Ristelä, 2003).

Assessing the Potential Benefits of Teamwork for Oneself

In order to undertake the following activity, you will need the opportunity to work with at least one, and preferably two or three other colleagues. The activity will take around one hour, and has five parts.

1 Each member working on his or her own, and under 'examination conditions', should write a list of pros and cons concerning the use of group work in self-esteem enhancement work with primary children. (They can refer to the material of Chapter 3 of this text if you wish.) Spend no less than 10 minutes, and no more than 15 minutes, on this task.

2 Working on their own, and again under 'examination conditions', each member should write a few paragraphs on how it felt to do the first exercise. They should be as honest as they can be, and be sure to record any negative reactions that they might have had, no matter how trivial these might appear to be. Again, this task should take no less than 10 minutes, and no more than 15 minutes.

3 Together as a group, members should compare the lists that they made in point 1 of this activity. The group members should then try to come up with a definitive list that suits them all. Again, this should take no less than 10 minutes, and no more than 15 minutes.

4 Again, working together as a group, members should compare the lists that they made in point 2 of this activity. They should try to come up with definitive statements to the following:
   - What were the commonalities in positive responses to the 'individual condition' exercise?
   - What were the commonalities in negative responses to the 'individual condition' exercise?
   - What were the differences between undertaking a task alone (point 1 of this activity), and undertaking the same task in a group (point 3 of this activity)?
   - Which did they prefer, and why?
   - Which did they find to be most academically beneficial, and why?

5 Finally, with your experiences of this activity in mind, spend some time reflecting (in the group and on your own) about students' experiences of and feelings concerning individual and teamwork-based teaching methodologies.

Implications for Educators

In this chapter, we have reviewed a range of approaches within education, most of which probably did not apply to an educator's remit when we ourselves were school students, and almost certainly did not apply when our parents were school students. Yet positive methods of discipline, the teacher's role in resolving student-to-student and student-to-teacher conflict, the necessity to think about group behaviour, and classroom methodologies based on co-operative learning approaches are features of almost every pre-service teacher-training programmes, and quite possibly most teachers' working days. Whilst it is important to embrace new ideas in improving the professional practice of educators, it is also important to reflect upon the genesis and potential applications of such ideas, and it has been an aim for the activities, case study (see above) and points for discussion (see below) of this chapter to help the reader to do this.

Please think about, write short notes on, but above all take the opportunity to discuss with colleagues the following pair of questions:

1 Take a moment to reflect upon your own teaching practice, after having undertaken the activities of this chapter. Would you say that your approaches to discipline and learning may best be characterised as 'positive' and 'co-operative' respectively, or otherwise? What ideas from this chapter, if any, might you incorporate into your professional practice?

2 Which approaches to discipline, conflict resolution and learning prevailed when you were a school student yourself? How have things changed (if they have changed) in between that time and now?

Joliffe, W. (2007) *Co-Operative Learning in the Classroom: Putting it into Practice.* London: Sage. An up-to-date and well-written overall examination of this area, which as we have seen has increased in importance and influence in recent years.

Mindell, A. (1995) *Sitting in the Fire: Large Group Transformations Using Conflict and Diversity.* Portland, OR: Lao Tse Press. This text contains plenty of case material and also has descriptions of key skills, yet is probably most useful for those who are interested in the psychological aspects and large-scale potential for conflict resolution and management approaches.

Rogers, B. (2011) *Classroom Behaviour: A Practical Guide to Effective Teaching, Behaviour Management and Colleague Support,* 3rd edn. London: Sage. An excellent and very practical book on planning and implementing behaviour management strategies, including areas such as positive discipline, dealing with conflict and supporting colleagues.

Peaceful Schools International (2011). *Conflict Resolution in Schools: Every Child Should Feel Respected.* Available at www.peacefulschoolsinternational.org. International network, based at Nova Scotia, Canada, of 340 member schools, committed to organising events and international projects to help schools around the world become more peaceful places.

Thinking about Special Educational Needs

This chapter does *not*, and indeed within its confines, *could not* provide an overview of the substantial body of literature and practice concerning the area of meeting special educational needs in schools. Rather, and in keeping with the goals advanced in other chapters of this text, the aim for this chapter is to help the reader *think through* some key issues in the area of special educational needs. This is made chiefly through the *activities* of this chapter: *challenging oneself as to how one thinks about special educational needs*, the question of *neurodiversity*, and taking a *critical view of research into special educational needs*. In undertaking this, reference is made to just three specific special educational needs areas: *general and specific learning difficulties*; *autistic spectrum disorders*; and *attention deficit hyperactivity disorder*. This chapter concludes with an examination of some *implications for educators*, *points for discussion*, and a selective and an annotated list of *further reading* and *useful websites*.

Challenging Oneself as to How One Thinks about Special Educational Needs

When my former colleague Dr Deirdre O'Neill began teaching her undergraduate students of education about special education needs, she would stress that it was imperative to start by challenging oneself (and accordingly, start the class with such an exercise). So with grateful acknowledgement for the idea, we can do the same here. When a student presents with special educational needs, ask yourself the following questions:

- What do I understand by terms like 'disability', 'learning difficulties' and 'special educational needs'?
- Who has identified that a 'disability', 'learning difficulty' or 'special educational need' exists in a student? What is this identification based upon? Observation? Formal assessment? Anything else (e.g. reading an article on the Internet)? How did this first identification first arise? How have things progressed since?
- What is the student's own understanding of the 'disability', 'learning difficulty' or 'special educational need'? What is the understanding of his or her parents/guardians/teachers/peers?
- What are the concerns of the student, and his or her parents/guardians/teachers/peers? What are your own concerns?
- What are the limits of your own training/professional role? How can you access the collegial support, resources and training that are necessary to assist you in your professional role?
- Is everyone clear about the terminology that is being used in describing the 'disability', 'learning difficulty' or 'special educational need'?
- What questions now remain?

General and Specific Learning Difficulties

When we begin to speak of special education needs such as *general learning difficulties*, the problem of terminology presents itself. As recently as 1995, Arthur Reber noted that 'the favoured cover term is now mental retardation' (p. 451), a term that he contrasted favourably with older lexical categories such as 'mental deficiency', 'mental handicap' and 'feeblemindedness'. The term 'mental retardation' was based purely on IQ scores, with no assumptions being made about abilities, causes, prognoses or supports, and was used to refer to those individuals with IQ scores of two standard deviations or more below the mean; hence, below 70 points. Four categories of mental retardation, again based purely on IQ categories, were distinguished:

> *Mild mental retardation*: 50–55 to 69 IQ points; can develop reasonable social and communication skills and be self-supporting as adults, although may need supervision and guidance; however, do not usually progress beyond the sixth year of schooling.
> *Moderate mental retardation*: 35–40 to 50–55 IQ points; can communicate reasonably well, but show poor awareness of social conventions and need

supervision for living and (unskilled and semi-skilled) work as adults; schooling is rarely successful beyond the second year.

> *Severe mental retardation*: 20–25 to 35–40 IQ points; show poor motor development in childhood, minimal speech, no acquisition of social skills, although can perform simple tasks in closely supervised settings.

> *Profound mental retardation*: usually involves an identifiable neurological disorder, below 20–25 IQ points; minimal sensorimotor functioning is evident in childhood, although as adults, there can be some speech and motor development; can occasionally be taught some limited aspects of self-care, but usually need a highly structured environment with constant supervision by an individual caregiver. (Reber, 1995)

The reader who recalls what was said in Chapter 3 of this text can perhaps acknowledge the power that terms used by educators, psychologists and wider society to *label* individuals have. A poll conducted in the United Kingdom (see Rohrer, 2008) found that 'retard' was the most offensive disability-related word; and in 2006, the American Association on Mental Retardation renamed itself the American Association on Intellectual and Developmental Disabilities (although this was partly because many of its members worked with individuals with developmental disorders, most of whom show no intelligence deficit – see section on 'Autistic Spectrum Disorders', below). It is worth remembering too that some terms which are now used purely as offensive epithets were originally precise psychological terms. A 'moron' (first coined in 1910) once referred specifically to an adult with a mental age of between 8 and 12 years, equating to an IQ of between 51 and 70 points; an 'imbecile' had an IQ of between 26 and 50 points, and an 'idiot' had an IQ of 0 to 25 points (Zenderland, 2001) – therefore, equating to 'mild', 'moderate'/'severe' and 'profound' mental retardation respectively. In a small way, I have witnessed the tendency that descriptor terms for individuals with learning difficulties have to become terms of abuse – moments after explaining the 'mild' to 'profound' categories of mental retardation to an A-Level Psychology class around 15 years ago, I recall hearing a student in the class insult a classmate by calling him 'profound'.

In the American Psychiatric Association (APA)'s *Diagnostic and Statistical Manual of Mental Disorders*, which has been used in the United States and to varying extents in other countries worldwide since it first appeared in 1952, the fifth version (DSM-V) of which is due to be published in May 2013, *intellectual disabilities* are rendered distinct from *learning disorders*. An *intellectual disability* is defined as 'a disorder that includes both a current intellectual deficit and a deficit in adaptive functioning with onset during the developmental period', in which all three of the following criteria must be met:

1 Deficits in general mental abilities such as reasoning, problem-solving, planning, abstract thinking, judgment, academic learning and learning from experience.

2 The deficits in general mental abilities impair functioning in comparison to a person's age and cultural group by limiting and restricting participation and performance in one or more aspects of daily life activities, such as communication, social participation, functioning at school or at work, or personal independence at home or in community settings. The limitations result in the need for ongoing support at school, work, or independent life. Thus, intellectual disability also requires a significant impairment in adaptive functioning.

3 [Have an] onset during the developmental period. (APA, 2011)

It is also noted that coding is no longer based on IQ level, so that 'functionality [should be] improved', 'inaccuracy of testing [should] no longer [be] a factor', and that the 'old criteria failed to consider adaptive behaviours in setting thresholds' (APA, 2011).

Being as the severity of general learning difficulties can vary considerably, and that those individuals most severely affected usually have an identifiable neurological condition, it is difficult to say definitively what 'causes' general learning difficulties. To use American averages, heredity or pre-natal causes can be involved in about 5 per cent of cases (chromosomal aberrations, such as Fragile X syndrome; or an error in chromosome replication, such as Down's syndrome). In about 30 per cent of cases, an early alteration of the embryonic environment is implicated (a maternal infection, such as rubella; pre-natal exposure to toxins, such as foetal alcohol syndrome; and low birth weight, a *risk* factor that does not *inevitably* cause problems, which may result from maternal malnutrition). In about 10 per cent of cases there may be a perinatal cause, such as a lack of oxygen at birth (may cause cerebral palsy). Medical conditions in infancy and childhood account for about 5 per cent of cases, such as those stemming from neglect, poisoning, accidents and malnutrition; and environmental influences account for a further 15–20 per cent of cases. However, this still leaves somewhere around 30–35 per cent of cases where no clear cause is attributable (from APA, 2011; Gleitman, 2010; Reber, 1995; Vander Zanden, 1989).

It is important to distinguish *general* learning difficulties from *specific* learning difficulties, in which an intellectually normal child may have specific problems. In previous versions of the DSM, there were no general criteria for *learning disorders*. Under DSM-V, learning disorders are seen as those that 'interfere with the acquisition and use of one or more of the following academic skills:

oral language, reading, written language, mathematics. These disorders affect individuals who otherwise demonstrate at least average abilities essential for thinking or reasoning' (APA, 2011). It is also stated that the diagnostic criteria for learning disorders 'do not depend upon comparisons with overall IQ and are consistent with the change in [federal] regulations which state that, "the criteria adopted by the State must not require the use of a severe discrepancy between intellectual ability and achievement for determining whether a child has a specific learning disability"' (APA, 2011).

An example of a specific learning difficulty with which educators, teachers and students of education will probably be familiar is *dyslexia*. In defining this, John Stein (2001) differentiated developmental dyslexia from the rather more common problems with literacy: 'low literacy is termed "developmental dyslexia" when reading is significantly behind that expected from the intelligence quotient in the presence of other symptoms – inco-ordination, left–right confusions, poor sequencing – that characterize it as a neurological syndrome' (p. 12), and notes that between 5 and 10 per cent of children are found to be dyslexic, with this being more common in boys (Stein, 2001). Somewhat similar is the specific learning difficulty *dysgraphia*. Again, there is no overall intellectual deficit or general learning difficulty, but as Smits-Engelsman and Van Galen (1997) state, 'even with the proper amount of instruction and practice, [dysgraphic students] fail to make sufficient progress in the acquisition of the fine motor task of handwriting . . . Dysgraphic handwriting lacks consistency that is not due to carelessness or ignorance . . . [these] problems are typically of a motor nature and are not caused by poor spelling or other psycholinguistic problems' (p. 165). They note that 'it is estimated that 5–20 per cent of all children show some form of non-optimal fine motor behavior, including writing disorders' (p. 165).

As well as these literacy-related specific learning difficulties, there is a numeracy-related specific learning difficulty called *dyscalculia*. Landerl et al. (2004) note that traditional (American Psychiatric Association) definitions state that the child must 'substantially underachieve on a standardised test relative to the level expected given age, education and intelligence, and must experience disruption to academic achievement or daily living'. However, they note that mathematical achievement tests 'generally test a range of skills, which may include spatial and verbal abilities, before collapsing the total into one global score of "maths achievement"' (p. 100). Nevertheless, they argue that researchers 'agree that dyscalculia manifests itself as a problem in learning arithmetic facts and calculation procedures [but] the question which remains unanswered relates to the underlying deficits which cause these problems' (p. 101).

It is equally important to distinguish general and specific learning difficulties from developmental and emotional/behavioural disorders, which, as we shall see, often have no implications regarding intellect (see sections on 'Autistic Spectrum Disorders' and 'Attention Deficit Hyperactivity Disorder' below).

National Legislature for Additional Support for Learning (Scotland)

Although it remains, at present, part of the United Kingdom, Scotland has devolved powers of legislature through her own Parliament, which sat for the first time in 1999. The Education (Additional Support for Learning) (Scotland) Act was introduced in October 2003, and received Royal assent on 1 April 2004. Amongst other provisions, the Act:

- replaced 'the concept of Special Educational Needs with Additional Support Needs, which will include children and young people, who, *for whatever reason* require support to access and benefit from education' (my emphasis)
- 'promotes the integrated working of education, health and social work to combine support for children and young people'
- 'aims to increase the involvement of parents in decisions affecting their child's education and to support the involvement of children and young people in their own learning'
- 'aims to safeguard the rights of those with the most significant and enduring needs'
- 'provides for a new Co-ordinated Support Plan (CSP) for children and young people who have enduring needs arising from complex or multiple factors and require support from more than one agency. It places duties on education authorities to identify and assess whether children and young people have additional support needs or require a Co-ordinated Support Plan'
- places 'a duty on education authorities to establish independent mediation services for the purpose of avoiding or resolving disputes'
- ensures that 'any child, young person or parent will be able to have an advocate present during any discussions with the education authority'. (SPICe, 2008)

Although the passage of time since this very significant piece of legislature has been too short to properly judge its impact at the time of writing, its combination of a move away from the restricted definitions of special educational needs used in the past, its strong focus on the policy of inclusion and its presumption of mainstreaming are all progressive (SPICe, 2008), and featured in legislature at a national level for the first time. This Act provides the framework for Scotland to act as a model for good legislative and policy practice on special educational needs into the future.

Autistic Spectrum Disorders

Autism has been defined as 'a developmental disorder characterised by deficits in social interaction and communication, and restricted, repetitive interests and behaviours, beginning in infancy and toddler years' by Gardener et al. (2009), who estimate its prevalence as being 13/10,000 and believed to be rising. It is more common in boys than girls (4.3:1) (Newschaffer et al., 2007), and is unconnected to race, ethnicity or socioeconomic background (Bertoglio and Hendren, 2009). There is no known 'cure', although some individuals have recovered and lost their diagnoses (Helt et al., 2008). The *autistic spectrum* is usually given as including (infantile) autism and two similar disorders: *Asperger Syndrome* (similar to autism; including deficits in social interaction and restricted, repetitive interests and behaviour, but without the communication/language deficits) and *Pervasive Developmental Disorder, Not Otherwise Specified* (PDD-NOS), which may be diagnosed when the conditions necessary for the diagnosis of autism or Aperger syndrome are not all present (APA, 2011). It is debatable as to who first used the term 'autism' in its modern, clinical sense; in the US, Leo Kanner described 11 children under his care as having *early infantile autism* in 1943; however, Hans Asperger had used the term *autistic psychopathy* in a lecture (to a German-speaking audience) in 1938. Whether Kanner knew of Asperger's usage of the term is unknown (Lyons and Fitzgerald, 2007).

The term 'autism' (*aut-* = self; *-ism* = orientation or state) *literally* refers to a tendency to be absorbed in oneself; a condition in which one's thoughts, feelings and desires are governed by one's internal apprehensions of the world (Reber, 1995). However, when used in its non-literal, clinical/educational sense, because the term implies pathology, it refers to an internal state that is not consonant with a shared reality – hence, not mere introversion, as the literal meaning might suggest. Because the term 'autism' has acquired this clinical/educational usage, the term *autic* is preferred when the literal meaning is required. Neuropsychologist Marie T. Banich (1997) stated that children with autism 'seem to avoid interacting with the environment and people, and act as if the world around them is intrusive [which] leads to both social isolation and cognitive deprivation' (p. 481). Confusingly, the term 'autism' was first coined in the mental health literature in 1910 by the Swiss psychiatrist Eugen Bleuler as a suggested term (never widely taken up) for what was the condition that was then referred to as *dementia praecox* and is now called *schizophrenia* (the term that Bleuler settled on) (Cahn, 2004). It is extremely important to note that autism and schizophrenia, of course, are *not* the same.

Under DSM-V, autism spectrum disorder is to be categorised as a neuro-developmental disorder, and it is proposed (APA, 2011) that for it to be diagnosed, four criteria should be met:

1 'persistent deficits in social communication and social interaction across contexts, not accounted for by general developmental delays', manifested by 'deficits in social-emotional reciprocity', 'deficits in non-verbal communicative behaviours used for social interaction' and 'deficits in developing and maintaining relationships, appropriate to developmental level (beyond those with caregivers)'
2 'restricted, repetitive patterns of behaviour, interests, or activities', for example 'stereotyped or repetitive speech, motor movements, or use of objects'; 'excessive adherence to routines, ritualized patterns of verbal or non-verbal behaviour, or excessive resistance to change'; 'highly restricted, fixated interests that are abnormal in intensity or focus'; and, 'hyper- or hypo-reactivity to sensory input, or unusual interest in sensory aspects of environment'
3 'symptoms must be present in early childhood (but may not become fully manifest until social demands exceed limited capacities)'
4 'symptoms together limit and impair everyday function'.

(APA, 2011)

Previously, autism was sometimes divided into low-, medium- or high-functioning autism, depending on IQ scores (Baron-Cohen, 2006). Estimations of the proportion of autistic individuals who may also be categorised as mentally retarded vary between 25 and 70 per cent, a finding that has been interpreted as showing the difficulties of assessing the IQ scores of individuals with autism (Dawson et al., 2008). It is proposed that under DSM-V, three severity levels ('requiring support', 'requiring substantial support' and 'requiring very substantial support'), based on social communication, and restricted interests and repetitive behaviours, and should be specified (APA, 2011). An estimated 60 to 80 per cent of people with autism show motor difficulties, including poor muscle tone, poor motor planning, and toe walking (Geschwind, 2009), and unusual patterns of eating (selectivity, eating rituals and food refusal) occur in around 75 per cent of children with autistic spectrum disorders (Dominick et al., 2007).

Gardener et al. (2009) report that the causes of autism remain unknown; however, the estimated 60–92 per cent concordance rate between identical twins, compared with the estimated 0–10 per cent concordance rate between non-identical twins, indicates a strong genetic influence, but the fact that the concordance rate between identical twins is not perfect shows that environmental factors also play a role. They argue that it is likely that multiple genes are involved, and that environmental factors may interact with genetic factors to increase the risk of autism. Hence, the original theories that autism was caused somehow by 'cold mothering' (e.g. Bettleheim, 1967) have been shown to be groundless. Whilst the precise constellation of brain areas involved is not clear, some specific areas have been implicated (Banich, 1997), in terms of both structure and function, and it seems that it is the prenatal period of brain development that is critical (Gardener et al., 2009). However, whilst Gardener et al.'s (2009) systematic review and meta-analysis of the literature on the relationship between pregnancy complications, pre-natal development and autism indicated that over 50 pre-natal risk factors have been studied, 'there is insufficient evidence to implicate any one pre-natal factor in autism aetiology, although there is some evidence to suggest that exposure to pregnancy complications may increase the risk' (p.7). The factors associated with autism risk were 'advanced parental age at birth, maternal prenatal medication use, bleeding, gestational diabetes, being first-born versus third or later, and having a mother born abroad' (Gardener et al., 2009, p. 7).

As autism is evident in infancy; it tends to be noticed first by parents/caregivers, who notice signs such as lower eye-contact, lower turn-taking, less use of gestures (such as pointing), and delays in language development, usually in the first two years of life (Ozonoff et al., 2008). Filipek et al. (1999) cite no babbling or gesturing (pointing, waving) by 12 months, no single words by 16 months, no two-word spontaneous phrases by 24 months, and any loss of previously acquired language or social skills at any age to be 'an absolute indication to proceed with further evaluations'. However, it should be noted that claims that intervention by around age 3 years is crucial are *not* substantiated (Howlin et al., 2009).

Worryingly, even though more than half of American children with autistic spectrum disorders are prescribed drug treatments (Oswald and Soneklar, 2007), there is little in the way of hard evidence for either their effectiveness or their safety (Broadstock et al., 2007). However, educational interventions have demonstrated effectiveness in enhancing the global functioning and improving the intellectual performance of young children (Eikeseth, 2009; Rogers and Vismara, 2008). For example, Alloway (2011) asserts that 'the primary area of memory weakness in a student with ASD is verbal short-term memory' (p. 94), and recommends teaching strategies that reduce the amount of effort involved in switching between tasks, where those with autistic spectrum disorders will have difficulty determining which is the more relevant. This can include offering only one task at a time; limiting the number of assignments that deal with abstract concepts; providing as much structure as possible; encouraging students with ASD to develop their own learning and memory strategies; and connecting new information to their long-term memory base. As students with ASD can react differently to certain physical stimuli (such as noise, light, crowding), it is also important to attend to the physical and social aspects of the classroom/learning environment (Alloway, 2011).

Applied Behaviour Analysis (ABA) is an approach that involves using techniques derived from the psychological discipline known as behaviourism (see this text, Chapter 1) to modify behaviours. Whilst articles in the *Journal of Applied Behaviour Analysis* evidence its application in such diverse areas as safety in open-pit mining (Fox et al., 1987) and zoo management (Forthman and Ogden, 1992), ABA is best known for its use in treating autistic spectrum disorders (Eldevik et al., 2009). According to Baer et al.'s (1968) original article on the subject, ABA has seven dimensions: it is applied (i.e. focussed on areas of social and long-term significance); it is focussed on behavioural change; it is analytical (i.e. behavioural scientists have credible control); it is technological (i.e. replicable by other researchers using the same procedures); it is conceptually systematic; it is effective; and it exhibits generality (i.e. it should produce long-lasting effects in areas not directly treated by the intervention, and outlast the intervention period).

In Eikeseth's (2009) substantive review of the effectiveness of methods of early intervention for children with autism, it is demonstrated that 'children receiving ABA made significantly more gains than control group children on standardized measures of IQ, language and adaptive functioning' (p. 173), and that some studies have shown the positive effects of ABA with children with autism on maladaptive behaviour, personality, school performance and changes in diagnosis. ABA treatment has also been demonstrated as effective in enhancing global functioning in children with PDD-NOS. However, Eikeseth (2009) also notes that ABA treatment is effective in enhancing global functioning in children with autism 'when treatment is intensive and carried out by trained therapists (p. 176)', and for children who are up to 7 years old at the beginning of the intervention, thus emphasising both the importance of early intervention and the role of specialist practitioners.

Ortega (2009) notes that although ABA is 'for many parents, the only therapy that leads autistic children to make some progress in the form of establishing visual contact and performing limited cognitive tasks' (p. 429), it has been attacked by autism advocates who consider that autism is *not* an illness, and resent a 'cure' strategy that they see as repressing autistic people's natural modes of expression. As Ortega (2009) points out, autism advocacy has been 'largely organised around the neurodiversity movement, which emerged during the 1990s' (p. 426), and it is towards this movement that we shall turn our attention now.

Neurodiversity

The first autistic parents' association to appear was the UK's National Autistic Society (in 1962), and Ortega (2009) argues that one of the earliest online parent lists, the Autism and Developmental Disabilities List (AUTISM List), contributed to the spread of ABA. However, as Ortega notes, 'while most pro-cure parent and professional associations refuse to identify positively with the condition (because they see autism as a disease, and therefore something one is afflicted with), autistic self-advocates take pride in the condition. This is epitomised in their rejection of the term "person with autism" and the adoption of labels such as "autie" or "aspie"' (2009, p. 427). Rather than a treatable disease, they believe that ASD is a human continuum, due to a variant neurological organisation, that must be equally respected. The chief features of the neurodiversity argument are:

- The acknowledgement that neurodiverse people do not need a 'cure'.
- The changing of the language from the current medical-based nomenclature.
- Broadening the understanding of healthy or independent living and the acknowledgement of new types of autonomy.
- Giving neurodiverse individuals more control over their treatment, including the type, timing, and whether there should be treatment at all. (Fenton and Krahn, 2007)

On a critical note, however, Ortega (2009) notes that 'the neurodiversity movement constitutes a minority within the total spectrum of autism' (p. 427); and that the movement has been 'dominated by people diagnosed with Asperger Syndrome and other forms of high-functioning autism [and that] it would be hypocritical to subsume all forms of the autistic continuum under the "high-functional", and then happily consider that autism is a lifestyle' (p. 426).

Consider the above as you think about, and preferably discuss with colleagues, the implications that the concept of neurodiversity has for the way in which we, as both educators and members of society, think about people with autistic spectrum disorders. How does this contrast with the approach taken by advocates of ABA treatment? Which (neurodiversity or ABA) do you find the more convincing, and why? What might the implications of each be for the way in which students with autistic spectrum disorders are educated?

Attention Deficit Hyperactivity Disorder

Attention Deficit Hyperactivity Disorder (ADHD) is one of the most common psychiatric disorders diagnosed in children (Goldman et al., 1998), involving a combination of symptoms relating to inattention, hyperactivity and impulsivity

(APA, 2011). The worldwide-pooled prevalence rate for ADHD has been found to be 5.29 per cent (Polanczyk et al., 2007), and is between twice and four times more frequently diagnosed in boys (Goldman et al., 1998; Southall, 2007). ADHD is also a controversial disorder; Jadad et al. (1999) stated that professional opinions vary from those who see it as a biologically-based medical condition to those who see it as a myth. Southall (2007), for example, asserts that 'ADHD is not only contentious but also a highly political diagnosis' (p. 2). Jadad et al. (1999) argued that 'several features of ADHD contribute to the controversy' (p. 1026), including:

> It is a clinical diagnosis for which there are no laboratory or radiological confirmatory tests or specific physical features.
> Diagnostic criteria have changed frequently.
> There is no curative treatment, so patients require long-term therapies.
> Therapy often includes stimulant drugs that are thought to have abuse potential.
> The rates of diagnosis and of treatment substantially differ across countries, particularly Britain, Australia, Canada, and the United States (US). (Jadad et al., 1999, p. 1026)

A more recent review of 303 full-text articles worldwide concerning ADHD amongst those aged less than 18 years was conducted by Polanczyk et al. (2007) in order to investigate discrepancies in the diagnosis rates for ADHD worldwide. They found that geographical location plays only a limited role in accounting for these discrepancies: variations were significant between North America and Africa/the Middle East, but not between North America and Europe, and the variability is better explained by the differing methodologies used in the studies. This seems to indicate that diagnostic rates have been brought into line between the US and UK in particular; it is possible that this is attributable to the rapid increase in the frequency of the diagnosis of ADHD in the UK over the last decade (Southall, 2007).

Fourteen years after Jadad et al.'s (1999) paper, the diagnostic criteria for ADHD are set to undergo a substantive revision, although not in a way that will incorporate the 'laboratory or radiological confirmatory tests or specific physical features' that Jadad et al. (1999) referred to. Under the DSM-V, it is proposed that ADHD should be listed under the diagnostic category of Disruptive, Impulse Control and Conduct Disorder. ADHD is described as consisting of 'a characteristic pattern of behavior and cognitive functioning that is present in different settings where it gives rise to social and educational or work performance difficulties' (APA, 2011). In the proposed revisions for the diagnosis of ADHD in DSM-V, two broad groups of symptoms are listed: those pertaining to *inattention* and those pertaining to *hyperactivity/impulsivity*. For a diagnosis to be made, six or more of the symptoms in either group (or four or more for those over the age of 17 years) should have been present for at least six months, and to a degree that is 'inconsistent with developmental level and that impact directly on social and academic/occupational activities' and not be due to 'oppositional behavior, defiance, hostility, or a failure to understand tasks or instructions' (APA, 2011). The symptoms of the *inattention* group are:

> Often fails to give close attention to details or makes careless mistakes in schoolwork, at work, or during other activities.
> Often has difficulty sustaining attention in tasks or play activities.
> Often does not seem to listen when spoken to directly.
> Frequently does not follow through on instructions.
> Often has difficulty organizing tasks and activities.
> Characteristically avoids, seems to dislike, and is reluctant to engage in tasks that require sustained mental effort.
> Frequently loses objects necessary for tasks or activities.
> Is often easily distracted by extraneous stimuli.
> Is often forgetful in daily activities, chores, and running errands.

(APA, 2011)

The symptoms of the *hyperactivity/impulsivity* group are:

> Often fidgets or taps hands or feet or squirms in seat.
> Is often restless during activities when others are seated.
> Often runs about or climbs on furniture and moves excessively in inappropriate situations.
> Is often excessively loud or noisy during play, leisure, or social activities.
> Is often 'on the go,' acting as if 'driven by a motor'.
> Often talks excessively.
> Often blurts out an answer before a question has been completed.
> Has difficulty waiting his or her turn or waiting in line.
> Often interrupts or intrudes on others.
> Tends to act without thinking, such as starting tasks without adequate preparation or avoiding reading or listening to instructions.
> Is often impatient, as shown by feeling restless when waiting for others and wanting to move faster than others.
> Is uncomfortable doing things slowly and systematically and often rushes through activities or tasks.
> Finds it difficult to resist temptations or opportunities, even if it means taking risks.

(APA, 2011)

For a diagnosis of ADHD to be made, symptoms should be present by age of 12 years, and apparent in two or more settings (e.g. at home, school or work), and should 'not occur exclusively during the course of schizophrenia or another psychotic disorder and are not better accounted for by another mental disorder' (APA, 2011). At the time of writing (June 2011), severity criteria for ADHD are listed as 'forthcoming' (APA, 2011).

The specific causes of ADHD are not known. An explanation that has captured the public imagination is Thom Hartmann's 'hunter-farmer' theory (Hartmann, 1995, 2003) in which it is argued that human beings were hunter-gatherers for much of their history, but since the development of agriculture have become 'farmers'. Those with ADHD have not psychologically adapted to this 'farmer' existence, but retain previously useful (for survival) 'hunter' characteristics, which are not deemed as useful in the context of a classroom.

However, for the most part, Southall (2007) reports that 'pharmaceutical companies have helped to promote an increasingly biological understanding of mental health problems'. The analysis of twin studies suggests that genetics are a factor in about 75 per cent of cases, but there are indications that both genes and the environment are involved in a complex set of predispositions and interaction effects (Acosta et al., 2004). Nevertheless, stimulant drugs remain the treatment of choice in the United States (Southall, 2007), although under the National Institute for Health and Clinical Excellence's (NICE) guidelines in the United Kingdom, this is recommended in moderate and severe, and not mild, cases for school-aged people and adults, and never for pre-school children. NICE acknowledges concerns regarding safety and the potential for misuse of such drugs, and recommends that parents of young people affected by ADHD should attend training or education programmes, and that trained teachers should provide behavioural classroom interventions (Kendall et al. 2008). On the basis of short-term memory being unaffected by ADHD, but visual-spatial memory and time-management skills being affected, Alloway (2011) suggests that when teachers are working with ADHD students, lists of classroom instructions should be kept short (one or two items fewer than the average limit for the students' age); study periods should be kept short (e.g. in a 20-minute reading task, take a break of three minutes half way through); opportunities for rehearsal of material (i.e. pop quizzes) are provided; and that the physical energy of students with ADHD should be harnessed by relating learning tasks to physical actions.

A Critical View of Research into Special Educational Needs

As we have seen in the section immediately above, ADHD is a controversial area in terms of how it is conceptualised, diagnosed, caused and treated, and whether it exists at all. All of these questions also relate to how ADHD has been researched, about which British clinical psychologist Angela Southall (2007) has grave concerns. In her *The Other Side of ADHD*, she reports that:

> It has been suggested that over 70 per cent of research into [the] drug treatment [of ADHD] is funded by the drug companies themselves. Whilst not necessarily invalidating the research in question, such funding surely raises an important question about conflict of interest. Critics of drug company-sponsored research point out that whoever pays for the research is crucial. The paymaster, they suggest, determines not only how the research is conducted, but also what gets reported (and what does not) once the study is completed (p. 40).

Southall gives as an example the National Institute for Mental Health Multimodal Treatment Study for ADHD (also known as the MTA study), one of whose researchers, Dr Russell Barkley, considered to be a world authority on ADHD, 'admits to taking money from drug companies for consultancy and speaking engagements [but] does not see this as problematic because it represents only a small proportion of his income'.

It is to be acknowledged that Southall is not a neutral party in the debate; she says of her *The Other Side of ADHD* that 'my sole purpose [was not] to challenge the view that ADHD exists (although I hope that through a wider discussion it will help readers to consider this possibility)' (2007, p. 2).

Consider the above as you think about, and discuss with colleagues and perhaps even family members and friends, whether research into the treatment of special educational needs is, should be, or even can be free of political and financial interests.

Implications for Educators

It was acknowledged at the beginning that this chapter could not and did not attempt to provide an overview of the area of special educational needs. However, we have promoted *challenging oneself as to how one thinks about special educational needs* through the examination of *general and specific learning difficulties*; considered the question of *neurodiversity* through the examination of *autistic spectrum disorders*; and taken a *critical view of research into special educational needs* through the examination of *attention deficit hyperactivity disorder*. Some further and especially critical implications are elicited in the 'Points for Discussion' below.

Please think about, write short notes on, but above all take the opportunity to discuss with colleagues the following pair of questions:

1 Consider the breadth of the proposed criteria in the DSM-V diagnostic categories for ASD and ADHD, as outlined above, and the issues arising from the activities of this chapter. If the diagnosis of these areas of special educational needs becomes more frequent, and the provision of additional supports to schools is diminished, is the likelihood of educators being asked to do 'more with less' due to become an inevitability? Could this in turn prompt the 'easy fix' of the medication route?

2 Most educational professionals these days are careful in the terminology they use around the area of special educational needs. It could be argued that how we speak about differences is rooted in how we think about these differences, which in turn affects how we are likely to act on them. To what extent do you think that this 'carefulness' is attributable to genuine changes in how educators think about and treat those with special educational needs, and to what extent do you think it may be attributable to other factors (such as 'political correctness')?

Alloway, T.P. (2011) *Improving Working Memory: Supporting Students' Learning*. London: Sage. Contains evidence- and theory-based practical strategies, based on the concept of working memory, to assist educators in working with students with dyslexia, dyscalculia, speech and language difficulties, dyspraxia, ADHD and autistic spectrum disorders.

Cline, T. and Frederickson, N. (2009) *Special Educational Needs, Inclusion and Diversity*. Buckingham: Open University Press. An excellent contemporary review of the area of special educational needs.

Thomas, G. and Loxley, A. (2007) *Deconstructing Special Education and Constructing Inclusion*. Buckingham: Open University Press. A stimulating and lively critical examination of a range of issues surrounding special education and inclusion.

TES Connect. *Special Needs Teaching Resources*. Available at www.tes.co.uk/
sen-teaching-resources (accessed June 2011). Free learning resources for special
educational needs (SEN) teachers, including lesson plans, activities, games, teaching
ideas, classroom resources and worksheets.

7

Preventing and Countering Bullying Behaviour and Cyber-bullying in Schools

The primary goal for this chapter is to provide the reader with an introduction to bullying and cyber-bullying: how these areas have been researched, and how inroads can be made into preventing and countering these behaviours in schools and school communities. In order to be effective in accomplishing this, we must first consider *what is school bullying*? We then examine the different *types of bullying behaviour*, including cyber-bullying, and empirical research *evidence* into these areas. The chapter then takes a more practical turn: *key issues for schools and school staff* emerge, and *practical ideas for anti-bullying work in schools* are presented. These include ideas for action at the classroom, school and broader community levels: a deep consideration of how the whole-school approach is applied. This chapter concludes with a reflective examination of some *implications for educators*, *points for discussion*, and a selective and annotated list of *further reading* and *useful websites*.

What is School Bullying?

As I have argued elsewhere (Minton, 2010a), if we wish to be effective in reducing the incidence of school bullying, the first thing to do is to work out precisely what we mean by the term. If one works at a practical level in school communities, one must be aware that at the outset, students, parents and school staff are not always 'singing from the same hymn sheet'. Younger children will tend to over-apply the word 'bullying'; parents, particularly those who grew up in a time when less was known and done about bullying behaviour in schools, may be more sensitive to bullying when they perceive that their children are on the 'receiving end' than they would be were their children involved as perpetrators (O'Moore and Minton, 2004). Likewise, teachers' knowledge and skills regarding the prevention and countering of bullying behaviour in schools may vary, according to where and perhaps most of all *when* they were trained – as we shall see, the development of specific knowledge and school resources really is a feature only of the last two decades. So it is important to be clear what we mean; ambiguities ultimately mean that the vulnerable may 'fall through the gaps'.

Arriving at One's Own Definition of Bullying

Either working on your own as a thought exercise, or in discussion with colleagues, please answer the following questions:

- How would you approach defining school bullying behaviour?
- Which words or phrases would you include?

Now try to write a working definition of bullying behaviour, suitable for use in school communities, in four sentences or less.

If you haven't already done so, consider the ideas of repetition and power imbalance as distinguishing features of bullying behaviour, and answer the following questions:

- Is it always necessary for behaviour to be repeated to be considered as bullying? If not, why not? Is there some bullying that isn't characterised by repetition, and if so, how is such bullying behaviour characterised?
- Does there have to be a power imbalance between the perpetrator(s) and the target(s) to characterise the behaviour as bullying?
- Are other factors important to consider in characterising behaviour as bullying? Intentionality, perhaps? Is there any bullying that is unintentional (consider the different perspectives of the perpetrator(s) and target(s), perhaps with specific reference to younger children)?

Now revisit the definition of bullying you provided before. Can you improve upon it?

Through working on the activity above, you can perhaps understand that there are many possible definitions of bullying behaviour, but it will suffice to say that most experts acknowledge a number of key aspects in approaching a definition (Minton, 2010a). Hence, bullying behaviour is:

> *aggressive* (verbally, psychologically or physically)
> *deliberate* on the part of the perpetrator(s)
> generally *unprovoked* on the part of the target(s) of the bullying
> repeated, or *systematic* in nature
> characterised by an *imbalance of power in favour of the perpetrator(s)* – this could be physical power (such as superior size and strength); social power (e.g. a popular person deliberately manipulating friendship groups in order to exclude someone); or, in the case of cyber-bullying, technological power (a person using his or her superior knowledge of or access to technological systems in order to abuse or harass someone).

When all of these things are present, we may reasonably refer to the behaviour in question as *bullying* (Minton, 2010a). An established expert definition that I have found helpful in a variety of contexts, which incorporates most of the 'key aspects' I have outlined above – generated in Norway (Roland, 1989) and used there as well as in Scotland (Mellor, 1999) and Ireland (Minton, 2010b) – is as follows:

> Bullying is long-standing violence, mental or physical, conducted by an individual or a group against an individual who is not able to defend himself or herself in that actual situation. (Roland, 1989; in Mellor, 1999, p. 93–94)

Types of Bullying Behaviour

Traditionally, two broad types of school bullying behaviour have been discerned. They are referred to as *direct* and *indirect* bullying (Olweus, 1978). *Direct* bullying involves relatively overt, or open attacks on a target; it includes, but is not limited to, *verbal* bullying (teasing, name-calling, use of unwelcome nicknames, non-good-natured 'slagging', direct threats), *physical* bullying (from minor but persistent physical irritations to serious assaults), *gesture* bullying (threatening, intimidating or insulting non-verbal communication) and *extortion* (possessions and resources being stolen or deliberately damaged) (O'Moore and Minton, 2004). *Indirect* bullying is more hidden, or covert; it usually involves the deliberate manipulation of friendship and peer groups to leave a target out, to exclude him or her, to make him or her unpopular, or to damage his or her reputation. It may be characterised, therefore, by the spreading of gossip, rumours or lies, nasty notes, pictures or graffiti, strategic inclusions and invitations and so on (O'Moore and Minton, 2004). As a general rule, male and female students have been found to be involved to differing extents in the various types of bullying behaviour: female students have been found to be significantly more likely to use indirect forms of bullying and aggression, and male students have been found to be significantly more likely to use physical forms (Minton, 2010b). It is important to note that there are, of course, some boys who bully indirectly and some girls who bully physically.

Cyber-bullying has been defined as

> an aggressive, intentional act carried out by a group or individual, using electronic forms of contact, repeatedly over time against a victim who cannot easily defend him- or herself. (Smith et al., 2006)

Smith et al. (2006) identified seven sub-categories of cyber-bullying behaviour: text-message bullying; bullying by the taking, sending and publication of photographs or film-clips via mobile telephone cameras; telephone call bullying; e-mail bullying; chat-room bullying; bullying through Instant Messaging (IM); and bullying via websites (defamatory blogs, personal websites, online personal polling sites, general polling sites and social networking sites) (O'Moore and Minton, 2011). In a point that has ramifications for how we characterise and deal with both bulling and cyber-bullying, Vandebosch et al. argue that there are important differences between cyber-bullying and non-cyber forms of bullying:

> With cyber-bullying, it is not necessarily the case that the victim is harassed repeatedly. A defamatory website, for example, will often stay online for a longer period of time and can, moreover, be read by many individuals. A spoken insult, by contrast, disappears from the moment it is uttered, and is only heard by those present at the time. (2006, p. 1)

This line of argument prompts one to consider 'where the "repetition" lies; in cyber-bullying, the *perpetrator's act* of posting offensive material is a one-off event, but due to the possibility of multiple viewers and viewing, the *target's experience* of being abused is one of repetition' (O'Moore and Minton, 2011, p. 4).

I would now like to make some points about my *general approach* to the issue of bullying in schools and school communities. It is not helpful to 'label' someone as a *bully* (O'Moore and Minton, 2004); if the reader recalls what was said in Chapter 3 of this text concerning the communication of negative expectancies, and the likelihood of a subsequent 'self-fulfilling prophecy', it is easy to see why. Similarly, *victimhood* is a psychological response; if one has sufficient self-esteem and resilience, one might be the *target* of someone else's unacceptable behaviour without adopting a *victimised* standpoint. Therefore, in my own work, I have endeavoured to use the word 'bully' as a *verb* only, and *not* a noun (e.g. O'Moore and Minton, 2004); whereas some will talk about 'bullies' and 'victims', I prefer to talk about 'perpetrators' and 'targets' of bullying behaviour, or 'those who bully' and 'those who are bullied'.

Practical approaches to dealing with bullying behaviour in schools have moved towards what has been called a 'no-blame' (Robinson and Maines, 1997) or 'problem-solving' (O'Moore and Minton, 2004) approach. Instead of the ineffective reliance on sanctions *alone*, which provide no insight into the root of the problem, and potentially prompt only a resentment of sanctioning bodies and vengefulness, a focussed challenging and changing of the inappropriate behaviour is advocated in this newer approach (O'Moore and Minton, 2004). This approach also rests on the assumption that young people who are involved in bullying, aggressive behaviour and harassment as targets, perpetrators, both targets and perpetrators, or bystanders, need the coordinated help, support and intervention of both school personnel and parents/guardians. Preventing and countering bullying behaviour can usefully be viewed as a *community issue*; hence, although we focus on the behaviour that goes on *between students* in this chapter, other potential dyads are important and have been considered by researchers, including teacher-on-teacher, teacher-on-student, student-on-teacher and parent-on-teacher (see Smith, 2003, for reviews).

Bullying Behaviour and Cyber-bullying in Schools: The Evidence

There has been an awareness of the issue of bullying in schools for many years; Rigby et al. (2004) note that, 'there was much animated public discussion of bullying in English private schools in the mid-nineteenth century, following the publication of the famous novel *Tom Brown's School Days* (Hughes, 1857)' (p. 1). However, the formal scientific investigation of the issue of school bullying dates back less than four decades. One of the first sets of data on school bullying was accrued via Michael Rutter's classic studies (1964–1974) of psychiatric epidemiology amongst children on the Isle of Wight (1964–1974) (Rutter, 1976). However, it was in Scandinavia, largely through the pioneering work of Dan Olweus, that the large-scale empirical investigation of school bullying and subsequent design of evidence-based intervention programmes was first developed. Olweus initiated a survey of bullying behaviour in the greater Stockholm area in 1970 (Olweus, 1973; in Olweus, 1978) and, in a subsequent nationwide survey of bullying behaviour conducted in Norway in 1983, showed that 15 per cent of 7- to 16-year-old students were involved in bullying behaviour: 9 per cent as targets, 7 per cent as perpetrators and 1.6 per cent as both perpetrators and targets (Olweus, 1993).

The methods and ideas of Olweus and other researchers in the Nordic countries spread to other countries throughout the late 1980s and 1990s. The European Seminar for Teachers on Bullying in Schools was held in Stavanger, Norway, in 1988; O'Moore (1997) judged that the seminar was 'instrumental . . . in awakening Europe to the need for research into school bullying' (p. 136). In 1999, although Vettenburg reported that it was still almost impossible to say how common bullying behaviour was in European schools, Smith et al. (1999) published a collection of 21 national reports on what was known about bullying in schools in different countries worldwide. For example, in a survey undertaken in Scotland in 1989, it was found that that 6 per cent of 12- to 16-year-old students reported that they had been bullied, and that 4 per cent reported that they had been involved in bullying others (Mellor, 1990). In a study of over 6,700 participants in England (in Sheffield, South Yorkshire, in 1990) it was found that 27 per cent of primary school students and 10 per cent of secondary school students reported having been bullied 'sometimes' or more frequently (Smith, 1997). In Ireland, a nationwide study of 20,422 students undertaken in the school year 1993–1994, found that 31.2 per cent of primary students and 15.6 per cent of secondary school children reported having been bullied within the last school term (O'Moore et al. 1997). In Australia, studies have permitted an estimate that 'one child in six or seven is being bullied in Australian schools with quite unacceptable frequency, that is, on a weekly basis or more often' (Rigby and Slee, 1999). Knowledge and data in this area is still accruing: in a study of 5,569 students in the school year 2004–2005, it was found that bully/victim problems appear to be persistent in Irish schools, with 35.3 per cent of primary students and 36.4 per cent of post-primary students reporting having been bullied in the last school term (Minton, 2010b).

The history of systematic studies of *cyber-bullying*, of course, is far shorter – somewhere in the order of five years or so (at the time of writing). In 2006, studies undertaken in the United Kingdom (amongst 92 students aged 11–16 years by Smith et al.) and in Canada (amongst 177 seventh-graders by Li) were published showing that 25 per cent and 54 per cent respectively reported having been cyber-bullied within the last few months. A larger Flemish study published the same year (involving 636 primary school students and 1,416 secondary school students) showed that when the 'number of youngsters who [had] come into contact with at least one form of potentially offensive behaviour over the Internet or mobile phone that can be classified as being related to cyber-bullying over the last three months' (p. 5) was examined, 61.9 per cent reported having been targets, 52.5 per cent reported having been perpetrators, and 76.3 per cent reported having been bystanders (Vandebosch et al., 2006). Two years later, a larger study still in Ireland involving 2,794 students aged 12–16 years, and using similar definitions to Smith et al.'s (2006), found that around one in seven (14.2 per cent) reported having been cyber-bullied, and around one in eleven (8.7 per cent) reported having taken part in the cyber-bullying of others, within the past couple of months (O'Moore and Minton, 2011).

O'Moore and Minton (2004) recorded that being made the target of bullying behaviour can 'destroy a person's confidence and self-esteem [and] cause physical, emotional and psychological damage of the potentially most serious and long-lasting kind' (p. 1). This was based on studies such as those in Finland where Kumpulainen et al. (2001), in a study of 423 parents and 420 children, found that children involved in bully/victim problems were more likely to have psychiatric disorders (most frequently, attention deficit disorder, oppositional/conduct disorder and depression) than those who were not so involved, and Kaltiala-Heino (1999) found that having been bullied was associated with depression and suicidal ideation. Furthermore, Neil Marr and the late Tim Field estimated that *16 children a year* in the United Kingdom take their own lives as a result of literally having been 'bullied to death' (p. 3). In their book on the subject of 'bullycide', the earliest case they describe dates back to 1967; the youngest victim was, tragically, just nine years old (Marr and Field, 2001).

Cyber-bullying too has been unequivocally linked to cases of adolescent suicides in many countries, such as Belgium (see Boylan, 2008), Ireland (Riegel, 2007), New Zealand (Bramwell and Mussen, 2003), the United Kingdom (Fleming, 2004) and the United States (Toppo, 2006). Hence the question as to whether bullying or cyber-bullying can 'push young people over the edge' is very readily answered by the fact that it already has done. Therefore, let no-one underestimate the serious nature of school bullying and cyber-bullying.

Key Issues for Schools and School Staff

A way to consider what the key issues are for schools and school staff, and to make suggestions as to how they should be addressed, is to review the aspects that should be included in school anti-bullying policy. Since evidence-based anti-bullying action began in the form of designing anti-bullying programmes for schools (see Olweus, 1999; O'Moore and Minton, 2004), attention has been given over to first establishing a strong policy document that serves to underpin and direct the practical and day-to-day implementation of anti-bullying procedures and strategies in the school. However, even before such policy is formulated or revised, O'Moore and Minton (2004) have suggested that those responsible for the task should consider the following questions:

> Who will take the responsibility for the formation and implementation of anti-bullying policy and strategies?
> What are the overall goals for the anti-bullying policy?
> Should we focus exclusively on bullying, or cover related issues such as aggressive behaviour, harassment or indiscipline?
> Who should this policy serve? Students? Teachers? Everyone?
> How can we find practical ways of involving classroom staff, parents and students in the policy formation process?
> What are the relevant legal, curricular and policy issues to be aware of? (p. 10–11)

It should then be borne in mind that a good anti-bullying policy in a school should specify:

> How bullying is defined, and the forms it takes.
> How incidents of alleged bullying behaviour are to be reported, investigated and recorded.
> How incidents of bullying behaviour are to be dealt with, including support and intervention; strategies for those involved (both perpetrators and targets) and, where necessary, the specification of sanctions for perpetrators.
> Preventative strategies in the school and classroom.
> The role of school management staff, classroom staff, parents/guardians, students and relevant others in the above.
> Measures for dissemination, evaluation and review. (O'Moore and Minton, 2004, p. 88)

Regarding the last point, it has been argued that 'a school should be proud of its pro-active stance against bullying behaviour. To act publically against bullying behaviour is not an admission of past problems; it is, rather, a statement that the school is finding practical ways to safeguard the people of the community of which it is a part' (O'Moore and Minton, 2004, p. 20). Indeed, in the 'Zero' anti-bullying programme in Norway (Roland et al., 2010), the logo of the programme sometimes appear upon the soccer team shirts of the participating schools, and is emblazoned on the high-visibility vests that teachers in the participating schools wear on yard/playground duty (Ytre-Arne and Dirdal, 2004). I would also argue that a school's anti-bullying policy statement needs to provide sufficient clarity on the school's position on cyber-bullying (see below), and on race/ethnicity-related, homophobic and alterophobic bullying (see this text, Chapter 8). It has also been advised that the written anti-bullying statement should be 'construed as a matter of public record; displayed on school notice boards as a permanent poster; available to all school students in a language they can understand; given to all members of staff, especially new and non-permanent members; given to all parents, especially those "new" to the school; distributed to all relevant groups in the school community; and evaluation and review measures should be "built in" – reviews must be made at least annually' (O'Moore and Minton, 2004, p. 88).

The School's Anti-Bullying Policy Statement

Equip yourself with a copy of your school's anti-bullying policy statement. Does it provide sufficient clarity for the school's management and classroom staff to act effectively in countering and preventing incidents of school bullying? If not, please think about what you can do in order to facilitate its review and update.

Practical Ideas for Anti-bullying Work in Schools

Action at the Classroom Level

Classroom staff members can make great contributions to their schools' anti-bullying actions via promoting preventative strategies. The most basic way to create an awareness of bullying and its problems with one's students is to have a talk with them about it. But what things should a classroom teacher emphasise in such a talk? O'Moore and Minton (2004) deem the following points to be key:

> What bullying is, and the different forms that it can take.
> That bullying is, and is seen in the school, as an unacceptable form of behaviour.
> That we all have a responsibility to safeguard the wellbeing of others.
> That if we are being bullied, or if we know about someone else being bullied, the best way to get help is to tell a member of school staff.
> That violent retaliation will only make things worse in the long run.

> That everyone has a right to a school that is free of bullying and harassment, and we all have to play our part in achieving this. (p. 92)

It is argued that as is the case with all important learning, repetition is essential, and a guideline could be that young people in school should hear such a talk at least once per school term (O'Moore and Minton, 2004).

Talking to Young People about Bullying

Using the above points as a base structure, design a preventative talk (of 40 minutes to 1 hour's duration) to be delivered to the students under your care, using age-appropriate and local exemplifiers to illustrate the points. Consider discussing this with your school management, and if encouraged to do so, take the opportunity to deliver such a presentation.

As well as such introductory talks, it is possible for classroom staff to conduct anti-bullying activity classes; generally, whole class groups should be used, and the work should emphasise a focus on self-esteem (see this text, Chapter 3) and inclusiveness, utilising a combination of creative media – film, visual arts (posters, pictures and sculpture) and performance arts (musical composition and performance, drama) – and facilitated discussion work, (perhaps in the familiar 'circle time' set-up (Mosley, 1996, 1999)). Such sessions provide excellent opportunities to facilitate students' input into aspects of school anti-bullying policy and strategy, through the public display of students' creative contributions and other anti-bullying work, and the construction and use of class charters (O'Moore and Minton, 2004). Classroom staff should recognise that it is possible to convey an anti-bullying message through one's day-to-day teaching practise, too – it has been advised that teachers 'take the issue of bullying behaviour in schools seriously, and then take every opportunity, using [their] own creativity and ingenuity to convey a pro-social and anti-bullying message' (O'Moore and Minton, 2004, p. 93).

Action at the School and Broader Levels
A good deal of advice regarding countering strategies for bullying behaviour is usually based on using the same core principles that underpin *conflict resolution*

and conflict management (e.g. Mosley, 2006, 2007; see also this text, Chapter 5). However, it must be recognised that many incidents of bullying do not, in fact, stem from a situation of conflict – which, after all, involves mutual antagonism, dislike or distrust – but may more often be connected to the perpetrator's desire to manipulate and exert power over the target(s) (O'Moore and Minton, 2004). O'Moore and Minton (2004) have specified guidelines on *countering strategies*, which are summarised below:

> Schools should recognise that there can be enormous social pressure against reporting incidents of bullying behaviour.
> Alleged perpetrators and targets of bullying behaviour, and witnesses to it, are to be interviewed separately at first.
> Targets will need to be reassured, in the first place, that they will be safeguarded from future incidents of bullying behaviour, especially acts of retribution.
> When talking to targets of bullying behaviour, it is not necessary to communicate your unhesitating belief, but only acceptance that what that person says is true from their point of view. One should listen actively – without interpreting – and record specific grievances.
> When talking with perpetrators of bullying behaviour it is advisable to investigate as soon as is possible, and when a group is involved to interview members of that group separately at first. An accusatory tone is not helpful; one needs to assure alleged perpetrators that their sides will be heard before a decision is made. It is not necessary to tell the alleged perpetrator who has reported the incident – only that the incident has come to the attention of the school authorities, and that bullying behaviour is not tolerated in the school.
> 'After investigation, perpetrators of bullying behaviour should be informed (in good faith) that his or her behaviour constituted an unambiguous incident of bullying behaviour, and that this contravenes school policy; that he or she must refrain from bullying, and the particular forms of bullying behaviour experienced by the target, in future; that specified sanctions, in line with the anti-bullying policy, will be implemented if future instances occur; and that acts of retribution against the target will be dealt with by the severest possible applications of these sanctions' (O'Moore and Minton, 2004, p. 89).
> Many schools use standardised reporting forms and standardised written behavioural agreement forms in order to clarify in writing actions taken on bullying behaviour in the school.

Dan Olweus designed, implemented and evaluated the world's first nationwide *anti-bullying programme* in Norwegian schools from the autumn of 1983 (Olweus, 1999). An overview is provided below (where + + denotes a core component, and + denotes a highly desirable component):

General prerequisites
+ +   Awareness and involvement on the part of adults

Measures at the school level
+ +   Questionnaire survey
+ +   School conference day
+ +   Better supervision during break periods
+   Formation of co-ordinating group

Measures at the class level
+ +   Class rules against bullying
+ +   Regular class meetings with students
+   Class PTA meetings

Measures at the individual level
+ +   Serious talks with bullies and victims
+ +   Serious talks with parents of involved students
+   Teacher and parent use of imagination

(Olweus, 1999)

Olweus' evaluation of the effects of the 1983 intervention programme was based on data from 2,500 students (modal ages 11–14 at the outset) from 42 primary and lower secondary schools in Bergen, who were followed for a period of 2½ years (from 1983–1985 inclusive) (Olweus, 1999). Reports of being victim to direct and indirect bullying fell by 50 per cent or more. However, it should be noted that a second evaluation of the programme, conducted by Roland in 1986 in the neighbouring county of Rogaland, recorded that there had been considerably less success than Olweus had indicated (Roland, 1989, 1993).

Olweus' anti-bullying programme, which he and his team at the University of Bergen, Norway have continually refined (see Olweus, 2004), exemplifies a *whole-school* approach. As bullying is a complex, multi-factorial problem, in order to prevent and counter it, a sophisticated and multi-level strategy is required (O'Moore and Minton, 2004). We have already seen, in Chapter 3 of this text, how such approaches have been applied to the area of self-esteem enhancement in schools. Broadly speaking, in a whole-school anti-bullying programme, work is simultaneously carried out with school management staff (largely, working on school policies and resources); teaching and non-teaching staff (training and resources in countering and preventing bullying); parents (awareness raising and input into school anti-bullying policies and strategies); and students (awareness-raising and practical work) (Minton, 2008a; Minton and O'Moore, 2008; O'Moore and Minton, 2004, 2005). The whole-school design and ethos has been massively influential on subsequent nationwide programmes in Norway – the Second

Nationwide Programme to Prevent and Manage Bullying in Norwegian Schools (Roland and Munthe, 1997); the 'Respekt' Anti-Bullying Programme (Ertesvåg and Vaaland, 2007; SAF, 2004); and the 'Zero' Anti-Bullying Programme (Roland et al., 2010) – and large-scale interventions conducted elsewhere (see Farrington and Ttofi, 2010; Smith et al. 2004 for reviews), and most recently, the 'KiVa' Nationwide Anti-Bullying Programme in Finland, which was implemented in 1,400 secondary schools (about half of those in the country) from autumn 2009 (Salmivalli et al., 2010a, 2010b).

Given that different levels of success, even within the same programme, have been reported from the start (see Olweus, 1999; Roland, 1989, 1993), are the benefits of implementing a whole-school anti-bullying programme in schools supported by research evidence? The answer would appear to be 'Yes'. In March 2010, an updated report on the systematic evaluation and meta-analysis of the effectiveness of various anti-bullying programmes worldwide was published (Farrington and Ttofi, 2010). School-based anti-bullying programmes were effective in reducing bullying (by 20–23 per cent) and victimisation (being bullied) (by 17–20 per cent). Farrington and Ttofi (2010) concluded that 'results obtained so far in evaluations of anti-bullying programmes are encouraging' (p. 6), and recommend that 'a system of accrediting anti-bullying programmes should be developed' (p. 7).

In order to implement a whole-school anti-bullying approach, it is necessary to arrange in-service training for management, teaching and non-teaching staff; evening talks or open days with parents/community members; and classroom work with students. All of these groups will need input on what bullying is, and the forms it takes; the 'problem-solving' philosophy and approach; conceptualising bullying behaviour as a community issue; the school's policies and thinking around investigating, recording, countering and preventing bullying behaviour; and the roles and responsibilities, legal and otherwise, of different groups within the school community regarding these issues (O'Moore and Minton, 2004).

Elsewhere, I have noted that although there are a 'number of points upon which the principles of dealing with cyber-bullying coincide with those pertaining to dealing with more "traditional" (i.e. non-cyber-) forms of bullying' (Minton, 2008b, p. 20-21) (the whole-school approach is warranted; 'schools, parents, community interest groups, health, educational and psychological professionals, and young people themselves all have a role to play'; 'awareness-raising of bullying and cyber-bullying as real problems is a key "first step"; and changing attitudes towards oppression and violence are outcome goals'), cyber-bullying raises issues of its own. For example, 'those targeted can be attacked (via electronic means) outside conventional space and time limits'; cyber-bullying is easily hidden; 'potentially intervening adults may be far less familiar with technical media than are the young people involved'; the ready distribution of cyber-bullying material means that each episode of bullying can reach a much wider 'audience' than 'traditional' forms of bullying; and as cyber-bullying usually takes place outside of school hours and premises, the question as to who has responsibility for the investigation of and dealing with such incidents may be unclear (Minton, 2008b, p. 21). Smith et al. suggest that:

> Cyber-bullying should be included in school anti-bullying policy, which should include the input of parents and students. Schools should work with police and other support agencies on preventing and dealing with cyber-bullying.
> School managers should ensure that teachers have enough knowledge to deal with cyber-bullying, and can tell students about cyber-safety. Classroom staff should be familiar with their roles and responsibilities in implementing anti-bullying policies, and be able to take action if a child is cyber-bullied, and to teach young people about cyber-safety.
> Parents should make sure that they and their children are aware of the risks of technology use, and that they know what to do if the child is bullied, and consider the use of control software for home computers.
> Targeted young people should not ignore bullying behaviour, or just react, but try to keep calm – in the case of phone call, e-mail, text-message and video-clip bullying, messages and images should not be deleted, but kept as evidence.
> It may be worth turning off incoming texts for a few days, or changing one's number. If one is being bullied via phone calls, the advice is not to hang up right away (this may gratify the caller's sadistic need to cause fear) but to walk away, and to hang up after a few minutes. It should be recalled that almost all telephone calls can be traced, and that malicious calls and texts are illegal in many countries.
> Young people should not respond to unwanted e-mails, nor should they open files from unknown sources – for e-mail bullying, incidents should be reported to the Internet Service Provider.
> For Internet-based bullying, follow the online safety links. In using Instant Messaging, chatrooms or social networking sites, never give out personal details. For preference, use a nickname, and recognise that who you think you are communicating with online might not actually be that person. Young people should think very carefully about what they write, and tell their parents or teachers if they are worried.

Gran School (Norway)

Norway is a world leader in anti-bullying research and action, and has been so for many years (Minton, 2010b; Roland, 2000); it is thus surprising to hear reports of a Norwegian school that had lost control, and was in the grip of violence. Yet this is what was reported concerning Gran School in January 1997. Roland et al. (2003) recorded that an article in *Aftenposten* ('The Evening Post', a conservative national newspaper) described 'how violence, the use of weapons, threats towards pupils and teachers, disruption and vandalism had become part of everyday life at Gran. Groups of pupils controlled the school with terror, and the leadership and staff were in desperate need of help . . . the head teacher and staff had lost control' (p. 209). Gran School is a combined primary and lower secondary school, located in Furuset, a multi-cultural district of Oslo, and enrols around 450 students aged 6–15 years. In 1998, 62 per cent of the students at Gran school were from a non-Norwegian background (Soløy, 1998), and in August 2001, 68.3 per cent of the students spoke a mother tongue other than Norwegian (O'Moore and Minton, 2002). So given these concerns – school violence and cross-cultural communication – what could be done to help Gran School?

Following collaboration between the school's management team and the Senter for atferdsforskning (SAF) ('Centre for Behavioural Research') at Stavanger University College (now the University of Stavanger), and funding from national and local educational bodies, a new four-year programme called the 'Home/School/ Environment Project' was launched in August 1997. Interventions included: (i) the provision of training of school staff by SAF; (ii) improved parent–school and interprofessional cooperation; (iii) activities for pupils; (iv) improvements in the aesthetics of the physical environment; (v) recruitment of specialist personnel and non-Norwegian staff; (vi) the introduction of a pupil mediation service; (vii) the establishment of school traditions, and the positioning of the school as a 'Culture House'; and (viii) a general focus on social competence (O'Moore and Minton, 2002, 2006).

As part of a pan-European research project into tackling violence in schools in Europe (see Smith, 2003), an independent evaluation of the Home/School/ Environment Project at Gran School was undertaken by an Irish team (see O'Moore and Minton, 2002, for complete details). Records provided by the school principal in the course of that evaluation evidenced reductions in: (i) violence against adult school personnel; (ii) pupil injuries caused by violence; (iii) gang-characterised violence in the school; (iv) cases of exclusion; and (v) vandalism, and improvements in (a) collaboration with parents, (b) staff recruitment and retention, and (c) pupils' evaluations of the school (O'Moore and Minton, 2002, 2006). Furthermore, the three annual reports of the working group of the project and master report reflect five underlying success factors: (i) the introduction of mediation services; (ii) the use of pupils' creative work; (iii) the use of specialist subject teachers; (iv) cooperative work with parents; and (v) training to work with pupils and parents from ethnic minority groups (O'Moore and Minton, 2002, 2006).

The approach undertaken at Gran was characterised as a 'broad approach' by Roland et al., who quote the school's principal thus: 'It was not one, single ingenious thing that made the great difference, but the sum of many small moves' (2003, p. 211). In their evaluation of the project, O'Moore and Minton (2002, 2006) found there was 'no reason whatsoever to dispute the innovative solutions to the most serious of problems previously experienced at the school which have been generated by this project', and recorded that Gran School, through the Home/School/Environment Project, has been given several awards and prizes. Finally, after just 14 months of intervention efforts, *Aftenposten*, the same newspaper whose afore-mentioned article had caused such concern in January 1997, reported that 'Gran school has found the antidote to daily violence' (Soløy, 1998; in O'Moore and Minton, 2002, 2006).

Implications for Educators

Given the serious nature of the issues of bullying behaviour and cyber-bullying in school communities, we can say that in terms of implications for educators, much of what has been documented in this chapter is self-explanatory. However, the reader may like to think a little about the following quotes, which I believe draw one's attention to the broader societal implications for anti-bullying work:

> The twentieth century will be remembered as a century marked by violence, [but] violence can be prevented. Violent cultures can be turned round . . . Governments, communities and individuals can make a difference . . . We owe our children – the most vulnerable citizens in society – a life free from violence and fear . . . We must address the roots of violence. Only then will we transform the past century's legacy from a crushing burden into a cautionary lesson. (Nelson Mandela, in his foreword to the World Health Organisation's *World Report on Violence and Health*, 2002, p. ix).

So, as teachers:

> To prevent the cycle of violence going from one generation to the next, adults in all possible bullying situations must intervene. Failure to act gives a silent but powerful message that aggressive, violent or abusive behaviour is appropriate and acceptable. Moreover, valuable opportunities are lost for shaping society's general attitude to violence and oppression. (O'Moore, 1996)

Please think about, write short notes on, but above all take the opportunity to discuss with colleagues the following pair of questions, which are designed to focus the reader on further 'big picture' aspects of the problems of school bullying and violence:

1 Bullying behaviour thrives in an atmosphere of silence; many targets of bullying are too afraid to report it, and yet schools and teachers can do very little about problems they are unaware of. Please write down some concrete ways in which your schools could help to increase the likelihood of bullied students reporting such incidents to the school.
2 Why do you think that expert-designed anti-bullying programmes have, to date, only been partially effective in reducing the incidence rates of school bullying?

Farrington, D. P. and Ttofi, M.M. (2010) *School-Based Programs to Reduce Bullying and Victimization*. Oslo: Campbell Systematic Reviews. The meta-analysis of anti-bullying programmes referred to in the text above; the most complete treatment of its kind to date, and fascinating reading for those who want to understand what does and does not work regarding school bullying and why.

O'Moore, A.M. and Minton, S.J. (2004) *Dealing with Bullying in Schools: A Training Manual for Teachers, Parents and Other Professionals*. London: Sage. A very practically-written book designed to act as a 'one-stop' resource for school communities in setting up whole-school anti-bullying initiatives, with chapters for management staff, classroom staff, parents and young people.

Anti-Bullying Alliance. Available at www.anti-bullyingalliance.org.uk (accessed June 2011). An organisation that has developed from a network of anti-bullying charities, advocacy and support groups, research centres and like. It provides many excellent resources, and supports the Anti-Bullying Week held in UK schools each year.

Northern Ireland Anti-Bullying Forum. Available at www.niabf.org.uk (accessed June 2011). A small, yet highly productive organisation that provides many high-quality resources, especially for school and classroom use. This important work has been consistently supported by the Northern Ireland Executive.

Teach Today. Available at www.teachtoday.eu (accessed June 2011). A collaboration of the ICT Industry and European Schoolnet (a network of 31 European Ministries of Education) with the support of the European Commissioner for Information Society and Media. It offers advice and resources on technology in education, including a variety of resources on bullying, cyber-bullying and cyber-safety.

8

Dealing with Prejudice – Racism, Homophobia and Alterophobia in Schools

The goal for this chapter is to provide the reader with an understanding and knowledge of dealing with prejudice in schools and school communities. Prejudice takes many forms; we shall focus on just three – *racism*, *homophobia* and *alterophobia* (prejudice directed towards members of alternative sub-cultures, featured in this chapter's case study) – as well as examining the *psychology of prejudice and attitude formation*. This chapter concludes with a reflective examination of some *implications for educators*, *points for discussion*, and a selective and annotated list of *further reading* and *useful websites*.

Examining Prejudice in Ourselves

Let us begin in a reflective mode – by challenging ourselves before we ask others to challenge themselves. So I invite the reader, privately, to begin by identifying her or his own prejudices and biases.

First, think about the religious background(s), family type(s), geographical region(s), nation(s), and culture(s) into which you were born, or into which you may have become affiliated. How did this process inform your identity, your social behaviour, your expectations and aspirations, and the 'moral code' or values by which you live? Focus particularly on how these things might have been influenced by your passage through life.

Next, pick a 'rite of passage' – marriage, childbirth, death and funeral customs, for example. How do people from your own background perform this 'rite'? Does what normally happens within your 'home culture' always seem 'normal' and 'natural' to you? Have you ever been surprised, shocked or offended by the way people from other cultures, religions and countries perform this 'rite'? Why do you think this is? These questions should give a sense of your own ethnocentricity (which we are *all* subject to).

Then, think about the religious background(s), family type(s), geographical region(s), nation(s) and culture(s) – your own, perhaps, and those other than your own – that you are drawn to, or feel favourably disposed towards. This gives us an indication of our positive biases. Are there accents you prefer? Places you visit on holidays for the 'people', perhaps? Are there strangers from other places/cultures/religions that you 'give a break' to because they come from that place/culture/religion? National sports teams that you cheer for in international competitions? What generalisations do you make about people according to these positive biases? When and how did you acquire these positive biases? What are the implications, personal and professional, of your holding these positive biases?

Now think about the religious background(s), family type(s), geographical region(s), nation(s), and culture(s) that we or feel unfavourably disposed towards. This gives us an indication of our negative biases. Are there accents you dislike? Places you avoid visiting on the grounds that certain people, or certain 'types of people', live there, perhaps? Are there strangers from other places/cultures/religions that you make life more difficult for when you get the opportunity to do so, simply because they come from that place/culture/religion? Are there national sports teams that you would cheer any other nation against in international competitions? What generalisations do you make about people according to these negative biases? When and how did you acquire these negative biases? What are the implications, personal and professional, of your holding these negative biases?

Racism, Ethnic Bias and Schools

Racism/ethnic bias would seem to be, from an even cursory glance at the history books, an age-old problem. This prejudice underpins and is found in acts of war, invasion, conquest and imperialism; it takes its forms in colonisation, forced labour, slavery, genocide, physical and cultural apartheid, feudalism, and many forms of discrimination, as well as acts of individual, group, collective and societal violence. Predictably, the academic study of racial and ethnic bias has a long history in social science literature. In the early 1930s, a sociologist named Richard LaPiere spent two years driving around the continental United States by car with a couple of Chinese ethnicity, visiting 251 hotels and restaurants. They were refused service only once. Afterwards, LaPiere wrote to all of the establishments that they had visited, asking, 'Will you accept members of the Chinese race in your establishment?' Of the 128 establishments that responded to his letter, 92 per cent answered 'No' (LaPiere, 1934). The study was influential in highlighting the inconsistency that often exists between expressed (internal) attitudes and exhibited (external) behaviours – the restaurateurs and hoteliers of LaPiere's study *expressed* more anti-Chinese racism than they actually *demonstrated*. These days, it may be the case that the *opposite* is true; we may be *more* prejudiced than we are prepared to outwardly *express*. In a study of whether and how 37 seventh to twelfth-grade high-school students across two school districts in Canada identified difference as a factor in bullying, using the innovative method of photo elicitation, Walton and Niblett (2011) asserted that their analysis revealed that a culture of political correctness 'strongly shapes how students describe various forms of social difference . . . political correctness can function as a hindrance from speaking about racial differences lest one be labelled a racist'.

Genocides, the horrific extreme of racism and ethnic bias, have been studied by psychologists, who have perhaps paid most attention to the Holocaust. They have attempted to illuminate our understanding of what happened – of how apparently cultured and reasonable European people had been willing to take their part in genocide. With the Nuremberg trials, having taken place less than two decades previously, at which many defendants attempted to evade their responsibility for their crimes on the basis of having simply 'followed orders', Stanley Milgram (1965) sought to answer this via an experimental demonstration of obedience to authority.

Milgram's experiment involved duping genuine participants into believing that they were acting as 'teachers' in delivering electric shocks of increasing severity to 'learner' out-of-view participants next door (in reality, the 'learners' were actors, and associates of the experimenter), according to the learners' 'errors' in a 'word-association' learning task. The genuine participants' apparently 'random' assignation to the 'teacher' role was fixed; the 'shock equipment' was bogus; the people under investigation were the genuine participants, who were instructed to give the 'learner' a 'shock' each time he made a mistake. The 'shocks' were to increase by 15 volts each time; the 'shock machine' had levers up to '450 volts', followed by three more levers marked only by large 'X's. At 120 volts, the 'learner' would complain of pain; at 210 volts, of a heart condition, and make repeated requests to be able to get out of the room; after 330 volts, there was only an ominous silence. From the experimenter, the genuine participant received prompts such as, 'It's essential to the experiment that you continue' and latterly, 'You have no choice, you have to go on'. How many participants would go 'all the way' to the third 'X' after '450 volts'?

Astonishingly, over 60 per cent of participants did so. Milgram proposed that the citizens of countries that had been 'Allies' or neutral in the Second World War had contented themselves with the ideas that 'Germans are different' and that 'the same thing couldn't happen here'. These were dangerous falsehoods, according to Milgram (1965, 1974). In his famous experiment, he demonstrated that normal American people rejected or ignored their own feelings of sympathy or empathy for an apparently suffering fellow participant in favour of obedience to authority – even if this seemed to result in the death or serious injury of that fellow. Sadly, events in Cambodia, the Balkans and Rwanda since Milgram's original study have shown that the Nazi genocide nightmare could indeed happen anywhere.

The crowd mentality, then, explains why some people behave anti-socially, as the crowd gives people somewhere to hide – to use a term employed by both Goffman (1961) and Latané (1981), people within the crowd 'deindividuate'. Apparently as a consequence of anonymity within the crowd, the individual's own sense of *social responsibility* becomes 'diffuse'; under such circumstances, impulsive anti-social behaviours (such as aggression) that are usually kept in check may become disinhibited (Latané, 1981). It should perhaps be reflected upon that military organisations require their members to wear a uniform for more than reasons of identification by one's fellows in battle. It is far easier, as a largely nameless, faceless member of a uniformed unit to kill someone who has been defined as an enemy of you and your cause or country, as at times of war, society condones acts of violence if they can somehow be seen as serving 'the greater good'. Yet this same deindividuation, and its immediate social correlate, 'mob behaviour', underlies a great deal of aggressive anti-social behaviour at times when countries are 'at peace'. It is not coincidental that many gang members, like military personnel, wear a 'uniform' of sorts – the anonymity of members of the Ku Klux Klan was protected not only socially by ingrained patterns of inequality and corruption, but physically by the Klansmen's robes and hoods.

Again during the 1960s, Bibb Latané and John Darley investigated why people fail to intervene and to help in an emergency. They used deceptive experimental situations, where participants would find themselves (say) outside a door in a 'waiting room', and smoke would pour over the top of the door, or a female scream or a crash could be heard from behind the door. What influences whether they intervened (at least, pushed open the door) or not? Essentially, two things are important: first, the presence of others (the more people there are around, the less likely we are to act – this is 'social loafing', and underpins what is called either 'bystander apathy' or the 'bystander effect'); and second, the apparent ambiguity of the situation (the more clearly defined the situation is as an emergency, the more likely we are to act). It seems that in uncertain situations, the initial response of human beings is to look for what others are doing, and then to behave in a similar way (see Gleitman, 2010; Zimbardo, 1992, for reviews).

As much of the nineteenth century had been a time in which some European nations colonised large portions of the globe, the twentieth century, and the period after the Second World War in particular, was marked by the formerly colonised countries struggling for and gaining their independence. Some of the people of the newly independent, and developing nation-status former colonies, came to Europe seeking improved work and life opportunities in the country of their former colonial 'masters', sometimes after having contributed to the war effort. It is sad to acknowledge that the attitudes of many people in the countries that had fought against Nazism owed more to that of the colonist than the guardian of individual liberties. The popular US-born writer, Bill Bryson, describes viewing a 'hopelessly moronic' sitcom on his first visit to Britain in March, 1973: 'the gist of it [was] that there was something richly comic in the notion of having black people living next door' (1995, p. 23). (Bryson did not recall the title of the sitcom, but having grown up in Britain in the 1970s, I can think of a number of possible candidates). Should accusations of hypocrisy be forming in the reader's mind, it is worth remembering that Bryson has unflinchingly documented and condemned his native land's historical acts of racism (Bryson, 1994). It is to be remembered that such portrayals in television 'comedies' constitute only the mildest example of the indignities and injustices that were inflicted upon immigrants from the former colonies in Africa, the West Indies and the Indian subcontinent, and their descendants, by sections of British society in the latter half of the twentieth century.

Unfortunately, there is some evidence that racial divisions in certain areas of the UK seem to have deepened with time, and again, schools are under the spotlight. Racial riots in Oldham, Lancashire, in 2001 were both the product and the cause of divisions between white and Asian populations, with the Home Office stating that Oldham was a place of 'deep-rooted segregation, with communities living parallel lives' (BBC News, 2010). A recent BBC television documentary traced the attempt to merge two schools in the town that had since *become* effectively racially segregated – an extraordinary situation in twenty-first-century Britain –

and the fears, concerns and sometimes direct opposition that existed around this attempt, which extended to local children and their parents, and the principal of the 'white area' school who expressed that he would favour integration at an earlier age, and raised concerns around the merger's being an 'experiment with children'.

Of course, ethnicity is not only demarked by differences in skin colour or religion. In Ireland, the only historically ethnically distinct group has been the Travelling Community, although Travellers have only been legally recognised as a distinct ethnic group in Ireland since 1989, with the passing of the Prohibition of Incitement to Racial, Religious and National Hatred Act (Government of Ireland, 2010). Whilst being white, Irish and almost entirely Roman Catholic, Travellers are rendered distinct from settled people due to their shared culture and traditions (including a historically nomadic existence). According to Carlson and Casavant (1995), Travellers are 'frequently the victims of prejudice and discrimination in Ireland, which appears to extend into school life'. Some schools have refused to enrol Traveller children (Noonan, 1994); Carlson and Casavant (1995) argue that there also exists a low expectation of attainment amongst those teaching Travellers, which produces a 'reverse Pygmalion effect'. As a result of this, the general incompatibility of a nomadic lifestyle with regular school attendance, and other conflicts between Traveller and settled culture, absenteeism amongst Traveller children remains high (O'Connell, 1989), whilst scholastic attainment remains low (Noonan, 1994). Traveller children – boys in particular – have a reputation for fighting and classroom indiscipline. In understanding this, Carlson and Casavant (1995) refer to the cultural differences that exist between the settled and the Travelling communities in terms of their respective attitudes towards aggression: 'aggression is part of Traveller culture and is frequently rewarded in boys because it is felt that life is brutal and children must learn to fight to survive' (p. 101). They also report that 'because of their nomadic lifestyle, and the extreme prejudice of settled people, Traveller children are often intimidated by settled classmates' (p. 103); however, whether this intimidation includes physical violence is unclear from their literature, although 'name-calling' (Noonan, 1994) has been mentioned.

And now for a 'good news' story! Journalist Neil Marr, and the much-missed anti-bullying campaigner and author, the late Tim Field (2001), described how a well-known child of immigrant parents overcame racist harassment and bullying. Naseem Hamed, better known (to boxing fans at least) by his ring persona, 'Prince Naseem', was one of nine children born in Sheffield, England, of Yemeni immigrant parents. Like the rest of his family, he was (indeed, still is) devoutly Muslim; as a child, he was also short for his age, and skinny. Mr Hamed was physically and verbally abused (he was nicknamed 'chocolate drop'); his family was seriously harassed by members of the National Front, including attacks on their home. As a teenager, Mr Hamed took up boxing, along with two of his brothers, and their harassment stopped – not due to their 'fighting their way out of trouble', but due to their increased self-esteem and the recognition of the effort they had made. Mr Hamed said to Marr and Field that 'Boxing is not bullying, it's sport'. It was clearly a sport in which he excelled – he went on to win, and to successfully defend, the world featherweight title. He described the arrogant ring persona that he developed as 'just the face I wear for the job'. Marr and Field (2001) recorded that following his retirement from boxing, Mr Hamed spent much of his time counselling targets of bullying, particularly racist bullying, telling them:

> Go through life with dignity. Never let it enter your head to lose. Leave the bullies where they belong, kicking their downtrodden heels on a street corner wondering why they are now standing alone.

The Psychology of Prejudice and Attitude Formation

The literal root of the word 'prejudice' is *pre-judgement*, that is to say, a premature judgement being made, without sufficient evidence to support it. In literal sense of the word, prejudice could be either positive or negative, and it is quite possible to see how we might form a favourable opinion prematurely. However, when we use the word 'prejudice', we almost invariably mean it in a *negative* way: Vander Zanden defines prejudice as 'a system of negative conceptions, feelings and active orientations regarding the members of a particular religious, racial or nationality group' (1989). Similarly, Reber (1995) defines prejudice as 'a negative attitude toward a particular group of persons based on negative traits assumed to be uniformly displayed by all members of that group'.

Prejudicial *attitudes*, like any other attitudes, are held by psychologists to have both 'internal' (affective/cognitive, i.e. feelings and thoughts) components, and 'external' (behavioural) components (Maio and Haddock, 2009). The internal components of prejudicial attitudes, as long as they remain as unexpressed thoughts and feelings, cannot possibly be countered by either policy or education. However, the 'external' components can be and have been acted against in systems of law. For example, discrimination that is underpinned by prejudices such as racism and homophobia can be countered in employment law, and laws prohibiting hate crimes and the incitement to hatred. Another clear behavioural manifestation of prejudice in schools is bullying, although bullying has been more frequently conceptualised by researchers in that field purely as a sub-category of aggressive behaviour (e.g. Olweus, 1999) than as an outcome of prejudice. In Ireland, for example, progress in acting against homophobia has been made in the last 20 years. As recently as 1993, male homosexuality was illegal in Ireland (Bacik, 2004); yet in 2010, schools were officially instructed to specifically reference homophobic bullying in their anti-bullying policies, and civil partnerships between same-sex couples were legally recognised (O'Higgins-Norman et al., 2010).

Although best known for his famous experimental study of obedience to authority (1965; discussed above), Stanley Milgram also contributed an ingenious method of investigating prejudice in a non-intrusive way – the 'lost-letter technique' (Milgram et al., 1965). In the original study, 400 stamped letters addressed to four fictional addressees – 'Friends of the Nazi Party', 'Friends of the Communist Party', 'Medical Research Associates' and 'Mr Walter Carnap', all at the same P.O. Box number rented out by the experimenters – were 'misplaced' around town in four types of location: under car windshield wipers, on pavements, in shops and telephone booths. Did the type of 'addressee' affect whether people who found the 'lost-letter' posted it on or not? Indeed it did. Most of the envelopes that were addressed to either 'Mr Carnap' or the 'favourable' organisation ('Medical Research Associates') were posted by their finders (71 per cent and 72 per cent respectively); however, most of the letters (75 per cent in each case) addressed to 'Friends of the Nazi Party' and 'Friends of the Communist Party', were not (Milgram et al., 1965).

Liggett et al. (2010) note that since Milgram et al.'s original lost-letter study, there have been numerous investigations using the lost-letter technique in order to assess attitudes toward members of minority groups. With this chapter in mind, examples can be found of it being applied in the study of racial, sectarian and homophobic prejudice. Montanye et al. (1971) showed that return rates were lower for 'lost-letters' addressed to an African American equal rights movement than they were for those addressed to a medical research association. Kremer et al. (1986) used the lost-letter technique in six 'sensitive' urban areas in Northern Ireland, and found that the return rates were influenced by the assumed religion (derived from the addressee's name) of the intended recipient. Finally, Bridges et al. (2002) showed that return rates were lower for 'lost-letters' addressed to homosexual organisations than they were for letters addressed to other groups (in their study, creationists and Darwinists).

Homophobia and Schools

When the suffix -*phobia* is used in a psychological sense, it usually refers to an irrational and specific object-related anxiety, such as the very common *arachnophobia* (the fear of spiders), the familiar but rather less common *agoraphobia* (the fear of open spaces), and the rather unusual *phobophobia* (the fear of fear). The -phobia suffix is used correctly in describing prejudice towards those of non-heterosexual orientation, as it refers to the irrational fear affective component that underlies the prejudice: Blumenfeld and Raymond (1992) define homophobia as 'the fear of being labelled homosexual and the irrational fear, dislike or hatred of gay males and lesbians' (in Norman et al., 2006, p. 36).

In his fascinating study of 'sexual bullying' in four post-primary schools in central England (each were co-educational local authority comprehensive schools, urban, had multi-ethnic populations and enrolled between 850 and 1,100 students), Neil Duncan (1999) presented results from a series of interviews with year 7 (11–12-year-olds) and year 10 (14–15-year-olds) students. One interesting feature to emerge from Duncan's data was the discourse around homophobia. Although the term 'gay' was the most frequently used put-down amongst boys in the study, this term was not used in an absolutely literal sense. As Duncan noted, 'actual homosexual activity was found incomprehensible by the majority, and some of the boys were so appalled at its existence they baulked at defaming even "gays" with that level of alien depravity' (p. 124). He found that in all four schools, a virulent homophobia permeated from the older boys down throughout the entire school student community. Boys unanimously claimed that they would beat up their best friend (or have him beaten up) if he confided that he was homosexual ('There is no way I'd be mates with a poof . . . I'd slap him, I would. I would not have him coming near me'; 'It's right. I would do the same, not hit him, but tell our mates and we'd probably all get him. Let him know . . . But like you say, it's what we would do but we're not gay. We're not gay' (p. 108–109.). Girls were more tolerant, if not approving ('Well I'd think she was still my friend whatever she is 'cos she hasn't changed . . . They would have to be quite close friends for them to tell you in the first place, it's hardly the sort of thing you'd tell everyone' (p. 124.). Hence, conformity to the heteronormative student cultures in the schools was rigidly enforced, through the discourse and the imminent threat of physical violence that such 'gender policing' involved.

Homophobic bullying, defined as taking place when 'general bullying behaviour, such as verbal and physical abuse and intimidation, is accompanied by, or consists of the use of terms such as gay, lesbian, queer or lezzie by perpetrators' (Warwick et al., 2001; in Norman et al., 2006), is a clear behavioural manifestation of this attitude in schools. Elsewhere, we have found it helpful to render distinct heteronormative bullying – which may include frequent use of homophobic language and epithets, and contributes to a general climate of discomfort for lesbian, gay, bisexual and transgendered (LGBT) individuals, whether their orientation is known to others or not – the sort of behaviour that Duncan (1999), above, described – and sexual orientation-based bullying (attacks on persons known to have a non-heterosexual orientation), although there are, of course, considerable overlaps (Minton et al., 2008).

The biggest empirical study of the relationship between sexual orientation and bullying to date was conducted in Norway (Roland and Auestad, 2009): 3,046 (1,583 male and 1,463 female) tenth-grade students (ca. 17–18 years of age) in Norwegian schools participated. They were asked to complete a study-specific questionnaire: 94.2 per cent of the males identified as heterosexual (and 2.7 per cent as bisexual, and 3.2 per cent as homosexual); 90.8 per cent of the females identified as heterosexual (and 6.6 per cent as bisexual, and 2.7 per cent as homosexual). Results revealed that 7.3 per cent of heterosexual boys, 23.8 per cent of bisexual boys, 48.0 per cent of homosexual boys, 5.7 per cent of heterosexual girls, 11.5 per cent of bisexual girls, and 17.7 per cent of homosexual girls reported having been bullied in the last two to three months. Both depression and anxiety were higher amongst bisexual and homosexual students than they were amongst heterosexual students, and higher amongst bullied students than amongst non-bullied students. Roland and Auestad (2009) concluded that their study had 'shown that bisexual and homosexual students, especially boys, are very strongly over-represented in both being bullied and bullying others' (p. 80; my own translation from the original Norwegian).

In 2006, my colleagues and I conducted an exploratory survey of the experiences of homophobic bullying amongst 123 young LGBT people. We found that half of all the respondents had been bullied at school within the last three months (Minton et al., 2008); as the general population figure for post-primary aged people in Ireland is generally taken to be one-in-six (based on the nationwide study by Mona O'Moore et al., 1997), we concluded that one can consider the LGBT population to be 'at risk' in the school population, in terms of being bullied. This initial finding was verified by the far more extensive 'Supporting LGBT Lives' project (Mayock et al., 2009), which comprised 1,100 participants completing online surveys, and 40 participants being interviewed in-depth, and examined a huge array of factors that impinged upon the mental health and wellbeing of LGBT people. Of the current school-goers in their sample, over half reported having been called names relating to their sexual orientation or gender identity by fellow students, and 8 per cent reported being subjected to the same by members of school staff. Twenty per cent of their sample had missed school because they felt threatened or were afraid of getting hurt at school because they were LGBT; 5 per cent had actually left school early because of homophobic bullying. Outside of school, 80 per cent of the sample reported that they had been verbally abused, 40 per cent that they had been threatened with physical violence, and 25 per cent had been punched, kicked or beaten because of their LGBT identity. As was the case in Roland and Auestadt's (2009) study, psychological effects of such harassment and abuse were evident: 86.3 per cent of the sample had suffered from depression, 27 per cent of their sample had self-harmed, and 18 per cent of their sample had attempted suicide (Mayock et al., 2009). In an earlier study of 362 LGBT individuals under the age of 25 conducted in Northern Ireland (Carolan and Redmond, 2003), findings were broadly similar, with 44 per cent of the sample reported having been bullied at school because of their sexual orientation; 35 per cent of their sample had been physically abused, and 65 per cent had been verbally abused. Again, 21 per cent of the sample had been medicated for depression, 26 per cent had self-harmed, and 29 per cent had attempted suicide.

The BeLonG To Youth Project, 'Ireland's first and only designated lesbian, gay, bisexual and transgender youth project' (Barron and Collins, 2005, p. 7), has been operational since 2002, and provides both one-to-one and group-based support for young (14–23-years-old) LGBT people, and has an ongoing 'Stop Homophobic Bullying in Schools' campaign, which is backed by secondary school principals' and teachers' trade unions, parents councils and An Garda Síochána (the Irish national police force) (BeLonG To/The Equality Authority, 2006). In April 2010, BeLonG To launched Stand Up! in which young people were encouraged to 'show your support for your lesbian, gay, bisexual and transgender friends' and 'don't stand for homophobic bullying' (BeLonG To, 2010). Furthermore, a recent joint publication of the Irish government's Department of Education and Science and the Gay and Lesbian Equality Network (GLEN) advocated that 'specific reference to homophobic bullying within the school's Anti-Bullying Policy' be included, and that schools should 'develop and/or maintain a zero tolerance approach to the use of anti-gay language that is pejorative or derisive in all areas of school' (2010, p. 13).

Helping Students to Stand against Prejudicial Behaviour

Much of this chapter thus far has been devoted to the documentation of problems – the roots and manifestations of prejudice, and the negative effects it has on people. Within this chapter, however, there have been two success stories – where people have challenged and helped others to deal with racist behaviour (the story of Naseem Hamed) and homophobia (the BeLonG To 'Stand Up!' campaign) (see above). From what we have learned from the social psychologists such as Milgram and Latané, anti-social behaviour is more likely when people are anonymous, or shirk their responsibility to intervene positively due to the force of numbers, or because some 'authority' tells us to act in such a way. Naseem Hamed's and BeLonG To's 'Stand Up!' intervention success rests on the power that emerges when people take the responsibility for doing what they can to counter behaviour that they believe to be wrong – when they decide that, in the words of the sign that former US president Harry S. Truman kept on his desk in the Oval Office, 'The buck stops here' (Harry S. Truman Library and Museum, 2011).

Think now of the prejudices or biases that exist amongst students and the broader school community where you work. How would you characterise these? Find out as much as you can about the origins, prevalence and manifestations of these. Does this provide you with cause for concern? If so, start a resource file and think about what you, personally, can do; then talk the matter over with your colleagues and school management staff. Think also of how your school community could develop a campaign, involving the students in a central role, along with staff and parents, to promote 'standing up' against the prejudice that you have identified. Then, if you do have a cause for concern and the support of your school management, try to implement such a campaign.

The Murder of Sophie Lancaster and the Sophie Lancaster Foundation (England)

On the morning of Saturday, 11 August 2007, at around 1.30 a.m., Sophie Lancaster (20) and her boyfriend, Robert Maltby (21), were walking through the skateboarding area of Stubbylee Park, Bacup, Lancashire, England, when they were attacked, without provocation, and kicked unconscious, by a gang of teenagers who had been drinking in the park (Butt, 2007). It was reported that at the time of the attack, Ms Lancaster and Mr Maltby had been dressed in the 'goth' style (Butt, 2007; Garnham, 2008; Wainwright, 2008; Watkinson, 2009), and it was this that had 'provoked' the attack. Mr Maltby was attacked first; the gang then attacked Ms Lancaster, who was trying to protect Mr Maltby (Wainwright, 2008). Both Mr Maltby and Ms Lancaster were left comatose, with bleeding on the brain; Mr Maltby has since physically recovered. Tragically, Ms Lancaster did not – on 24 August 2007, her family agreed to switch off life support after a brain stem scan showed that there was no chance of her making a recovery (Butt, 2007). Horrifyingly, witnesses to the incident attested that afterwards, the attackers boasted that they had 'done summat [something] good', saying that 'there's two moshers nearly dead up Bacup park – you wanna see them – they're a right mess' (Wainwright, 2008). Police officers reported that one of those eventually sentenced for Ms Lancaster's murder laughed and joked with his mother about what he had done during initial interviews (Garnham, 2008). Murder charges were secured against two of the attackers; they were sentenced to life imprisonment (Watkinson, 2009).

Since Ms Lancaster's murder, her family and friends have established a charity in her name – the Sophie Lancaster Foundation – with the acronym 'S.O.P.H.I.E.' standing for 'Stamp Out Prejudice, Hatred and Intolerance Everywhere'. Ms Lancaster's mother, Sylvia Lancaster, has become an in-demand speaker and an advisor to various bodies on these issues, as well as a campaigner to extend UK hate crime laws to cover hatred towards members of sub-cultures. An animated short film, *Dark Angel*, in which the attack on Mr Maltby and Ms Lancaster is represented in a moving 4-minute production, was released to mark what should have been Ms Lancaster's 23rd birthday, and to raise awareness of the Foundation's aims and work. Since then, an educational game has been developed for and used in some schools; a BBC Radio 4 play, *Black Roses* (a eulogy that combined the poetry of Simon Armitage, read by Rachel Austin, and Sylvia Lancaster's reminiscences of her daughter's life and death) was broadcast on Friday, 11 March, 2011, and in Spring 2011, the Foundation held a creative writing competition in Manchester and East Lancashire schools. The Facebook and My Space groups set up in Ms Lancaster's memory show that support for the Foundation's work amongst alternative music lovers in particular, and others, has been substantial in the UK and beyond.

Alterophobia and Schools

The term 'alterophobia', which may be defined as 'prejudice directed towards members of alternative sub-cultures' (Minton, submitted), is a neologism seemingly modelled after another form of prejudice that utilises a '–phobia' suffix, homophobia (see this chapter, above). 'Alterophobia' has no entry in the *Oxford English Dictionary,* and a Google Scholar search undertaken in June 2011 recorded only a handful of peripheral mentions of the term in articles on other subjects. However, the term has made appearances online since 2006, when the 'phobic' component of the attitude was emphasised:

> Alterophobia is the phobia of the Other. In Latin, alter = other, like in alternative (another way to take) or alter-ego (another [my]self) . . . [alterophobia] feeds all kinds of intolerance against everything which is not like us. To be unable to recognize the legitimacy of different cultures having different values or moral codes, to believe that one's own way of life is the better or the only possible way of life, are all inspired by alterophobia. (World Association of International Studies, 2011)

A more specific conception, one more in accordance with how I and most others use the term, is provided by the 'Alterophobia Blogspot', the setting up of which was 'motivated by the death of Sophie Lancaster':

> Members of alternative subcultures [which the blog lists as including 'a wide range of groups, such as goths, punks, emos, skaters and fans of heavy metal] and those who listen to any type of alternative music, frequently face intolerance and even physical attacks all over the world . . . This intolerance is based on the way they look and that their musical and other interests differ from the mainstream. Media distortion and inaccurate descriptions of subcultures usually intensify and support this prejudice . . . This blog aims to document this problem and by doing so to help reduce it. (Alterophobia Blogspot, 2011)

From the case study outlined above, it is clear that alterophobia has been manifest in criminal cases. But is it also evident in schools? I know of only one such empirical study – I undertook a survey of 820 fifth-year students (males and females, aged ca. 16–17 years), at nine secondary schools in Ireland, who completed a short questionnaire concerning membership of sub-cultures and bullying behaviour. It was found that self-identified members of sub-cultures reported having been bullied more frequently than did members of the general sample. The participants expressed that members of 'alternative' sub-cultures (moshers/rockers, goths and emos) were more likely to be bullied, and that members of 'non-alternative' sub-cultures (chavs and D4s) were more likely to bully others. (N.B. 'D4' describes an Irish liberal elitist attitude, based on the perceived opinions and characteristics of some residents of this area, referring to the alleged wealth and posh life-style of residents. D4s bear some resemblance to 'jock' and 'preppy' sub-groups in US high-schools.) On the basis of the results, I concluded that alterophobic bullying was indeed a reality for teenagers in Ireland, and that members of 'alternative' sub-cultures may be considered to be 'at risk' of being bullied (Minton, submitted).

Prejudice in the Broader Sense

Alterophobia, and the case study referred to above, can give us pause for thought, and cause us to consider prejudice in the broader sense. Racism/ethnic bias and homophobia are long-standing problems, to which a great deal of attention has been paid; thus far, the same cannot be said for alterophobia, which is one reason why I have included it as an exemplar in this chapter. So for the last of the activities in this chapter, I would ask that you view the *Dark Angel* short film referred to above (link via the Sophie Lancaster Foundation website; see 'Useful Websites' section below). If you are a secondary school teacher, after viewing it yourself, please also consider showing it to and discussing it with your students and colleagues.

Implications for Educators

Whilst we examined the important role of intelligence, learning and educational attainment in Chapter 4, once more we have been reminded – as we have seen elsewhere in this book – that school and schooling is, or can and should be, about so much more than the development of young people's cognitive abilities. In the previous chapter, we looked at one area that blights the lives of many young people – bullying behaviour – and in the present chapter we have examined another – prejudice.

Modern education systems now stress the value of developing the 'whole' student – this is exemplified in the United Kingdom in the focus on Social and Emotional Aspects of Learning (Department for Education and Skills, 2010). When we educate young people, we have the opportunity to do far more than directing the development of cognitive acuity, or cram students full of abstract knowledge – we have the opportunity to shape attitudes, for better or for worse. Political movements characterised by prejudice and mass psychology saw the opportunities that educators have to do this – think of the Third Reich's 'Hitler Youth', for example. Educators should be mindful of the influence they exert upon developing young minds, and consequently on young people's behaviour, and to take opportunities as they rise to make the social and emotional lessons we learn at school to contain something of real value.

Please think about, write short notes on, but above all take the opportunity to discuss with colleagues the following pair of questions:

1 If you have close colleagues with whom you can discuss your thinking around teaching practice ask them to undertake the first (To Think About) activity of this chapter, and then compare your results.
2 In this chapter, we have focussed on just three areas of prejudice that can exist in schools and school communities – racism/ethnic bias, homophobia and alterophobia – but, of course, many other types of prejudice exist. Make a note of what these types of prejudice are; how they might manifest themselves in schools and school communities; and practical ways in which how such prejudice could be countered and dealt with. Think about these points with reference to school policies, school and classroom practice, implications for staff pre- and in-service training, and the development of positive relationships between school personnel and the communities that schools serve.

Brown, R. (2010) *Prejudice: Its Social Psychology*, 2nd edn. London: Wiley-Blackwell. A very complete consideration of both the theoretical and applied ideas around prejudice, including ways to combat prejudice.

Gillborn, D. (2008) *Racism and Education: Coincidence or Conspiracy?* London: Routledge. A clearly written examination of race, racism and the English education system from the standpoint of critical theory.

Alterophobia Blogspot. Available at http://alterophobia.blogspot.com (accessed June 2011). This blog documents cases of alterophobia and alterophobic bullying and violence worldwide.

The Sophie Lancaster Foundation. Available at www.sophielancasterfoundation.com (accessed June 2011). The homepage of the charity set up by Ms Sophie Lancaster's friends and family (see case study, above). The site provides an account of Ms Lancaster's murder, the Foundation's aims and news of its activities, contact details, links to supporting organisations, and a link to the animated short film, *Dark Angel*, mentioned above.

9

Stress and Stress Management for Teachers and Educators

The goal for this chapter is to provide the reader with an introduction to stress, its causes and manifestations, and how it can be managed by teachers and educators in themselves and others. We shall consider both the *physiology* and *psychology of stress*. Having completed this general overview, we then examine *psychological and physical ways of coping with stress*, and *stress and the teaching profession: avoiding burnout*. This chapter concludes with a reflective examination of some *implications for educators*, *questions for discussion*, and a short annotated list of *further reading*.

The Physiology of Stress

All forms of strong human emotional arousal, including psychological stress, are physiologically associated with what is known as the *alarm response*, which in itself is underpinned by the activity of the autonomic nervous system. The human nervous system (the brain, spinal chord and all other nervous tissue in the body) may be divided on the basis of either *structure* (location) or *function*. Structurally, a division is made between the *central* (brain and spinal chord) and *peripheral* (everything else) nervous systems. Functionally, the first division that one can make is between the *voluntary* and *involuntary* (also known as *autonomic*) nervous systems.

The autonomic nervous system can be divided into the parasympathetic (which is active when the organism is at rest) and the sympathetic branch (which primes the organism for attacking or evasive action). The major sympathetic responses are *increases* in the diameter of pupil, heart rate, breathing rate, blood supply to the limbs, muscular tension and the release of adrenalin, and *decreases* in the blood supply to the viscera, the capacity of bladder, and the rate of peristalsis. Exactly the same set of nervous/hormonal responses is operational in the bodies of both carnivorous (hunting) and herbivorous (hunted) animals in predator/prey behaviour. This is why this response is sometimes known as the *fight/flight* response (Gleitman, 2010), reflecting its 'biological utility'. As we have already seen, it is also known as the 'alarm response'; it is sometimes known as the *autonomic response* or the *sympathetic response*; and in certain clinical settings, as the *orientating response*. (The reader can perhaps understand why I advised the purchase of a dictionary of psychology early on in this text.) Humans show the same response when afraid, angry, stressed, excited (i.e. emotionally charged in any way), but as we are conscious animals, we *cognitively label* our emotions depending on context. Hence, we *don't* feel stress, then experience an alarm response; we *do* experience an alarm response and interpret this as stress (Gleitman, 2010).

Understanding the Psychology of Stress

Can the Content of Emotions be Understood?

Towards the end of his *Women, Fire and Dangerous Things* (1987; the deliberately provocative title comes from a declension category in Dyirbal, an Australian aboriginal language), George Lakoff argues that:

> Emotions are often viewed as feelings devoid of any conceptual content. But in addition to feeling, we also impose an understanding on what it is that we feel (p. 377) . . . A topic such as the logic of emotions would seem to be a contradiction in terms . . . I would like to argue that the opposite is true, that emotions have an extremely complex conceptual structure, which gives rise to a wide variety of non-trivial inferences. (p. 380)

Lakoff (1987) provides an analysis of the wide variety of verbal expressions used in modern (American) English when people talk about *anger*, beginning with a consideration of what he calls the 'folk theory' of the physiological effects of anger:

> The physiological effects of anger are increased body heat, increased internal pressure [blood pressure, muscular pressure, agitation and interference with accurate perception].

> As anger increases, its physiological effects increase.

> There is a limit beyond which the physiological effects of anger impair normal functioning.

This folk theory yields a system of metonymies for anger: *body heat* ('Don't get hot under the collar'), *internal pressure* ('When I found out, I almost burst a blood vessel'), *redness in the face and neck area* ('She was scarlet with rage'), *agitation* ('She was shaking with anger') and *interference with accurate perception* ('She was blind with rage'). This gives rise to what Lakoff calls the 'most general metaphor for anger': *anger is heat*, either applied to *solids* ('After the argument, Dave was smouldering for days') or *fluids in a container* (a general metaphor for the body is *a container for the emotions* – hence, 'I had reached the boiling point'). There are other principal metaphors for anger, too: *insanity* ('You're driving me crazy!'), an *opponent in a struggle* ('I've been wrestling with my anger all day'), a *dangerous animal* ('He unleashed his anger'), a *physical annoyance* ('Don't be a pain in the ass'), *trespassing* ('This is where I draw the line!') and a *burden* ('He has a chip on his shoulder'). These metaphors and metonyms, according to Lakoff, 'converge on a certain prototypical cognitive model of anger' (p. 397–398):

> Stage One: Offending Event

> Stage Two: Anger

> Stage Three: Attempt at Control

> Stage Four: Loss of Control

> Stage Five: Act of Retribution

The act of retribution must equal to the original offending event in terms of intensity in order for the scales to be balanced again, and the intensity of anger level to return to zero (Lakoff, 1987). He notes that he has 'shown that the expressions that indicate anger in American English are not a random collection but rather are structured in terms of an elaborate cognitive model that is implicit in the semantics of the language.'

Attempting to Understand the Conceptual Content of Stress through Linguistic Analysis

You could try a similar exercise to that of Lakoff's (above) in a discussion group, or perhaps even in a class with young people as a facilitated brain-storming session. Work from generating idioms referring to stress (rather than anger), and see if similar 'principal metaphors' appear. Is it possible to build up a 'prototypical cognitive model of stress', as Lakoff did for anger? Would you agree that, having read about anger and experimented yourself with stress as exemplifiers, 'emotions have an extremely complex conceptual structure, which gives rise to a wide variety of non-trivial inferences' (Lakoff, 1987, p. 380)?

Lakoff's approach to understanding the conceptual content of emotions is an interesting and innovative one. However, in terms of understanding stress in particular, most researchers have made reference to the biological aspects discussed in the section on 'The Physiology of Stress' (above). It is to this type of research that we now turn our attention.

Early Approaches to Understanding Psychological Stress

The first approach to understanding psychological stress was made by a Hungarian-Canadian endocrinologist called Hans Selye (1907–1982), who wrote the enormously influential *The Stress of Life* (1956). Using Walter Cannon's work on *homeostasis* (1932) – the idea that the living organism has mechanisms which regulate its internal environment in order to maintain a stable, constant condition – Selye (1956) proposed the now well-known General Adaption Syndrome (GAS) as a set of responses that exist when an organism is exposed to stress. The GAS has three phases: *alarm* (when we register the existence of a threat; here, adrenaline is released by the body in order to trigger and maintain the 'fight/flight' response); *resistance* (if the threat remains, we attempt to adapt or act in order to cope with it); and *exhaustion* (as we cannot cope indefinitely, our body's resources become depleted). The exhaustion phase, involving as it does long-term sympathetic autonomic nervous activity, leads to the development of stress-related symptoms and illnesses, such as digestive problems (including peptic ulcers), cardiovascular problems, diabetes, and mental health problems (such as anxiety and depression) (Selye, 1956, 1975).

In 1975, Selye published a paper in which he proposed that a difference exists between negative stress, which he termed *distress*, and positive stress, *eustress*, according to how we perceive a stressor (a thing that causes stress). Eustress is that which serves to enhance mental and physical functioning; therefore, includes that which can be seen as 'challenges', rather than threats. The idea that how we think about, or 'appraise', stressors is important had already been argued by another influential author in stress research, Richard Lazarus. In his *Psychological Stress and the Coping Process* (1966), both internal factors – personality, life experience, coping-styles and so on – and external factors (features of the stressor itself) are important in determining whether a stimulus will be appraised by an individual as a stressor or not (*primary appraisal*). What then follows is a *secondary appraisal* – an individual's assessment of whether he or she has sufficient resources to cope, which then in turn may affect the primary appraisal. Further to this, the person will attempt different coping strategies; these may be revised according to his or her assessment of how effective they are.

Lazarus' approach, although influential upon later theorists, caught the popular imagination at the time rather less than did an attempt to develop lists of items that were stressful to *all* people. Holmes and Rahe (1967) published the first version of their *Social Readjustment Rating Scale* (SRRS), based originally on the medical records of 5,000 medical patients, in which 43 stressful events that can contribute to illness are ranked in terms of 'life-change units' from 100 downwards. The death of a spouse is given the highest 'life-change units' rating (100); next is divorce (73), then marital separation (65) and imprisonment (63), and so on, down to 'change in sleeping habits' (16) and 'Christmas' (12). In order to measure stress according to the SRSS scale, one adds up the number of 'life-change units' that have applied to an individual in the past 12 months. Over 300 means that there is a definite risk of stress-induced illness; 150–299 means that there is a moderate risk of stress-induced illness; and a score of less than 150 means that there is a slight risk of stress-induced illness (Holmes and Rahe, 1967). Naturally, such lists (although intriguing) would seem to have weaknesses which are very readily exposed using Lazarus' arguments, which show that what is stressful to person A at one point in time is not necessarily what is stressful to him or her at another point in time, or to person B at all. Nevertheless, Holmes and Rahe's (1967) approach remains a popular one, and influential in many 'stress tests' that have been developed, particularly in the realms of popular psychology.

The Importance of Choices: Learned Helplessness

As we have seen, Selye (1956, 1975) provided a number of examples of what happens to human beings *medically* as they struggle with stress. But what can happen *psychologically*? One example is *learned helplessness*. This term is used in animal and human psychology to refer to a condition where an organism has learned to behave helplessly, even when the opportunity is restored for it to help itself by avoiding an unpleasant or harmful circumstance to which it has been subjected. It results from a perceived *absence of control over the outcome of a situation*. The theory dates to Martin Seligman and Steven Maier's (1967) experiments, where initially three groups of dogs were placed in harnesses. Dogs in Group One were simply put in the harnesses for a period of time and later released. Groups Two and Three consisted of 'yoked pairs'. A dog in Group 2 would be intentionally subjected to pain by being given electric shocks, which the dog could end by pressing a lever. A Group 3 dog was wired in parallel with a Group 2 dog, receiving shocks of identical intensity and duration, but his lever didn't stop the electric shocks. To a dog in Group 3, it seemed that the shock ended at random, because it was his paired dog in Group 2 that was causing it to stop. For Group 3 dogs, the shock was apparently 'inescapable'. Group 1 and Group 2 dogs quickly recovered from the experience, but Group 3 dogs learned to be helpless. In part two of the Seligman and Maier experiment, these three groups of dogs were tested in a shuttle-box apparatus, in which the dogs could escape electric shocks by jumping over a low partition. For the most part, the Group 3 dogs, who had previously 'learned' that nothing they did had any effect on the shocks, simply lay down passively and whined. Even though they could have easily escaped the shocks, the dogs did not attempt to do so (Seligman, 1975; Seligman and Maier, 1967).

Gleitman (2010) has commented on how 'learned helplessness' may explain the phenomenon of prisoners who had been liberated from the Nazi concentration camps remaining 'behind the wire', unable to comprehend their freedom, and having been conditioned into a system where their own actions had no effect whatsoever on their own survival prospects. Learned helplessness is presented here, because it can also account for *poor motivation* amongst *vulnerable children at school*. Individuals who have failed at tasks in the past conclude erroneously that they are incapable of improving their performance. This might set children behind in academic subjects and dampen their social skills (Stipek, 1988). Children with learned helplessness typically fail academic subjects, and are less intrinsically motivated than others. They may use learned helplessness as an excuse or a shield to provide self-justification for school failure. Additionally, describing someone as having learned to be helpless can serve as a reason to avoid blaming him or her for the inconveniences experienced. In turn, the student will give up trying to gain respect or advancement through academic performance (Ramirez et al. 1992). Learned helplessness, a concept rooted in the belief that the way in which we are rewarded or otherwise shapes our behaviour, could accordingly be combated by making positive reinforcements absolutely regular, and in the mean time showing great patience as the previously learnt behaviour diminishes. One of those who was liberated from Auschwitz, Primo Levi (1996), reported that it took many months of freedom before he lost the habit he had acquired in the camp of scanning the ground immediately in front of him for 'something' – any object of use or value. By extension, it may take many months for an emotionally neglected or traumatised child who has learned helplessness to understand that in *this* classroom, in *this* environment, his or her efforts will win him or her credit, but only the consistent experience of the teacher reinforcing his or her efforts will teach him or her that this is in fact the case.

A Cognitive/Psychophysiological Model of Stress

Psychologists have generated many models of psychological stress. I would like to describe just one, which I believe is a particularly useful one, given the course of the material this chapter, and in particular the latter half. It was produced and used by two of my former academic supervisors, the University of Glasgow's John Hinton and Richard Burton (1992, 1997, 2001a). The basic principle of this model is, at the centre, that there is a cognitive evaluation of whether one possesses more resources than demands. If demands on one outweigh one's resources, then one experiences the incapacity to cope – known as 'PCI' (perceived coping incapacity), and reminiscent of Lazarus, 1966, see above. One then experiences psychological stress (or, as Hinton and Burton, 1992, 1997, 2001a, 2001b term it, 'psystress'). Perceived coping incapacity is, of course, a subjective measure that varies between individuals. In Hinton and Burton's model (1992, 1997) as well as balancing 'resources' against 'demands', there are differentiations between 'perceived resources' and 'actual resources', and 'perceived demands' and 'actual demands'. An individual's perception of demands and resources will depend, of course, on people's individual personalities, coping mechanisms and cognitive styles, and may be quite different to what those demands and resources are in reality. Hinton and Burton's model (1992, 1997) also includes attention being given over to the outcome of perceiving an incapacity to cope, or the experience of 'pystress', and how these psychological and physical responses to stress feed into the way in which we perceive our resources and our demands in future. The process is essentially self-accelerating (as Selye's GAS (1956) suggests; see above); one might perceive one's demands as being greater than they actually are, and one's resources as being fewer than they actually are, and therefore become more prone to perceive an incapacity to cope, and therefore experience increasingly greater levels of psychological stress.

One innovative aspect of Hinton and Burton's (1992, 1997, 2001a) overall approach is their attention to the measurement of the psychophysiological correlates of stress. Because our psychological experience of stress is underpinned by the 'fight/flight' response (see above), which, as we have seen, is a co-ordinated nervous and hormonal response, it is possible to measure these physical reactions as signs of tonic (short-term) and chronic (long-term) stress (Hinton, 2001). Such correlates include heart rate, localised blood pulse volume (indications of increased circulation), breathing rate, localised electromyography (a measurement of muscular tension, usually in a specific muscle), skin conductance response (a measurement of perspiration), all of which can be measured in a relatively simple laboratory set-up using polygraph equipment (Andreassi, 2006; Hinton, 2001). Measurements of sodium and potassium ionic concentration in saliva, either whole (Hinton and Burton, 2001b) or parotid saliva (Minton, 1995), give an indication of hormonal changes in the body that result from exposure to especially chronic stress.

Psychological and Physical Ways of Coping with Stress

Insights from Rational Emotive Behaviour Therapy

In coping with stress, we can employ strategies from Rational Emotive Behaviour Therapy (REBT), which may itself be applied to any one or combination of problems with which a client may present in psychotherapy (Ellis and Harper, 1975; Ellis and Tafrate, 1999). Albert Ellis (1913–2007) believed that human beings have the tendency to hold beliefs strongly, regardless of whether they are rational or irrational, and it is, by and large, the holding of irrational beliefs that does us damage. Hence, much of the stress, anxiety and depression we experience in life is actually self-inflicted, and down to our telling ourselves that our irrational beliefs about ourselves and the world are true. Much influenced by the philosophy of Stoicism, Ellis frequently quoted Epictetus: people are not disturbed by what happens to them, but by their view of what happens to them (Ellis, 1961, 1962). Although he once publically opined that 'all humans are out of their fucking minds, every one of them' (Green, 2003), Ellis devoted much of his professional life to working with clients as a psychotherapist, and in a 1982 survey of North American psychotherapists was voted the second most influential psychotherapist of all time (behind Carl Rogers, first, but ahead of Sigmund Freud, third) (see Ramirez, 2006). A key part of his REBT is the therapist disputing, and educating the client in how to dispute his own, negative self-statements (Ellis, 1962; Ellis and Harper, 1975).

In his 'A, B, C' model of the emotions (Ellis and Tafrate, 1999), Ellis provides a way that we can examine and 'de-catastrophise' our negative self-statements (I have illustrated this model with my own pair of examples):

> A = Antecedent Event(s) – something in the world happens to us that upsets us.
  - Example 1 – We have a lengthy report to write.
  - Example 2 – An intimate romantic relationship breaks down.

> B = Beliefs – note that the antecedent events don't cause us stress, anxiety or depression in themselves. It is the negative beliefs that we develop in relationship to the antecedent events that causes us to experience such things.
  - Example 1 – We tell ourselves that we do not have sufficient time or resources to complete the report; and that whoever is requiring us to do so is being unreasonable.
  - Example 2 – Either we tell ourselves that we are blameless and that our former partner is a bad person; or that we are entirely at fault, and that this rejection proves what a useless person that we are.

> C = Consequences – always negative, and as a result of generalisations we have based on the faulty logic of our beliefs (negative self-statements).
  - Example 1 – We may end up experiencing difficulties at work.
  - Example 2 – We develop skewed expectancies of ourselves and others in relationships; we may end up socially isolated, as we may reject help from others.

> D = Dispute – the therapist (or the person himself, playing his own therapist) uses his or her full powers of logic to deconstruct the faulty beliefs/irrational self-statements.
  - Example 1 – Who says we are not able to do the report? Can we find time resources and assistance in helping us to do so?
  - Example 2 – Where is the evidence for any one of the irrational beliefs that we have about ourselves or others in relationships? Because one relationship has failed, does that mean all subsequent relationships are doomed to failure from the beginning?

> E = New Philosophy of Life – this is hopefully what emerges from our period of dispute; we can learn from negative experiences, and not be psychologically/ socially paralysed by them.

Working with the 'A, B, C' of Emotions

In discussion with colleagues if possible, or maybe on your own, try to come up with hypothetical examples of realistic issues that might cause stress in (i) students' and (ii) teachers' lives.

Working in pairs if possible, or as a thought exercise if you are working on your own, role-play how you could use Ellis's 'A, B, C' of Emotions approach, as outlined above, in order to address some of the hypothetical issues that you generated.

Physical Ways of Coping with Stress

We may also consider using physical methods of relaxation; because we cognitively label emotions, and the alarm response works on homeostatic biofeedback loops, if left unchecked, stress is self-accelerating. However, we can slow the whole alarm process down by actively relaxing using techniques such as *progressive muscular relaxation* (PMR).

The actual technique of progressive muscular relaxation is really rather simple, which is one reason why it is continually replicated in commercially available formats – for a while, from the 1990s, 'relaxation tapes/CDs' became rather popular. The techniques that are narrated via these formats typically involve the listener being encouraged to:

> physically relax
> become aware, mentally and physically, of his or her own breathing, its depth and its rate
> slow down, deepen and control his or her breathing rate
> visualise, in some form or another, muscular tension leaving his or her physical system, sometimes by performing physical exercises of stretching and relaxing individual muscle groups
> work up or down the body – either from the crown of the head to the soles of the feet, or vice versa.

Incidentally, some primary teachers of my acquaintance who use these or similar techniques have told me that there are physical benefits to such activities that are specific to them, in as much as they spend a good deal of their working lives putting their adult bodies into furniture and classroom spaces designed for much smaller frames.

Stress and the Teaching Profession: Avoiding Burnout

One of the more persistent complaints that I have heard from teachers in training – pre-service and in-service – is that their profession is perceived as an easy one by the general public. It has sometimes even been assumed that, as a non-teacher, I share this opinion. Let me say here for the record that I certainly do not! I have also heard numerous personal theories of why teaching is perceived as an 'easy' profession – erroneous perceptions of short working days and years; the belief that because everyone has been taught, that everyone knows how to teach (many people have been operated on, but few would claim to know more about such procedures than surgeons); and so on. My own belief is that the non-teaching public (and to some extent even teachers themselves) is not adequately aware of precisely *why* education is a profession of high stress and burnout. It is now time, perhaps, to cast a 'psychological eye' on why this is the case.

In terms of *burnout*, Heidi Ahonen-Eerikäinen (2002) asserted that the following things were true of the teacher who is in the 'danger zone'. He or she:

> is 'gifted, conscientious, and diligent'
> has a career which is 'a personal crusade to better the world'
> has very high goals and self-expectations
> has 'incorrectly estimated his or her potential to influence matters'
> 'sub-consciously hopes to receive positive feedback, thankfulness and admiration from his or her students'
> 'cannot face the truth that good teaching does not always bring good results'
> is 'over-responsible, will not define his or her work limits, is always available to everyone, and considers himself or herself irreplaceable'
> 'offers to carry the burdens of colleagues'
> 'carries alone the burdens of coping, saving face and all-knowingness'.

If I skim-read this list, I feel alarmed because many (but thankfully not all) of these items seem evident in a good proportion of the student teachers and newly-qualified teachers that I have met and taught in recent years, especially those young teachers who are trying to work their way into achieving permanent positions in schools. Yet, as a psychologist, I realise that there is much truth in this list, and I therefore encourage the reader to think through it.

Ahonen-Eerikäinen (2002) also argued that burnout is tangible in the atmosphere of a workplace; these 'environmental aspects' include an almost contagious sense of fatigue and despair, and a staffroom climate that is characterised by competition and internal hierarchy struggles. Those staff members who are having problems may be belittled, teased in a non-good natured way, or outright rejected, which contributes to the anxiety that they are already experiencing. When burnout threatens the entire staff body, all of their strength goes into just coping – this is manifested in long, disorganised meetings, which are characterised by lengthy discussion of unrelated matters; a high turnover of personnel, excessive sick days and increased pressures for permanent staff. Hence, organisational 'symptoms' of burnout include unhealthy competition; games and politics between people; aggression, irritability, inflexibility, dissatisfaction and vengefulness; as the group dynamics no longer work, due to non-confidence in each other, either individual work is emphasise, or responsibility for solutions is transferred entirely to the school management level; staff members not being encouraged or even given the chance to develop themselves. Furthermore, a poor workplace atmosphere may give rise to workplace bullying as one person or a small number of people become scapegoated – he, she or they get bullied and blamed whilst the rest feel that they (as individuals) are performing well (Ahonen-Eerikäinen, 2002).

Naturally, burnout (whether organisational or individual in its genesis) has effects on the individual, too. These individual symptoms include a diminishing of self-confidence as one begins to doubt one's own skills, intelligence and even mental health; and what Ahonen-Eerikäinen (2002) refers to as the *Teachers' Warrior Neurosis*, in which symptoms of post-traumatic stress disorder take hold – psychologically, emotional exhaustion, tension, irritability, passiveness, obsessive thought patterns, depression, guilt, cynicism and feelings of estrangement; physically, hypertension, ulcers, migraines, general malaise, aches and pains, use of 'calming medicines' (e.g. sleeping pills) and substance use and abuse.

Individual burnout can be traced in stages; in one model, similar to Selye's GAS (1956, also see above), a *warning stage*, in which the individual attempts to achieve impossible goals, thus over-exerting his or her physical boundaries, is followed by a *distress stage*, in which all of his or her free time is spent working, and fatigue and irritability set in; the subsequent *exhaustion stage* is marked by a change in behaviour and attitude – the individual becomes uninterested, mechanical, inflexible, detached and negative, and students become depersonalised (just 'cases'). In another model, which calls to mind Lakoff's work on understanding the emotions (1987, also see above), a *heating stage*, in which the individual does not receive positive feedback, and the glamour of the chosen career diminishes, resulting in feelings of dissatisfaction, rejection and isolation, is followed by a *boiling stage*, marked by diminished self-confidence, and feelings that one cannot accomplish anything, helplessness, meaninglessness, and the doubting of one's own intelligence, capabilities and choice of careers; the final *explosion stage* is one of giving up – a feeling that 'I've had it!' The individual becomes absolutely robotic, releasing pressures anywhere, and comes to see students as 'the enemy' who must be conquered daily (Ahonen-Eerikäinen, 2002). Having read Chapter 3 of this text, the reader can perhaps imagine the long-reaching knock-on effects on student self-esteem here.

Having charted the problems so carefully, what does Ahonen-Eerikäinen (2002) see as constituting a potential solution? The key would appear to be in attending to everyday patterns of communication. Blocks to communication exist when people refuse to think about matters, refuse to believe that a given situation is happening, or think along the lines of 'This will take care of itself'. Consequently, such people's communication is compromised; they filter information, perhaps saying only what they think the other wants to hear, or are selective in their own understanding. Such compromised communication is characterised by doubletalk, consistent use of comparisons (which interfere with listening), 'thought-reading', advice-giving, refusing to try out new ideas (instead, arguing and debating each point), having to always be 'in the right', hanging onto one's principles, and the consistent use of double-bind statements and changing the subject (2002). Genuine communication is marked instead by *active* and *empathic* listening, in which we make an attempt to accurately understand the other person's perspective, and to 'tune in' on his or her 'wavelength' – to experience the world in the way in which the other person does. *Direct communication* – marked by the acknowledgement that others cannot, and cannot be expected to read one's thoughts, or automatically understand us, is also extremely important.

Teaching Stress Management Techniques to Students

Throughout this chapter, we have focused on how stress affects us with reference being made mostly to adults, and in particular the educational professional. However, teachers may wish to teach stress management techniques to students. Think (if working alone) or discuss (if working with colleagues) how you might do this; how you might adjust, for example, the presentation of models in this chapter. Few younger children will be able to understand or appreciate the 'fight/flight' response as an explanation as to what happens in the body when emotionally charged; what concepts or metaphors could you use as substitute explanatory devices? How could you simplify, or substitute, Hinton and Burton's (1992, 1997) model? How might you teach the REBT and PMR techniques referred towards the end of this chapter? If you could achieve these things, and if you have contact at all with young people in a pastoral role, then you could perhaps teach stress management to young people, say, before exam periods – it could be very welcome!

Viktor Frankl's Story of Surviving the Illogical Extremes (Austria)

In the final case study of this text, I hope that the reader will excuse me in drawing not from the field of education, but rather from a true life story that I believe all human beings can find inspiration in. Viktor Emil Frankl (1905–1997) was a Viennese psychiatrist who founded a school of psychotherapy known as *logotherapy*, which is influential in its own right and as a component of many counselling and psychotherapy programmes in which students are trained eclectically. However, it is the story of how some of these logotherapeutic principles were formulated which made Frankl such a compelling author and personality. In his best-selling *Man's Search for Meaning* (1959), Frankl provides an overview of his psychotherapeutic approach ('logotherapy in a nutshell') after recounting his experiences in a concentration camp (he spent a total of three years in the Theresienstadt, Auschwitz and Türkheim camps). In his preface to the book, the great personality researcher Gordon W. Allport explains that Frankl 'found himself stripped to his naked existence . . . excepting his sister, his entire family perished in these camps . . . every possession lost, every value destroyed, suffering from hunger, cold and brutality, hourly expecting extermination . . . a psychiatrist who has faced such extremity is a psychiatrist worth listening to' (p. 9–10). I fully agree.

The book contains many interesting professional insights (notably, on the psychological 'career' of the prisoner), as Frankl concerned himself with the question 'How is it possible for life to retain its meaning under such circumstances?'. Frankl provides numerous examples of how giving up hope underlay many deaths in the camp, and the necessity of showing the despairing men some future goal in order to restore their inner strength; quoting Nietzsche, 'He who has a why to live can bear with almost any how' as a 'guiding motto for all psychotherapeutic and psychohygienic efforts regarding prisoners' (p. 97). This reaches its zenith in the book as Frankl recounts the speech he gave, reluctantly, to his comrades in his block in the middle of a blackout during a period of starvation enforced by the camp authorities. Although Frankl estimated his own chances at this time as being about 'one in twenty' (given that there was no typhus in the camp at the time), he told his comrades that he 'had no intention of losing hope and giving up. For no man knew what the future would bring, much less the next hour . . . human life, under any circumstances, never ceases to have a meaning' (pp. 103–104). He told them of a comrade who, 'on his arrival in camp had tried to make a pact with Heaven that his suffering and death should save the human being he loved from a painful end. For this man, suffering and death were meaningful; his was a sacrifice of the deepest significance' (p. 105).

Frankl's focus on finding a meaning in life continued into his professional life as a psychiatrist after his liberation from Auschwitz, which he described as having been down to chance. The challenge of his own times, he argued, was treating the so-called the *noögenic neurosis* – the individual's experience of the existential vacuum that may appear when he or she is confronted with his or her life's meaninglessness. Frankl, like many existentially orientated practitioners, stressed the capacities that human beings have to *choose*, even in the most stressful and hopeless of circumstances – '*things* determine each other, but *man* is self-determining. In the concentration camps, in this living laboratory and on this testing ground, we watched and witnessed some of our comrades behave like swine while others behaved like saints . . . Our generation is realistic, for we have come to know man as he really is. After all, man is that being who invented the gas chambers of Auschwitz; however, he is also that being who entered those gas chambers upright, with the Lord's prayer or the *Shema Yisrael* on his lips' (1959, p. 157).

Implications for Educators

When we reflect upon the material of this chapter, we have examined a number of models of understanding stress – conceptually, as is the case with anger, through language (Lakoff); physiologically (the 'fight/flight' response, and Selye's approach); in terms of an appraisal of demands against resources (Lazarus; Hinton and Burton). We have also seen some constructive ways of dealing psychologically (REBT) and physically (PMR) with stress, and reflected upon stress and burnout and how they may be combated in education through improved attention to organisation/environmental factors and communication (Ahonen-Eerikäinen). In these latter sections, we have faced a reality that stress is endemic in the profession of education and yet, through their understanding of this process, teachers are in an excellent position both to manage their own stress and potentially to teach students to manage theirs. Taking all of this into account, dealing with stress in ourselves and others, therefore, may be a consistent challenge, but it need not – if the issues are thought through and acted upon properly – be an overwhelming one.

Please think about, write short notes on, but above all, take the opportunity to discuss with colleagues the following pair of questions:

Using whichever of the models that have been mentioned in this chapter that you wish (the Holmes and Rahe SRRS is always tempting), work out the factors that cause you to experience stress in your working and personal life. Are these things likely to persist? Are there phases of one's career and life that are more stressful than others? Does teaching get easier when we achieve a position that offers us financial and job security? Or acceptable levels of challenge and support? Or when we learn that 'good teaching doesn't necessarily bring good results'?

Think back to the point that was made earlier around the perception of those outside the teaching profession about the work of those within it. Would you agree with the complaints that I have heard from my students regarding teaching being an 'easy' job? What are the stressors that those outside the profession are NOT aware of? Is it important that educators are supported in their work by societies at large? If so, why? Would it be a desirable thing to educate the general public about the realities of education? If so, how might this be accomplished?

Hartney, E. (2008) *Stress Management for Teachers*. London: Continuum. Practical information and strategies, firmly focused on the school context.
Vanslyke-Briggs, K. (2010) *The Nurturing Teacher: Managing the Stress of Caring*. Lanham, MD: Rowman and Littlefield Education. A journey through the causes of teacher stress, to the development of a stress management plan.

10

Conclusions

As we have progressed together through nine chapters of what have consisted of, for the most part, evidence-based theory and practice, the reader will perhaps allow me the indulgence of beginning this short, reflective chapter with a pair of personal anecdotes.

A senior colleague of mine told me once of a conversation that she had had with a student of education. Immediately after she had finished the final lecture, in a set of around 20, on the subject of educational psychology – a module within a higher diploma in education programme for secondary school teachers – a student approached her with a question. The student said, 'That [i.e. the course] was great, but couldn't you just put it all down on an A4 page?'

This reminded me of an incident that had happened to me some years earlier. I had been presenting some in-service training (on self-esteem enhancement) to a group of teachers in a school in Dublin. It is possible that, as at the time I was relatively inexperienced in this sort of task, I had been too enthusiastic concerning the opportunity to illustrate certain psychological models, and a little short on the practicalities of dealing with concrete situations. (I hope that things have changed!) In any event, a member of the audience said to me after the presentation: 'We're not too concerned about all that theoretical stuff here; what I want to know is, what am I going to do with my third years on Tuesday morning?'

It would be possible to interpret these two anecdotes as illustrating the 'theory-practice' gap in the psychology of education, and constituting evidence for the idea that the psychologist inevitably occupies the 'theory' (or 'academic', 'ivory tower' or 'pie-in-the-sky') part of the dyad, whilst the hard-worked, deeply practical teacher at the 'coal-face', in the 'real world' of education, occupies the 'practice' part. This is not, however, an idea to which I subscribe; first, it assumes a relationship between the two professions of psychology and education that is fundamentally unhealthy; and second, I find it unsatisfactorily limiting to professionals within the fields of psychology and education alike.

Nevertheless, we live in an age of assuming that 'quick fix' solutions exist (as the first anecdote, above, perhaps illustrates), and psychologists have sometimes either been given the responsibility for (see the second anecdote, above), or have arrogantly assumed the expertise to 'solve' educational problems. As we have seen in the chapters of this text that preceded this one, there is no shortage of problems in education in which certain insights from the world of psychology can be of assistance to the educational professional. Hence, I think that a book that promised 'quick psychological fixes' to problems in teaching would, in all probability, sell many more copies than this one will. But this is not the sort of book that I have written; nor do I believe that it is the sort of book that a psychologist who genuinely wishes to show how his or her discipline can constructively interface with the broad range of issues in education could honestly write.

Throughout this book, I have attempted to be true to my own discipline of psychology, which is, or at least has consistently strived to be, a science of the human mind and human behaviour, resting on empirical research methods and evidence-based arguments and models. Whilst I am a strong advocate that the subject matter of psychology can and indeed should be communicated in plain language, I do not believe that its content should be 'simplified' for audiences of non-psychologists. Nor would I insult the intelligence of my colleagues in the field of education by assuming that they needed psychology, or anything else for that matter, 'simplifying' for them! What I have tried to do in this book is, with the help of my experience of everyday contact as a psychologist working with educators, to identify some 'areas of contemporary concern' in education. Hence, I have been selective not on the basis of avoiding complexity, but rather in restricting the *scope* – I have focused upon the areas of psychology that I feel are most likely to be of use and interest to the educational professional at this point in time. There are, of course, many areas that could have been chosen, but after introducing the psychology of education itself (Chapter 1) and taking a topical overview of pre-adult development (Chapter 2), we have examined seven: intelligence and learning styles; self-esteem and self-esteem enhancement; positive discipline, conflict resolution and co-operative learning; special educational needs; bullying behaviour and cyber-bullying; dealing with prejudice; and stress management (Chapters 3–9 inclusively). It is quite possible that, had this book been written ten years ago, or if it were to be written ten years into the future, this list of 'areas of concern' would be different in certain or even fundamental respects. This is quite natural, I suppose, when one attempts to write a 'contemporary' text.

Having identified these 'areas of contemporary concern', I have attempted to show the reader how psychologists have thought or think about these issues and then, using the benefits of these insights, to encourage the reader to think through these issues for himself or herself in a similar way. That, to me, is the key aim I had for this book. I did not wish to produce a book of 'facts' for the reader to absorb or, worse still, 'tricks of the trade' for the reader to 'perform' – I wanted instead to produce an interesting and accessible book in which insights from psychology were *thought through* by the reader, in order that his or her professional practice as an educator could be usefully informed. This, to me, is what *genuinely* using psychology in the classroom is all about.

Having completed this book now, the reader, of course, and not I, will be in the best position to assess whether or not I have achieved my aims. Should he or she wish to offer me any feedback on this book, or address any query to me directly, then I would be grateful. My e-mail address is: mintonst@tcd.ie

I hope that you, the reader, enjoyed this book, and I wish you the very best of luck in your future career.

References

Abercrombie, N., Hill, S. and Turner, B.S. (2000) *The Penguin Dictionary of Sociology* (4th edition). London: Penguin.

Aceviper.net (accessed 17th January 2011) *Famous People IQs*. Available at http://aceviper.net/estimated_iq_of_famous_people.php.

Acosta, M.T., Arcos-Burgos, M. and Muenke, M. (2004) Attention deficit hyperactivity disorder (ADHD): Complex phenotype, simple genotype? *Genetics in Medicine*, 6(1): 1–15.

Adler, A. (1956) *The Individual Psychology of Alfred Adler* (H.L. Ansbacher and R.R. Ansbacher, eds) New York: Basic Books.

Ahonen-Eerikäinen, H. (2002) Working from oneself as a base. Presented at *Group Dynamics and Social Skills in the Classroom*, a week-long intensive European in-service training course (Comenius 3.1) provided by the Finnish Centre for Health Promotion in Kuusamo, Finland (August).

Alloway, T.P. (2011) *Improving Working Memory: Supporting Students' Learning*. London: Sage.

Alterophobia Blogspot (2011) Available at http://alterophobia.blogspot.com.

American Psychiatric Association (APA) (2011) DSM 5 Development. Available at www.dsm5.org.

Andreassi, J.L. (2006) *Psychophysiology: Human Behaviour and Physiological Response* (5th edition). London: Psychology Press.

Anti-Bullying Alliance (2011) Available at www.anti-bullyingalliance.org.uk.

Asch, S.E. (1956) Studies of independence and conformity: A minority of one against a unanimous majority. *Psychological Monographs*, 70(9): whole no. 416.

Atkinson, R.C. and Shifrin, R.M. (1968) Human memory: A proposed system and its control processes. In K.W. Spence and J.T. Spence (eds), *The Psychology of Learning and Motivation* (Vol. 2). New York: Academic Press.

Axline, V.M. (1947) *Play Therapy*. New York: Ballantine Books.

Axline, V.M. (1964) *Dibs: In Search of Self*. Boston, MA: Houghton-Mifflin.

Bachman, J.G. and O'Malley, P.M. (1977) Self-esteem in young men: A longitudinal analysis of the impact of educational and occupational attainment. *Journal of Personality and Social Psychology*, 35(6): 365–80.

Bacik, I. (2004) *Kicking and Screaming: Dragging Ireland into the 21st Century*. Dublin: O'Brien Press.

Baer, D.M., Wolf, M.M. and Risley, T.R. (1968) Some current dimensions of applied behavior analysis. *Journal of Applied Behaviour Analysis*, 1(1): 91–7.

Bandura, A., Ross, D. and Ross, S.A. (1961) Transmission of aggression through imitation of aggressive models. *Journal of Abnormal and Social Psychology*, 63: 575–82.

Banich, M.T. (1997) *Neuropsychology: The Neural Bases of Mental Function*. Boston, MA: Houghton Mifflin.

Baron-Cohen, S. (2006) The hyper-systemizing, assortative-mating theory of autism. *Progress in Neuropsychopharmacology and Biological Psychiatry*, 30(5): 865–72.

Barron, M. and Collins, E. (2005) Responding to the needs of vulnerable lesbian, gay, bisexual and transgendered youth. Presented to the Irish Association of Suicidology Fifth Annual Conference, Dublin, December 2005.

Baskett, L.M. (1985) Sibling status: Adult expectations. *Developmental Psychology*, 21: 441–5.

Baumeister, R.F., Campbell, J.D., Krueger, J.I.D. and Vohs, K. (2003) Does high self-esteem cause better performance, interpersonal success, happiness, or healthier lifestyles? *Science in the Public Interest*, 4(1): 1–44.

BBC News (2008) SDLP hits out at new exam plans. Tuesday, 13 May. Available at http://news.bbc.co.uk/2/uk_news/northern_ireland/ 7399606.stm.

BBC News (2010) Oldham merges schools segregated by race. Thursday, 5 August. Available at http://news.bbc.co.uk/2/hi/programmes/ newsnight/8881030.stm.

Beckett, C. (2007) *Human Growth and Development*. London: Sage.

Bee, H. and Boyd, D. (2010) *The Developing Child* (12th edition). London: Pearson Education.

BeLonG To (2010) BeLonG To Professional: Supporting lesbian, gay, bisexual and transgender young people in Ireland. Available at www.belongto.org/pro.

BeLonG To/The Equality Authority (2006) Making your school safe for lesbian, gay, bisexual and transgender students. Available at www.glen.ie/education/pdfs/Making_Your_School_Safe_EN.pdf.

Bertoglio, K. and Hendren, R.L. (2009) New developments in autism. *Psychiatric Clinics of North America*, 32(1): 1–14.

Bettleheim, B. (1967) *The Empty Fortress: Infantile Autism and the Birth of the Self.* Oxford: Free Press of Glencoe.

Biesheuvel, S. (2002) An examination of Jensen's theory concerning educability, heritability and population differences. In A. Montagu (ed.), *Race and IQ: Expanded Edition*. Oxford University Press.

Blumenfeld, W.J. and Raymond, D. (1992) *Looking at Gay and Lesbian Life* (2nd revised edition). Boston, MA: Beacon Press.

Bly, R. (1999) *Iron John: A Book about Men*. Shaftesbury: Element Books.

Bongar, B.M. and Beutler, L.E. (eds) (1995) *Comprehensive Textbook of Psychotherapy: Theory and Practice*. Oxford: Oxford University Press.

Boylan, H. (2008) Ben X. Film review. *Sunday Business Post – 'Agenda'*, September 7.

Bracken, H.M. (1999) George Berkely. In R.H. Popkin (ed.), *The Pimlico History of Western Philosophy*. London: Pimlico.

Bradshaw, J. (1991) *Homecoming: Reclaiming and Championing Your Inner Child*. London: Piatkus.

Bradshaw, J. (1995) *Family Secrets: What You Don't Know Can Hurt You*. London: Piatkus.

Bramwell, S. and Mussen, D. (2003) Boy text bullied to death. *Sunday Star – Times*, November 30.

Bridges, F.S., Anzalone, D.A., Ryan, S.W. and Anzalone, F.L. (2002) Extensions of the lost letter technique to divisive issues of creationism, Darwinism, sex education, and gay and lesbian affiliations. *Psychological Reports*, 90: 391–400.

British Psychological Society (2010) 150 years of experimental psychology: special issue. *The Psychologist*, 23(12): 945–1024.

British Psychological Society (2011) The British Psychological Society. Available at www.bps.org.uk.

Broadstock, M., Doughty, C. and Eggleston, M. (2007) Systematic review of the effectiveness of pharmacological treatments for adolescents and adults with autism spectrum disorder. *Autism*, 11(4): 335–48.

Brody, N. (2004) What cognitive intelligence is and what emotional intelligence is not. *Psychological Inquiry*, 15: 234–8.

Bronfenbrenner, U. (1979) *The Ecology of Human Development: Experiments by Nature and Design*. Cambridge, MA: Harvard University Press.

Bronfenbrenner, U. (1989) Ecological systems theory. In R. Vasta (ed.), *Annals of Child Development*, Vol. 6: 187–249. Boston, MA: JAI Press.

Brown, R. (2010) *Prejudice: Its Social Psychology* (2nd edition). London: Wiley-Blackwell.

Brown, H. and Ciuffetelli, D.C. (eds) (2009) *Foundational Methods: Understanding Teaching and Learning*. Toronto: Pearson Educational.

Brown, R. and Kulik, J. (1997) Flashbulb memories. *Cognition*, 5: 73–99.

Bryson, B. (1994) *Made in America*. Reading: Black Swan.

Bryson, B. (1995) *Notes from a Small Country*. Reading: Black Swan.

Bulmer, M.G. (2003) *Francis Galton: Pioneer of Heredity and Biometrics*. Baltimore: Johns Hopkins University Press.

Burman, E. (1994) *Deconstructing Developmental Psychology*. London: Routledge.

Burt, C.L. (1945) *How the Mind Works*. London: Allen and Unwin.

Burt, C.L. (1958) The inheritance of mental ability. *American Psychologist*, 13: 1–15.

Burt, C.L. (1959) The examination at Eleven Plus. *British Journal of Education Studies*, 7: 99–117.

Butt, R. (2007) 'Tragedy beyond words' for family as woman, 20, dies after park attack. *Guardian*, August 25.

Cahn, C.H. (2004) Eugen Bleuler's concepts of psychopathology. *History of Psychiatry*, 15(3): 361–6.

Cameron, J.J., Stinson, D.A., Gaetz, R. and Balchen, S. (2010) In the eye of the beholder: Self-esteem and motivated perceptions of acceptance from the opposite sex. *Journal of Personality and Social Psychology*, 99(3): 513–29.

Canadian Mental Health Association (2011) *Children and Self-Esteem*. Available at www.cmha.ca/bins/content_page.asp?cid=2-29-68.

Cannon, W.B. (1932) *The Wisdom of the Body*. New York: Norton.

Carlson, H.M. and Casavant, C.M. (1995) Education of Irish Traveller children: Some social issues. *Irish Journal of Psychology*, 16(2): 100–16.

Carolan, F. and Redmond, S. (2003) shOUT. The Needs of Young People in Northern Ireland who Identify as Lesbian, Gay, Bisexual or Transgender. Belfast: YouthNet.

Charles, E. and McHugh, D. (2000) A whole school approach to culture and ethos. In C. Furlong and L. Monahan (eds.), *School Culture and Ethos: Cracking the Code*. Dublin: Marino Institute of Education.

Chiu, M.M. (2000) Group problem-solving processes: Social interactions and individual actions. *Journal for the Theory of Social Behaviour*, 30(1): 27–50.

Chiu, M.M. (2008) Flowing toward correct contributions during groups' mathematics problem-solving: A statistical discourse analysis. *Journal of the Learning Sciences*, 17(3): 415–63.

Cline, T. and Frederickson, N. (2009) *Special Educational Needs, Inclusion and Diversity*. Open University Press.

Community Links Programme (2011) Dublin Institute of Technology. Available at www.dit. ie/communitylinks.

Coopersmith, S. (1967) *The Antecedents of Self-Esteem*. San Fransisco, CA: Freeman.

Cowie, H., Jennifer, D., Chankova, D., Poshtova, T., Deklerck, J., Deboutte, G., Ertesvåg, S.K., Samuelsen, A.S., O'Moore, A.M., Minton, S.J., Ortega, R. and Sanchez, V. (2006) *VISTA: Violence in Schools Training Action*. Available at www.vista-europe.org/index.php.

Coyle, C. (2000) *Self-Esteem and Educational Disadvantage in Ireland: A New Way Forward*. Dublin Institute of Technology/'Pathways through Education' project document.

Craig, S. (2000) *Final Evaluation Report to the 'Pathways through Education' Project*. Dublin Institute of Technology/'Pathways through Education' project document.

Dallos, R. and Draper, R. (2010) *An Introduction to Family Therapy: Systemic Theory and Practice* (3rd edition). Maidenhead: Open University Press.

Darling-Hammond, L. and Bransford, J. (2005) *Preparing Teachers for a Changing World: What Teachers Should Learn and be Able to Do*. San Francisco, CA: Jossey-Bass.

Darwin, C.R. (1859) *On the Origin of Species by Means of Natural Selection, or the Preservation of Favoured Races in the Struggle for Life*. London: John Murray.

Davis, J.M. (2000) Multiple intelligences in the early childhood classroom. Available at www. galstar.com/~davii/mi.htm.

Dawson, M., Mottron, L. and Gernsbacher, M.A. (2008) Learning in autism. In H.L. Roediger (ed.), *Learning and Memory: A Comprehensive Reference*. New York: Academic Press.

De Beauvoir, S. (1949) *The Second Sex*. Harmondsworth: Penguin.

Deary, I.J. (2004) Intelligence differences. In R.L. Gregory (ed.), *The Oxford Companion to the Mind*. Oxford University Press.

Deboutte, G., Deklerck, J., O'Moore, A.M. and Minton, S.J. (2006) 'Verbondenheid': Creating a positive school ethos of non-violence and respect through 'Linkedness'. Available at http:// www.vistaeurope.org/downloads/English/B3f.pdf.

Deklerck, J., Deboutte, G. and Depuydt, A. (2003) The 'Linkedness' project. In *Conferência Internacional Prevenção da Violência na Escola* [International Conference on the Prevention of School Violence], eds L. Grave-Resendes and M.S.J. Caldeira, 321–325. Lisbon: Universidade Aberta.

Department for Education and Skills (2010) *Social and Emotional Aspects of Learning for Secondary Schools (SEAL): Guidance Booklet*. London: Department for Education and Skills.

Department of Education and Science (2000) *Exploring Masculinities: A Programme in Personal and Social Development for Transition Year and Senior Cycle Boys and Young Men*. Dublin: Department of Education and Science.

Department of Education and Science & GLEN (Gay and Lesbian Equality Network) (2010) *Lesbian, Gay and Bisexual Students in Post-Primary Schools: Guide for Principals and School Leaders*. Dublin: Department of Education and Science & GLEN.

Descartes, R. (1641/1996) *Meditations on First Philosophy*. Transl. J. Cottingham. Cambridge: Cambridge University Press.

Dominick, K.C., Davis, N.O., Lainhart, J., Tager-Flusberg, H. and Folstein, S. (2007) Atypical behaviors in children with autism and children with a history of language impairment. *Research into Developmental Disability*, 28(2): 145–62.

Duncan, N. (1999) *Sexual Bullying*. Abingdon: Routledge.

Dunn, R., Beaudry, S. and Klavas, A. (1989) A survey of research on learning styles. *Educational Leadership*, 46: 50–8.

Dweck, C.S. (1999) *Self-theories: Their Role in Motivation, Personality and Development*. Philadelphia, PA: Taylor & Francis.

Eaton, W.O., Chipperfield, J.G. and Singbeil, C.E. (1989) Birth order and activity level in children. *Developmental Psychobiology*, 25: 668–72.

Eikeseth, S. (2009) Outcome of comprehensive psycho-educational interventions for young children with autism. *Research into Developmental Disabilities*, 30(1): 158–78.

Eldevik, S., Hastings, R.P., Hughes, J.C., Jahr, E., Eikeseth, S. and Cross, S. (2009) Meta-analysis of early intensive behavioral intervention for children with autism. *Journal of Clinical Child and Adolescent Psychology*, 38(3): 439–50.

Elliott, S.N., Kratochwill, T.R. and Cook, J.L. (2000) *Educational Psychology: Effective Teaching, Effective Learning* (3rd edition). Boston, MA: McGraw-Hill.

Ellis, A. (1961) *A Guide to Rational Living*. Eaglewood Cliffs, NJ: Prentice-Hall.

Ellis, A. (1962) *Reason and Emotion in Psychotherapy*. New York: Lyle Stewart.

Ellis, A. and Harper, R.A. (1975) *A New Guide to Rational Living*. Hollywood, CA: Wiltshire.

Ellis, A. and Tafrate, R.C. (1999) *How to Control your Anger – Before it Controls You*. London: Robert Hale.

Erikson, E.H. (1963/1995) *Childhood and Society* (2nd edition). London: Vintage.

Ertesvåg, S.K. and Vaaland, G.S. (2007) Prevention and reduction of behavioural problems in school: an evaluation of the 'Respect' programme. *Educational Psychology*, 27(6): 713–36.

Eysenck, H.J. (2000) *Intelligence: A New Look*. New Brunswick, NJ: Transaction.

Eysenck, H.J. and Kamin, L. (1981) *Intelligence: The Battle for the Mind – H.J. Eysenck versus Leon Kamin*. London: Pan.

Eysenck, M.W. and Keane, M.T. (2010) *Cognitive Psychology: A Student's Handbook*. Hove: Psychology Press.

Farrington, D.P. and Ttofi, M.M. (2010) *School-Based Programs to Reduce Bullying and Victimization*. Oslo: Campbell Systematic Reviews.

Fechner, G. (1860/1966) *Elements of Psychophysics*. Transl. H. Adler. New York: Holt, Rinehart and Winston.

Felder, R.M. and Soloman, B.A. (2000) *Learning Styles and Strategies*. Available at www2.ncsu.edu/unity/lockers/users/f/felder/ public/ ILSdir/styles.htm.

Fenton, A. and Krahn, T. (2007) Autism, neurodiversity and equality beyond the normal. *Journal of Ethics in Mental Health*, 2(2): 1–6.

Filipek, P.A., Accardo, P.J. and Baranek, G.T. (1999) The screening and diagnosis of autistic spectrum disorders. *Journal of Autism and Developmental Disorders*, 29(6): 439–84.

Fleming, N. (2004) Mobile firms in talks to curb the text bullies. *Daily Telegraph*, July 17.

Flouri, E. (2006) Parental interest in children's education, children's self-esteem and locus of control, and later educational attainment: Twenty-six year follow-up of the 1970 British Birth Cohort. *British Journal of Educational Psychology*, 76(1): 41–55.

Fogel, A. and Melson, G.F. (1988) *Child Development: Individual, Family and Society*. St. Paul, MN: West Publishing.

Forrest, D.W. (1974) *Francis Galton: The Life and Work of a Victorian Genius*. London: Elek.

Forthman D.L. and Ogden, J.J. (1992) The role of applied behavior analysis in zoo management: Today and tomorrow. *Journal of Applied Behaviour Analysis*, 25(3): 647–52.

Fox, D.K., Hopkins, B.L. and Anger, W.K. (1987) The long-term effects of a token economy on safety performance in open-pit mining. *Journal of Applied Behaviour Analysis*, 20(3): 215–24.

Frank, G. (1983) *The Wechsler Enterprise: An Assessment of the Development, Structure, and Use of the Wechsler Tests of Intelligence*. Oxford: Pergamon.

Frankl, V.E. (1959/1985) *Man's Search for Meaning*. New York: Washington Square Press.

Freud, S. (1900) The interpretation of dreams. In the *Penguin Freud Library*, Vol. 3 (ed. and transl. J. Strachey) Harmondsworth: Penguin.

Freud, S. (1908) On the sexual theories of children. In the *Penguin Freud Library*, Vol. 7 (ed. and transl. J. Strachey) Harmondsworth: Penguin.

Freud, S. (1909) Analysis of a phobia in a five-year-old-boy. In the *Penguin Freud Library*, Vol. 8 (ed. and transl. J. Strachey). Harmondsworth: Penguin.

Freud, S. (1940) An outline of psychoanalysis. In the *Penguin Freud Library*, Vol. 15 (ed. and transl. J. Strachey). Harmondsworth: Penguin.

Furedi, F. (2004) *Therapy Culture: Cultivating Vulnerability in an Uncertain Age.* London: Routledge.

Gaarder, J. (1991/2000) *Sophie's World.* London: Phoenix.

Galton, F. (1869/1950) *Hereditary Genius: An Inquiry into its Laws and Consequences.* London: Macmillan.

Galton, F. (1883/1973) *Inquiries into Human Faculty and its Development.* London: Macmillan.

Gardener, H., Spiegelman, D. and Buka, S.L. (2009) Prenatal risk factors for autism: comprehensive meta-analysis. *The British Journal of Psychiatry*, 195: 7–14.

Gardner, H. (1999) *Intelligence Reframed: Multiple Intelligences for the Twenty-First Century.* New York: Basic Books.

Gardner, H. (2011) *Frames of Mind: The Theory of Multiple Intelligences* (3rd edition). London: Heinemann.

Garnham, E. (2008) Teenage boy guilty of goth murder. *Daily Express*, March 27.

Gathercole, S.E. and Alloway, T.P. (2009) *Working Memory and Learning: A Practical Guide for Teachers.* London: Sage.

Geake, J.J. (2005) The neurological basis of intelligence: A contrast with 'brain-based' education. Available at www.leeds.ac.uk/ educol/documents/156074.htm.

Gendron, B.P., Williams, K.R. and Guerra, N.G. (2011) An analysis of bullying among students within schools: Estimating the effects of individual normative beliefs, self-esteem and school climate. *Journal of School Violence*, 10(2): 150–64.

Geschwind, D.H. (2009) Advances in autism. *Annual Review of Medicine*, 60: 367–80.

Gillborn, D. (2008) *Racism and Education: Coincidence or Conspiracy?* London: Routledge.

Gleitman, H. (2010) *Psychology* (8th edition). London: Norton.

Goffman, E. (1961/1975) *Asylums: Essays on the social situation of mental patients and other inmates.* Harmondsworth: Pelican.

Goldberg, H. (1980) *The New Male: From Macho to Sensitive but Still All Male.* New York: Signet.

Goldman, L.S., Genel, M., Bezman, R.J. and Slanetz, P.J. (1998) Diagnosis and treatment of attention deficit hyperactivity disorder in children and adolescents. *Journal of the American Medical Association*, 279:1100–7.

Goleman, D. (1998) *Working with Emotional Intelligence.* New York: Bantam Books.

Gould, S.J. (1997) *The Mismeasure of Man* (revised edition). Harmondsworth: Penguin.

Government of Ireland (2010) Prohibition of Incitement to Hatred Act (1989). In the *Irish Statute Book.* Dublin: Office of the Attorney General.

Green, A. (2003) Ageless, guiltless. *The New Yorker*, October 13.

Gross, R.D. (2010) *Psychology: The Science of Mind and Behaviour* (6th revised edition). London: Hodder Education.

Gyatso, T. (1990) *Freedom in Exile: The Autobiography of the Dalai Lama.* London: Little, Brown.

Haney, C. and Zimbardo, P.G. (1977) The socialization into criminality: on becoming a prisoner and a guard. In J.L. Tapp and F.L. Levine (eds), *Law, Justice and the Individual in Society: Psychological and Legal Issues*, 198–223. New York: Holt, Rinehart & Winston.

Haralambos, M. (1989) *Sociology: Themes and Perspectives.* London: Unwin Hyman.

Harry S. Truman Library and Museum (2011) The 'Buck Stops Here' Desk Sign. Available at www.trumanlibrary.org/buckstop.htm.

Harter, S. (1987) The determinants and mediational role of global self-worth in children. In N. Eisenberg (ed.), *Contemporary Issues in Developmental Psychology*. New York: Wiley.

Hartmann, T. (1995) *ADD Success Stories*. Grass Valley, CA: Underwood.

Hartmann, T. (2003) *The Edison Gene: ADHD and the Gift of the Hunter Child*. Rochester, VT: Park Street Press.

Hartney, E. (2008) *Stress Management for Teachers*. London: Continuum.

Heidegger, M. (1927/1962) *Being and Time*. Transl. J. Macquarrie and E. Robinson. Oxford: Blackwell.

Helt, M., Kelley, E. and Kinsbourne M. (2008) Can children with autism recover? If so, how? *Neuropsychology Review*, 18(4): 339–66.

Herrnstein, R.J. and Murray, C. (1996) *The Bell Curve: Intelligence and Class Structure in American Life*. London: Simon & Schuster.

Hill, J. P. and Lynch, M.E. (1983) The intensification of gender-related role expectations during early adolescence. In J. Brooks-Gunn and A.C. Petersen (eds), *Girls at Puberty: Biological and Psychosocial Perspectives*. New York: Plenum.

Hinton, J.W. (2001) Physiological responses to stress. Invited presentation to the *Health and Safety Executive Research Workshop*, Manchester, UK, July 3–4.

Hinton, J.W. and Burton, R.F. (1992) Clarification of the concept of psychological stress – 'psystress'. *International Journal of Psychosomatic Medicine*, 39: 42–3.

Hinton, J.W. and Burton, R.F. (1997) A psychophysiological model of psystress causation and response applied to the workplace. *Journal of Psychophysiology*, 11: 200–17.

Hinton, J.W. and Burton, R.F. (2001a) Perceived mental coping incapacity as a central factor causing psychological stress. Proceedings of the *British Psychological Society Centenary Conference*, Glasgow, UK, pp. 199–200.

Hinton, J.W. and Burton, R.F. (2001b) Purported salivary indicators of psychological stress: Need for cross-validation. Proceedings of the *29th Annual Scientific Meeting of the British Psychophysiology Society*, Aston University, Birmingham, UK, September 17–29.

Holmes, T.H. and Rahe, R.H. (1967) The Social Readjustment Rating Scale. *Journal of Psychosomatic Research*, 11(2): 213–18.

Horn, J. L. and Cattell, R.B. (1966) Refinement and test of the theory of fluid and crystallized intelligence. *Journal of Educational Psychology*, 57 (5): 253–70.

Howard-Jones, P.A. (2010) *Introducing Neuroeducational Research: Neuroscience, Education and the Brain from Contexts to Practice*. Abingdon: Routledge.

Howard-Jones, P.A. (2011) From brain scan to lesson plan. *The Psychologist*, 24(2): 110–13.

Howard-Jones, P.A., Franey, L., Mashmoushi, R. and Liao, Y.-C. (2009) The neuroscience literacy of trainee teachers. Presented at the *British Educational Research Association Annual Conference*, University of Manchester, September 2–5.

Howlin, P., Magiati, I. and Charman, T. (2009) Systematic review of early intensive behavioral interventions for children with autism. *American Journal of Intellectual and Developmental Disabilities*, 114(1): 23–41.

Hughes, T. (1857/1994) *Tom Brown's Schooldays*. London: Penguin.

Hume, D. (1739/1967) *A Treatise of Human Nature*. Oxford: Oxford University Press.

Hume, D. (1751/1907) *An Enquiry Concerning the Principles of Morals*. In T.H. Green and T.H. Grose (eds), *David Hume: Essays Moral, Political, and Literary*. London: Longmans & Green.

Hume, D. (1777 / 1975) *An Enquiry Concerning Human Understanding*. Oxford: Clarendon Press.

Hyland, Á. (2000) (ed.). *Multiple Intelligences: Curriculum and Assessment Project – Final Report*. Cork: Multiple Intelligences, Curriculum and Assessment Project Document.

Irish National Teachers' Association (INTO) (1995) *Meeting the Needs of Children with Social and Emotional Problems*. Dublin: Irish National Teachers' Association.

Jadad, A., Booker, L., Gauld, M., Kakuma, R., Boyle, M., Cunningham, C.E., Kim, M. and Schachar, R. (1999) The treatment of attention-deficit hyperactivity disorder: an annotated bibliography and critical appraisal of published systematic reviews and metaanalyses. *Canadian Journal of Psychiatry*, 44(10): 1025–35.

James, W. (1890/1983) *The Principles of Psychology*. Cambridge, MA: Harvard University Press.

Jensen, A.R. (1969) How much can we boost IQ and scholastic achievement? *Harvard Educational Review*, 39(1): 1–123.

Jensen, A.R. (1980) *Bias in Mental Testing*. London: Methuen.

Jensen, A.R. (1981) *Straight Talk about Mental Tests*. New York: Free Press.

Jensen, A.R. (1998) *The g Factor: The Science of Mental Ability*. Westport, CT: Praeger.

Johnson, D. and Johnson, R. (1975) *Learning Together and Alone: Co-Operation, Competition and Individualisation*. Eaglewood Cliffs, NJ: Prentice-Hall.

Johnson, D. and Johnson, R. (1989) *Leading the Co-Operative School*. Edin, MN: Interaction.

Johnson, D. and Johnson, R. (1994) *Learning Together and Alone: Co-Operative, Competitive and Individualistic Learning*. Needham Heights, MA: Prentice-Hall.

Johnson, D., Johnson, R. and Holubec, E. (1988) *Advanced Co-Operative Learning*. Edin, MN: Interaction.

Johnson-Laird, P.N. (1980) Mental models in cognitive science. *Cognitive Science*, 4(1): 71–115.

Joliffe, W. (2007) *Co-Operative Learning in the Classroom: Putting it into Practice*. London: Sage.

Jung, C.G. (1921) Psychological Types. Vol. 3 of the *Collected Works of C.G. Jung* (H. Read, M. Fordham, G. Adler and W. McGuire, eds). London: Routledge.

Kaltiala-Heino, R. (1999) Bullying, depression, and suicidal ideation in Finnish adolescents: School survey. *British Medical Journal*, 319: 348–513.

Kanner, L. (1943) Autistic disturbances of affective contact. *Nervous Disorders of Childhood*, 2: 217–50.

Kaplan, R.M. and Saccuzzo, D.P. (2008) *Psychological Testing: Principles, Applications, and Issues* (7th edition). Belmont, CA: Wadsworth.

Kendall, T., Taylor, E. and Perez, A. (2008) Diagnosis and management of attention-deficit/hyperactivity disorder in children, young people, and adults: Summary of NICE guidance. *British Medical Journal*, 337: 1239.

Kohlberg, L. (1969) Stage and sequence: The cognitive-developmental approach to socialization. In D.A. Goslin (ed.), *Handbook of Socialization Theory and Research*. Chicago, IL: Rand McNally.

Kremer, J., Barry, R. and McNally, A. (1986) The misdirected letter and the quasi-questionnaire: Unobtrusive measures of prejudice in Northern Ireland. *Journal of Applied Social Psychology*, 16: 303–9.

Kuhn, T. (1962) *The Structure of Scientific Revolutions*. Chicago, IL: University of Chicago Press.

Kumpulainen, K., Räsänen, E. and Puura, K. (2001) Psychiatric disorders and the use of mental health services among children involved in bullying. *Aggressive Behaviour*, 27(2): 102–10.

Kutob, R.M., Senf, J.H., Crago, M. and Shisslak, C.M. (2010) Concurrent and longitudinal predictors of self-esteem in elementary and middle school girls. *Journal of School Health*, 80(5): 240–8.

Labouvie-Vief, G. (1982) Dynamic development and mature autonomy: A theoretical prologue. *Human Development*, 25: 161–91.

Lakoff, G. (1987) *Women, Fire and Dangerous Things: What Categories Reveal about the Mind*. Chicago, IL: University of Chicago Press.

Landerl, K., Bevan, A. and Butterworth, B. (2004) Developmental dyscalculia and basic numerical capacities: A study of 8–9-year-old students. *Cognition*, 93(2): 99–125.

LaPiere, R.T. (1934) Attitudes vs. Actions. *Social Forces*, 13(2): 230–7.

Latané, B. (1981) The psychology of social impact. *American Psychologist*, 36: 343–56.

Lawrence, D. (2006) *Enhancing Self-Esteem in the Classroom* (3rd edition). London: Sage.

Lazarus, R.S. (1966) *Psychological Stress and the Coping Process*. New York: McGraw-Hill.

Lazear, D. (2005) *Higher-Order Thinking the Multiple Intelligences Way*. Bethel, CT: Crown House.

Levi, P. (1996) *If This is a Man* and *The Truce*. Transl. S. Woolf. London: Vintage.

Lewis, M. and Brooks-Gunn, J. (1979) Toward a theory of social cognition. The development of self. *New Directions for Child and Adolescent Development*, 4: 1–20.

Li, Q. (2006) Cyberbullying in schools: A research of gender differences. *School Psychology International*, 27: 157–70.

Liggett, L.A., Blair, C. and Kennison, S.M. (2010) Measuring gender differences in attitudes using the lost-letter technique. *Journal of Scientific Psychology*, September: 16–24.

Locke, E.A. (2005) Why emotional intelligence is an invalid concept. *Journal of Organizational Behavior*, 26: 425–31.

Locke, J. (1689/1997) *An Essay Concerning Human Understanding*. Harmondsworth: Penguin.

Lorenz, K.Z. (1953) *King Solomon's Ring*. London: Methuen.

Lorenz, K.Z. (1966) *On Aggression*. Transl. M. Latzke. London: Methuen.

Luo, D., Thompson, L.A. and Detterman, D. (2003) The causal factor underlying the correlation between psychometric g and scholastic performance. *Intelligence*, 31: 67–83.

Lynch, M.E. (1991) Gender intensification. In R.M. Lerner, A.C. Petersen and J. Brooks-Gunn (eds), *Encyclopedia of Adolescence* (Vol. 1). New York: Garland.

Lynn, R. and Mikk, J. (2007) National differences in intelligence and educational attainment. *Intelligence*, 35: 115–21.

Lyons, V. and Fitzgerald, M. (2007) Asperger (1906–1980) and Kanner (1894–1981): The two pioneers of autism. *Journal of Autism and Developmental Disorders*, 37(10): 2022–3.

Mackintosh, N.J. (1995) *Cyril Burt: Fraud or Framed?* Oxford: Oxford University Press.

Maio, G.R. and Haddock, G. (2009) *The Psychology of Attitudes and Attitude Change*. London: Sage.

Marr, N. and Field, T. (2001) *Bullycide: Death at Playtime*. Oxon: Success Unlimited.

Maslow, A.H. (1954) *Motivation and Personality*. London: Harper and Row.

Maslow, A.H. (1968) *Toward a Psychology of Being* (2nd edition). Princeton, NJ: Van Nostrand.

May, M. and Doob, L. (1937) *Co-Operation and Competition*. New York: Social Sciences Research Council.

Mayock, P., Bryan, A., Carr, N. and Kitching, K. (2009) *Supporting LGBT Lives: A Study of the Mental Health and Well-being of Lesbian, Gay, Bisexual and Transgender People*. Dublin: GLEN and BeLonG To.

Mellor, A. (1990) *Spotlight 23: Bullying in Scottish Secondary Schools*. Edinburgh: Scottish Council for Research in Education.

Mellor, A. (1999) Scotland. In P.K. Smith, Y. Morita, J. Junger-Tas, D. Olweus, R. Catalano, and P. Slee (eds), *The Nature of School Bullying: A Cross-National Perspective*. London: Routledge.

Mellor, D., Fuller-Tyszkiewicz, M., McCabe, M.P. and Ricciardelli, L.A. (2010) Body image and self-esteem across age and gender: A short-term longitudinal study. *Sex Roles: A Journal of Research*, 63(9): 672–81.

Mensa International (2010) About Mensa International: How do I qualify for Mensa? Available at www.mensa.org/about-us#qualify.

Milgram, S. (1965) Some conditions of obedience and disobedience to authority. *Human Relations*, 18: 56–76.

Milgram, S. (1974) *Obedience to Authority: An Experimental View*. NY: Harper Collins.

Milgram, S., Mann, L. and Harter, S. (1965) The lost-letter technique: A tool of social research. *Public Opinion Quarterly*, 29(3): 437–8.

Mindell, A. (1995) *Sitting in the Fire: Large Group Transformations Using Conflict and Diversity.* Portland, OR: Lao Tse Press.

Minton, S.J. (1995) An investigation into the potential uses of ionic concentration in parotid saliva as a physical correlate of psychological stress. Unpublished B.Sc. (Hons). undergraduate thesis, University of Glasgow.

Minton, S.J. (2001) *Pathways through Education 2000–2001: End of Year Report.* Dublin Institute of Technology/'Pathways through Education' project document.

Minton, S.J. (2008a) Conducting anti-bullying awareness work with school students: an example of applying philosophical ideas in the classroom. *Practical Philosophy*, 9(1): 17–22.

Minton, S.J. (2008b) Cyber-bullying amongst young people in Ireland. *Child Links*, 1: 19–22.

Minton, S.J. (2010a) Parents and schools must unite to defeat the bullies. *Irish Independent*, 'Opinion', Monday 30 August, 2010.

Minton, S.J. (2010b) Students experiences of aggressive behaviour and bully/victim problems in Irish schools. *Irish Educational Studies*, 29(2): 131–52.

Minton, S.J. (2011) Поддршка На Училишните Психолози За Работа Со Ранливи Групи Ученици. Скопје: Македонски Центар За Грганско Образование. [*Supporting School Psychologists to Work with Vulnerable Students.*] Skopje: Macedonian Civic Education Centre.

Minton, S.J. (Submitted). Alterophobic bullying and pro-conformist aggression in a survey of upper secondary school students in Ireland.

Minton, S.J. and O'Moore, A.M. (2008) The effectiveness of a nationwide intervention programme to prevent and counter school bullying in Ireland. *International Journal of Psychology and Psychological Therapy*, 8(1): 1–12.

Minton, S.J., Dahl, T., O'Moore, A.M. and Tuck, D. (2008) An exploratory survey of the experiences of homophobic bullying amongst lesbian, gay, bisexual and transgendered young people in Ireland. *Irish Education Studies*, 27(2): 177–191.

Montagu, A. (ed.) (1975/2002) *Race and IQ.* Expanded edn. Oxford: Oxford University Press.

Montanye, T., Mulberry, R. F. and Hardy, K. R. (1971) Assessing prejudice toward negroes at three universities using the lost-letter technique. *Psychological Reports*, 29: 531–7.

Mosley, J. (1996) *Quality Circle Time in the Primary Classroom: Your Essential Guide to Enhancing Self-Esteem, Self-Discipline and Positive Relationships.* Wisbech: LDA.

Mosley, J. (1999) *Quality Circle Time in the Secondary School: A Handbook of Good Practice.* London: Fulton.

Mosley, J. (2006) *Helping Children Deal with Bullying.* Cambridge: LDA.

Mosley, J. (2007) *Helping Children Deal with Conflict.* Cambridge: LDA.

Newschaffer, C.J., Croen, L.A. and Daniels, J. (2007) The epidemiology of autism spectrum disorders. *Annual Review of Public Health*, 28: 235–58.

Noonan, P. (1994) *Travelling People in West Belfast.* London: Save the Children.

Norman, J., Galvin, M. and McNamara, G. (2006) *Straight Talk: Researching Gay and Lesbian Issues in the School Curriculum.* Dublin: Department of Education and Science Gender Equality Unit.

Northern Ireland Anti-Bullying Forum (2011) Available at www.niabf.org.uk.

O'Connell, J. (1989) Dublin Travellers' Education and Development Group (DTEDG): *Briefing Document on Irish Travellers.* Dublin: DTEDG.

O'Higgins-Norman, J., Goldrick, M. and Harrison, K. (2010) *Addressing Homophobic Bullying in Second-Level Schools.* Dublin: The Equality Authority.

O'Moore, A.M. (1996) *Anti-Bullying Centre: Research and Resource Unit.* Dublin: Trinity College, Teacher Education Department.

O'Moore, A.M. (1997) Foreword: Bullying behaviour in schools. *Irish Journal of Psychology*, 18(2): 135–7.

O'Moore, A.M. and Kirkham, C. (2001) Self-esteem and its relationship to bullying behaviour. *Aggressive Behaviour*, 27, 269–83.

O'Moore, A.M., Kirkham, C. and Smith, M. (1997) Bullying behaviour in Irish schools: A nationwide study. *Irish Journal of Psychology*, 18(2): 141–69.

O'Moore, A.M. and Minton, S.J. (2002) *Tackling Violence in Schools in Norway: An Evaluation of the 'Broad Approach'*. Available at www.gold.ac.uk/connect.

O'Moore, A.M. and Minton, S.J. (2004) *Dealing with Bullying in Schools: A Training Manual for Teachers, Parents and Other Professionals*. London: Sage.

O'Moore, A.M. and Minton, S.J. (2005) An evaluation of the effectiveness of an anti-bullying programme in primary schools. *Aggressive Behaviour*, 31(6): 609–22.

O'Moore, A.M. and Minton, S.J. (2006) Protecting children: Making the school environment safe. In C. Gittins (ed.), *Violence Reduction in Schools: How to Make a Difference*. Strasbourg: Council of Europe Publishing.

O'Moore, A.M. and Minton, S.J. (2011) *Cyber-Bullying: The Irish Experience*. Hauppage, NY: Nova Science.

Olweus, D. (1973) *Hackkycklingar och översittare: Forskning om skol-mobbning*. [Bullies and whipping-boys: Research on School Bullying]. Kungälv, Sweden: Almqvist & Wiksell.

Olweus, D. (1978) *Aggression in the Schools. Bullies and Whipping Boys*. Washington, DC: Hemisphere.

Olweus, D. (1993) *Bullying: What we Know and What we Can Do*. Oxford: Blackwell.

Olweus, D. (1999) Sweden, Norway. In *The Nature of School Bullying: A Cross-National Perspective*, P.K. Smith, Y. Morita, J. Junger-Tas, D. Olweus, R.F. Catalano and P. Slee (eds), 28–48. London: Routledge.

Olweus, D. (2004) The Olweus Bullying Prevention Programme: design and implementation issues and a new national initiative in Norway. In P.K. Smith, D. Pepler and K. Rigby (eds), *Bullying in Schools: How Successful Can Interventions Be?* Cambridge: Cambridge University Press.

Ortega, F. (2009) The cerebral subject and the challenge of neurodiversity. *BioSocieties*, 4: 425–45.

Oswald, D.P. and Sonenklar, N.A. (2007) Medication use among children with autism spectrum disorders. *Journal of Child and Adolescent Psychopharmacolo*gy, 17(3): 348–55.

Ozonoff, S., Heung, K., Byrd, R., Hansen, R. and Hertz-Picciotto, I. (2008) The onset of autism: Patterns of symptom emergence in the first years of life. *Autism Research*, 1(6): 320–8.

Peaceful Schools International (2011) *Conflict Resolution in Schools: Every Child Should Feel Respected*. Available at www.peacefulschoolsinternational.org.

Perry, W.G. (1981) Cognitive and ethical growth: The making of meaning. In A.W. Chickering (ed.), *The Modern American College: Responding to the New Realities of Diverse Students and a Changing Society*. San Fransisco, CA: Jossey-Bass.

Petrides, K.V. and Furnham, A. (2001) Trait emotional intelligence: Psychometric investigation with reference to established trait taxonomies. *European Journal of Personality*, 15: 425–48.

Petrides, K.V., Pita, R. and Kokkinaki, F. (2007) The location of trait emotional intelligence in personality factor space. *British Journal of Psychology*, 98: 273–89.

Phares, E.J. and Chaplin, W.F. (1997) *Introduction to Personality* (4th edition). Harlow: Longman.

Piaget, J. (1932/1965) *The Moral Judgement of the Child*. Glencoe, IL: Free Press.

Piaget, J. (1953) *The Origins of Intelligence in Children*. London: Routledge & Kegan Paul.

Piaget, J. and Inhelder, B. (1956) *The Child's Conception of Space*. London: Routledge & Kegan Paul.

Polanczyk, G., de Lima, M.S., Horta, B.L., Biederman, J. and Rohde, L.A. (2007) The worldwide prevalence of ADHD: A systematic review and metaregression analysis. *American Journal of Psychiatry*, 164: 942–8.

Popkin, R.H. (ed.) (1999a) *The Pimlico History of Western Philosophy*. London: Pimlico.

Popkin, R.H. (1999b) David Hume. In R.H. Popkin (ed.), *The Pimlico History of Western Philosophy*. London: Pimlico.

Popper, K. (1959) *The Logic of Scientific Discovery*. London: Routledge.

Ramirez, A. (2006) Despite illness and lawsuits, a famous psychotherapist is temporarily back in session. *New York Times*, December 10.

Ramirez, E., Maldonado, A. and Martos, R. (1992) Attribution modulate immunization against learned helplessness in humans. *Journal of Personality and Social Psychology*, 62, 139–46.

Reber, A.S. (1995) *The Penguin Dictionary of Psychology* (2nd edition). Harmondsworth: Penguin.

Reber, A.S., Allen, R. and Reber, E.S. (2009) *The Penguin Dictionary of Psychology* (4th revised edition). Harmondsworth: Penguin.

Riegel, R. (2007) Diary that broke the silence of torment of a suicide teen. *Irish Independent*, December 16.

Rigby, K. and Slee, P.T. (1999) Australia. In *The Nature of School Bullying: A Cross-National Perspective*, P.K. Smith, Y. Morita, J. Junger-Tas, D. Olweus, R.F. Catalano and P. Slee (eds), 324–39. London: Routledge.

Rigby, K., Smith, P.K. and Pepler, D. (2004) Working to prevent bullying: key issues. In *Bullying in Schools: How Successful Can Interventions Be?* P.K. Smith, D. Pepler and K. Rigby (eds), 1–12. Cambridge: Cambridge University Press.

Ristelä, P. (2003) *Ryhmätyö: mukavaa yhdessäoloa vai työskentelyä?* [Teamwork: effective activity or just having a nice time together?] Jyväskylä, Finland: Koulutuksen tutkimuslaitos.

Roberts, R.D., Zeidner, M. and Matthews, G. (2001) Does emotional intelligence meet traditional standards for an intelligence? Some new data and conclusions. *Emotion*, 1: 196–231.

Robinson, G. and Maines, B. (1997) *Crying for Help: The No Blame Approach to Bullying*. Bristol: Lucky Duck.

Rogers, B. (2007) *Behaviour Management: A Whole-School Approach*. London: Sage.

Rogers, B. (2011) *Classroom Behaviour: A Practical Guide to Effective Teaching, Behaviour Management and Colleague Support* (3rd edition). London: Sage.

Rogers, C.R. (1951) *Client-Centered Therapy: Its Current Practice, Implications and Theory*. London: Constable.

Rogers, C.R. (1967) *On Becoming a Person: A Therapist's View of Psychotherapy*. London: Constable.

Rogers, G.A.J. (1999) John Locke. In R.H. Popkin (ed.), *The Pimlico History of Western Philosophy*. London: Pimlico.

Rogers, S.J. and Vismara, L.A. (2008) Evidence-based comprehensive treatments for early autism. *Journal of Clinical Child and Adolescent Psychology*, 37(1): 8–38.

Rohrer, F. (2008) The path from cinema to playground. BBC New Magazine, September 22nd. Available at http://news.bbc.co.uk/2/hi/ uk_news/magazine/7629376.stm.

Roland, E. (1989) Bullying: The Scandinavian research tradition. In D.P. Tattum and D. Lane (eds), *Bullying in Schools*. Stoke-on-Trent, England: Trentham Books.

Roland, E. (1993) Bullying: A developing tradition of research and management. In D.P. Tattum (ed.), *Understanding and Managing Bullying*. Oxford: Heinemann Educational Books.

Roland, E. (2000) Bullying in school: Three national innovations in Norwegian schools in 15 years. *Aggressive Behaviour*, 26(1): 135–43.

Roland, E. and Auestad, G. (2009) *Seksuell orienteering og mobbing*. Universitetet i Stavanger: Senter for atferdsforskning. [*Sexual orientation and bullying*. University of Stavanger: Centre for Behavioural Research.]

Roland, E., Bjørnsen, G. and Mandt, G. (2003) 'Taking back adult control': A report from Norway. In P.K. Smith (ed.), *Violence in Schools: The Response in Europe*. London: Routledge-Falmer.

Roland, E., Bru, E., Midthassel, U.V. and Vaaland, G.S. (2010) The Zero programme against bullying: Effects of the programme in the context of the Norwegian manifesto against bullying. *Social Psychology of Education*, 13: 41–55.

Roland, E. and Munthe, E. (1997) The 1996 Norwegian programme for preventing and managing bullying in schools. *Irish Journal of Psychology*, 18(2): 233–47.

Rosenthal, R. and Jacobsen, L. (1968) *Pygmalion in the Classroom*. New York: Holt, Rinehart and Winston.

Rushton, J.P. and Jensen, A.R. (2005) Thirty years of research on race differences in cognitive ability. *Psychology, Public Policy and Law*, 11(2): 235–94.

Russell, B. (1946/1995) *History of Western Philosophy and its Connection with Political and Social Circumstances from the Earliest Times to the Present Day*. London: Routledge.

Ruth, S. (2006) *Leadership and Liberation: A Psychological Approach*. New York: Routledge.

Rutter, M. (1976) Isle of Wight studies 1964–1974. *Psychological Medicine*, 6(2): 313–32.

SAF (Senter for atferdsforskning) [Centre for Behavioural Research] (2004) *Connect Oslo: A Broad Approach. Information for Researchers, Politicians and School Staff* (English Language Version). Stavanger: Senter for Atferdsforskning, Høgskolen i Stavanger.

Salmivalli, C., Kärnä, A. and Poskiparta, E. (2010a) KiVa – A Finnish innovation to tackle bullying. In K. Österman (ed.), *Indirect and Direct Aggression*, 171–83. Frankfurt am Main: Peter Lang.

Salmivalli, C., Kärnä, A. and Poskiparta, E. (2010b) Development, evaluation, and diffusion of a national anti-bullying program, KiVa. In B. Doll, W. Pfohl and J. Yoon (eds), *Handbook of Youth Prevention Science*, 238–52). New York: Routledge.

Santrock, J.W. (1996) *Adolescence: An Introduction* (6th edition). Dubuque, IA: Brown & Benchmark.

Satir, V. (1983) *Conjoint Family Therapy* (3rd edition). Palo Alto CA: Science and Behaviour Books.

Schulte, M.J., Ree, M.J. and Carretta, T.R. (2004) Emotional intelligence: Not much more than g and personality. *Personality and Individual Differences*, 37: 1059–68.

Scottish Parliament Information Centre (SPICe) (2008) Education (Additional Support for Learning) (Scotland) Bill summary. Available at www.scottish.parliament.uk/business/bills/11-educationAdditional/11-AdditionalSupportforLearningScotlandBillsummary.pdf.

Sears, R. (1986) Catherine Cox Milles: 1890–1984. *American Journal of Psychology*, 99(3): 431–3.

Seligman, M.E.P. (1975) *Helplessness: On Depression, Development, and Death*. San Francisco, CA: Freeman.

Seligman, M.E.P. and Maier, S.F. (1967) Failure to escape traumatic shock. *Journal of Experimental Psychology*, 74(1): 1–9.

Selye, H. (1956) The Stress of Life. New York: McGraw-Hill.

Selye, H. (1975) Confusion and controversy in the stress field. *Journal of Human Stress*, 1: 37–44.

Sherif, M. (1967) *Group Conflict and Co-Operation: Their Social Psychology*. London: Routledge & Kegan Paul.

Sherif, M., Harvey, O.J., White, B.J., Hood, W.R. and Sherif, C.W. (1954) *Experimental Study of Positive and Negative Intergroup Attitudes between Experimentally Produced Groups: Robbers' Cave Study.* Norman, OK: Univ. of Oklahoma, 1954.

Skinner, B.F. (1938) *The Behavior of Organisms: An Experimental Analysis.* Cambridge, MA: B.F. Skinner Foundation.

Skinner, B.F. (1968) *The Technology of Teaching.* New York: Appleton-Century-Crofts.

Skinner, B.F. (1972) *Beyond Freedom and Dignity.* New York: Vintage.

Smith, P.K. (1997) Bullying in schools: The UK experience and the Sheffield Anti-Bullying project. *Irish Journal of Psychology*, 18(2): 191–201.

Smith, P.K. (ed.) (2003) *Violence in Schools: The Response in Europe.* London: Routledge-Falmer.

Smith, P.K., Mahdavi, J., Carvalho, M. and Tippett, N. (2006) An investigation into cyberbullying, its forms, awareness and impact, and the relationship between age and gender in cyberbullying. Research Brief No. RBX03-06. London: Department for Education and Skills.

Smith, P.K., Morita, Y., Junger-Tas, J., Olweus, D., Catalano, R.F. and Slee P. (eds) (1999) *The Nature of School Bullying: A Cross-National Perspective.* London: Routledge.

Smith, P.K., Pepler, D. and Rigby, K. (2004) *Bullying in Schools: How Effective Can Interventions Be?* Cambridge: Cambridge University Press.

Smits-Engelsman, B.C.M. and Van Galen, G.P. (1997) Dysgraphia in children: Lasting psychomotor deficiency or transient developmental delay? *Journal of Experimental Child Psychology*, 67: 164–84.

Snowman, J., McCown, R. and Biehler, R. (2009) *Psychology Applied to Teaching* (12th edition). Boston, MA: Houghton-Mifflin.

Soløy, M. (1998) Gran skole fant medisin mot hverdagsvold. [Gran school has found the antidote to daily violence.] *Aftenposten*, Friday 27 November.

Sophie Lancaster Foundation (2011) Available at www.sophielancasterfoundation.com.

Southall, A. (2007) *The Other Side of ADHD: Attention Deficit Hyperactivity Disorder Exposed and Explained.* Abingdon: Radcliffe.

Spiel, C., Reimann, R., Wagner, P. and Schober, B. (2008) Guest editorial: Bildung-Psychology: The substance and structure of an emerging discipline. *Applied Developmental Science*, 12(3): 154–9.

Stein, J. (2001) The magnocellular theory of developmental dyslexia. *Dyslexia*, 7: 12–36.

Stipek, D.E.P. (1988) *Motivation to Learn.* Boston, MA: Allyn & Bacon.

Szasz, T.S. (1978) *The Myth of Psychotherapy: Mental Healing as Religion, Rhetoric, and Repression.* Syracuse, NY: Syracuse University Press.

Tavris, C. (1992) *The Mismeasure of Woman: Why Women are not the Better Sex, the Inferior Sex or the Opposite Sex.* New York: Simon & Schuster.

Teach Today (2011) Available at www.teachtoday.eu.

TES Connect (2011) *Special Needs Teaching Resources.* Available at www.tes.co.uk/sen-teaching-resources.

Thomas, G. and Loxley, A. (2007) *Deconstructing Special Education and Constructing Inclusion.* Buckingham: Open University Press.

Thurstone, L.L. (1938) Primary mental abilities. *Psychometric Monographs*, 1.

Toppo, G. (2006) High-tech bullying may be on the rise. *USA Today*, April 12.

Trawick-Smith, J. (2010) *Early Childhood Development: A Multicultural Perspective.* Upper Saddle River, NJ: Merrill.

Turing, A.M. (1950) Computing machinery and intelligence. *Mind*, 59: 433–60.

Uhleman, J. (ed.) (2000) *Youthstart Prevent: The Report of the Transnational Project.* Helsinki: Helsinki University Press.

van den Berg, P.A., Mond, J., Eisenberg, M., Ackard, D. and Neumark-Sztainer, D. (2010) The link between body dissatisfaction and self-esteem in adolescents: Similarities across gender, age, weight status, race/ethnicity and socioeconomic status. *Journal of Adolescent Health*, 47(3): 290–6.

van Deurzen-Smith, E. (1988) *Existential Counselling in Practise*. London: Sage.

van Whye, J. (2011) The History of Phrenology on the Web. Available at www. historyofphrenology.org.uk.

Vandebosch, H., Van Cleemput, K., Mortelmans, D. and Walrave, M. (2006) *Cyberpesten bij jongeren in Vlaanderen*. [Cyberbullying amongst youngsters in Flanders]. Brussels: viWTA.

Vander Zanden, J. (1989) *Human Development*. New York: Knopf.

Vanslyke-Briggs, K. (2010) *The Nurturing Teacher: Managing the Stress of Caring*. Lanham, MD: Rowman & Littlefield Education.

Vettenburg, N. (1999) *Violence in Schools: Awareness-raising, Prevention, Penalties: General Report*. Strasbourg: Council of Europe Publishing.

VISTA (Violence in Schools Training Action) (2006) Available at www.vista-europe.org.

Wainwright, M. (2008) Woman dies after drunken gang attacked couple dressed as goths. *Guardian*, March 13.

Walton, G. and Niblett, B. (2011) Investigating the problem of bullying through photo elicitation. Presented at the *American Educational Research Association Annual Meeting: 'Inciting the Social Imagination: Education Research for the Public Good'*, New Orleans, LA, April 8–12.

Wang, L-Y., Kick, E., Fraser, J. and Burns, T.J. (1999) Status attainment in America: The roles of locus of control and self-esteem in educational and occupational roles. *Sociological Spectrum*, 19: 281–98.

Warwick, I., Aggleton, P. and Douglas, N. (2001) Playing it safe: Addressing emotional and physical health of lesbian and gay pupils in the UK. *Journal of Adolescence*, 24: 129–40.

Waters, J. (2000) 'Big Mac feminism' on the education menu. *Irish Times* 'Education & Living', October 24, pp. 8–9.

Watkinson, D. (2009) Sophie Lancaster's mum set to win tougher sentences for hate crimes. *Lancashire Telegraph*, May 7.

Watson, J.B. (1913) Psychology as the behaviourist views it. *Psychological Review*, 20: 158–77.

Wechsler, D. (1939) *The Measurement of Adult Intelligence*. Baltimore, MD: Williams & Witkins.

Woolfolk, A., Hughes, M. and Walkup, V. (2008) *Psychology in Education*. Harlow: Pearson Education.

World Association of International Studies. (2011) Available at http://cgi.stanford.edu/group/ wais/cgi-bin/?p=6082.

World Health Organisation (2002) *World Report on Violence and Health*. Geneva: World Health Organisation.

Wundt, W.M. (1874 / 1904) *Principles of Physiological Psychology*. New York: Macmillan.

Ytre-Arne, E. and Dirdal, I. (2004) Zero i Irland [Zero in Ireland]. *Monitor: Magasin for Høgskolen i Stavanger [Monitor: Magazine of Stavanger University College]*, No. 1, 2004.

Zenderland, L. (2001) *Measuring Minds: Henry Herbert Goddard and the Origins of American Intelligence Testing*. Cambridge University Press.

Zimbardo, P.G. (1992) *Psychology and Life* (13th edition). New York: Harper Collins.

Index

Adler, Alfred 74
Ahonen-Eerikäinen, Heidi 142–4, 146
aggression 9, 68
  learning from observation 68
aims for the book 11–13, 149–50
alarm response 132
Allport, Gordon W. 145
alterophobia 12
American Psychiatric Association 83
anger 133–4
  'folk theory' of 133–4
  metaphors and metonyms 134
anthropometrics 8
artificial intelligence 10
Asch, Solomon 70–1
attachment 9
attention 10, 15, 17
attention deficit hyperactivity disorder
    (ADHD) 81, 86, 91–5, 96
  causes, proposed 94
  controversies 92
    discrepancies in diagnosis 92
    pharmaceutical companies 94–5
    research 95
  diagnostic criteria 92–4
  'hunter-farmer' theory 94
  prevalence of 92
  symptoms 91
  treatment 94–5

educational interventions 94
  medication 94–5
attitudes 116, 122–3
  attitude-behaviour inconsistency 118
  components of 122–3
  psychology of attitude formation 116,
    122–3
autistic spectrum disorders 81, 83, 86, 87–91,
    95–6
  Asperger Syndrome 87
  autism 87–91
    and behaviour 87–9
    causes, proposed 88–9
    definitions of 87
    diagnostic criteria 88
    and eating problems 88
    and language 89
    and mental retardation 88
    and motor difficulties 88
    prevalence of 87
    and support needs 88
  as a continuum 91
  neurodiversity 90, 91, 95
  PDD–NOS 87
  treatment of 89–91
    applied behaviour analysis 90
    educational intervention 89–90, 91
    medication 89
autonomic nervous system 132

autonomic/orientating/sympathetic
   response 133
parasympathetic and sympathetic
   branches 133
Axline, Virginia 55, 62

Bandura, Albert 68
behaviourism 4, 8–9, 10
BeLonG To Youth project 126–7
Berkeley, George 3, 4, 6
Bildung 27
Bildung-Psychology 27–8, 29
birth order, effects of 74
Bly, Robert 21–2
Bradshaw, John 74
brain imaging 11
British Psychological Society 6–7, 13, 52
Bronfenbrenner, Uri 14, 26, 29
Bryson, Bill 120
bullying behaviour 12, 20, 28, 42, 45,
   98–115, 123, 130, 149
  anti–bullying policies 105, 106
    dissemination of 106
    formulation of 105
    and homophobic bullying 126
    key points of 105
    reviewing 106
  anti-bullying programmes 103, 105,
    108–10, 114
  in broader context 113–14
  countering strategies 108
  definitions of 98–100
  direct and indirect bullying 100–1
  effects of 104
  key issues for school staff 98, 104–6
  'no blame' approach 102
  practical anti-bullying work in schools 98,
    106–13, 114
    in the classroom 98, 106–7
    in the school community 98, 107–13
  'problem-solving' approach 102
  reporting by students 108, 114
  research into 98, 102–4, 108–10, 112– 13,
    114

sexual bullying 124
and sexual orientation 125
whole school/school community approach
   102, 108–10, 112–13
terminology 101–2
types of 98, 100–2
burnout 132, 142–4, 146
  avoiding 132, 142–4
  environmental aspects 142–3
  individual aspects 143–4
  organisational 'symptoms' 143
  potential solutions 144
    communication 144, 146
Burt, Cyril 51–2
bystander apathy 70, 120

Cannon, Walter 135
child and adolescent psychological
   development 12, 14–30, 149
  ecological approaches to 14
  functions of peer groups 73–74
  spheres of 14–15
  systematic and contextual models of
    development 26–9
  general texts on 29
circle time 75–6
cognition 10, 15, 57
cognitive development 15–20, 28
  atypical cognitive development 15
  qualitative approach 15–17
  quantitative approach 17–20
cognitive modelling 10–11
cognitive neuroscience 11
cognitive psychology 9
cognitive science 10
conflict management 64, 66–9, 108
conflict resolution 12, 64, 66–9, 79, 80, 107,
   149
  five-stage model 66
  objectivity 67–8
  skills 67–9
conformity 70–71
co-operative learning 12, 64, 75–8, 80, 149
Coopersmith, Stanley 39

critical thinking 6
crowd mentality 119
cyber-bullying 12, 98, 101, 115, 149
   comparison with non-cyber forms 101,
      110–11
   definitions of 101
   effects of 104
   research into 103–4
   strategies against 111
   types of 101

de Beauvoir, Simone 21
deindividuation 119
Descartes, René 3, 10
*Diagnostic and Statistical Manual of Mental
   Disorders* 83, 88, 92, 96
discrimination and the law 122
Duncan, Neil 124
dyscalculia 85
dysgraphia 85
dyslexia 85

educational attainment 12, 15, 29, 31, 41–2,
      45, 46, 47, 54–5, 61
   and intelligence 47, 54–5, 61
   and self-esteem 31, 41–2, 45, 46, 54, 61
Eleven Plus examination 52
Ellis, Albert 68, 139–41
   ABC of emotions 140–1
emotions, understanding content of
      133–5
empiricism, British 3–5
Epictetus 68, 139
Erikson, Erik 9, 36
ethology 9
eugenics 48, 51, 52
eustress and distress 136
expectancy effects 40–1, 45, 55
Exploring Masculinities programme 22
Eysenck, Hans 56

Fechner, Gustav 7–8
fight/flight response 133, 135, 138, 146
Frankl, Viktor Emil 145–6

Freud, Sigmund 8–9, 139
Furedi, Frank 33, 46

Galton, Francis 48, 51
gaming theory 71
Gardner, Howard 53, 56, 62
gender 20, 21
   social construction of 21–2, 29
gender intensification 21
gender role development 14, 20–2, 28, 29
genius 48
genocides 117, 118, 119
Goldberg, Herbert 21
Goleman, Daniel 56
Gould, Steven Jay 49–50, 52
Gross, Richard D. 2

Hamed, 'Prince' Naseem 121–2, 127
Heidegger, Martin 35
heteronormativity 124, 125
Hinton, John and Burton, Richard 138–9,
      144, 146
homeostasis 135
humanism 10, 32
Hume, David 3, 4, 9

ideal self 33–4
information processing approach 14, 15,
      17–20, 29
   child as a limited processor 17, 19, 28
intellectual disorders 83–4
intelligence 9, 12, 15, 47–63
   defining 48
   and educational attainment 47, 51, 54–5,
      61
   emotional intelligence 47, 56–7, 61
   heritability of 48–52, 61, 62
   intelligence tests and testing 47, 48–52,
      54, 60, 62
   intelligence quotient (IQ) 47, 49, 50, 54,
      55, 61, 62, 63, 82–3, 84
   multiple intelligences 47, 52–3, 61, 62
   nature-nurture debate 47, 49–52, 54, 61,
      62

and race 49–50, 61, 62
and teachers 50, 53, 61, 62
traditional views of 47–8, 61
intergendered people 29

James, William 8, 32
Jensen, Arthur 49–50
Johnson, David and Roger 75, 76
Jung, C.G. 32, 58

Kohlberg, Lawrence 23–5

knowledge 3, 4, 5
knowledge representation 10
Kuhn, Thomas 5, 6

labelling theory 40, 55, 83
Lakoff, George 133–5, 143, 146
LaPiere, Richard 118
Lancaster, Sophie 127–8, 129, 130, 131
Lancaster, Sylvia 128
Latané, Bibb and Darley, John 119–20, 127
Lawrence, Denis 33–4, 46
Lazarus, Richard 136, 138, 146
learned helplessness 136–8
    and concentration camp prisoners 137,
        138
    and motivation in vulnerable students
        137, 138
    Seligman's experiments 137
learning difficulties, general and specific 81,
        82–6, 95
    causes and risk factors 84
    and terminology 82–4
learning disorders 83, 85
learning styles 12, 15, 47, 57–60, 61, 62,
        63
    criticism of approach 59–60
    Felder and Solomon's approach 58–9,
        63
    neurological basis debate 59–60
    practical applications of 59, 60
    and teachers 59, 60
life-long learning 27

'linkedness' 26–7
Locke, John 3, 4, 9
logotherapy 145

Man's Search for Meaning 145–6
Marr, Neil and Field, Tim 121–2
Maslow, Abraham 10, 32
mass psychology 130
materialism 6
Mayock, Paula 125–6
memory 10, 14, 15, 17–20, 28
    'chunking' 17
    'flashbulb' memories 19–20
    long-term memory 18–19
        types of 19
    rehearsal 18
    short-term memory 17–18, 47
    two-process model 17–19
    working memory 18–19, 29
        and ADHD 18
        and autistic spectrum disorders 18
Mensa 49, 51, 55
men's movement 21–2
mental retardation 82–3
    categories of 82–3
Milgram, Stanley 70, 118–19, 123, 127
    'lost-letter' technique 123
mind 2, 6
    mind and brain 6
Mindell, Arnold 67, 68, 80
Minton, Stephen James 125–6, 128–9
Monk, Ray 2
moral development 14, 20, 22–5, 28
    Kohlberg's approach 23–5
        criticism of 25
        moral dilemmas 23, 24–5
        stage approach 23–5
    Piaget's approach 22–3, 25
        criticism of 25
        moral realism and relativism 22
    and research 23–5
    thought and behaviour 25
Mosley, Jenny 75

nature-nurture debates, 29, 47, 49–52, 54,
61, 62
and gender 29
and intelligence 47, 49–52, 54, 61, 62
Nietzsche, Friedrich 145
norms and roles 69–70

obedience to authority 118–19
Olweus, Dan 102–3, 108–10

paradigms 6
parenting 9, 39
positive parenting 39
Pathways through Education project 43–4, 46,
75–6
perception 10
personality 32, 47–8
Petrides, K.V. 57
phrenology 8
philosophy 2, 3, 5–6, 7, 9
and psychology 3, 7, 9
of science 5–6
Western philosophy 2, 3
physical development 15
Piaget, Jean 9, 14, 15–16, 22–3, 25, 26, 28, 29
concrete-operational stage 15, 16
conservation 15, 16
criticism of 16, 25, 26
egocentrism 15, 16
formal-logical stage 15, 16
model of cognitive development 15–16, 28
and moral development 22–3, 25
pre-operational stage 15–16
sensorimotor intelligence 15
planning 10, 15
play therapy 55
Popper, Karl 5
positive discipline 12, 64–6, 79, 149
prejudice 20, 28, 116–31, 149
alterophobia 116, 127–30, 131
definitions of 128–9
broader sense 130
dealing with 116–31
definitions of 122

examining in ourselves 116–17
facilitating student action against 127, 131
homophobia 12, 116, 123, 124–7, 130, 131
definitions of 124
homophobic bullying 124, 125–127
racism and ethnic bias 116, 117–22, 130,
131
and schools 120–2
psychology of 116, 122–3
and schools and school policies 131
primary recapitulation 74
Prisoner's Dilemma 71–2
and the 'panicky' crowd 72
problem solving 10, 15, 65–7
pseudoscience 8
psyche 2
psychoanalysis 8–9, 10
psychology 1, 2, 5, 6–7, 8–9, 10, 11–12, 13
applied 10
areas of enquiry 1, 6–7
definitions of 1–2
and education 2, 10, 11–13, 148–50
of education 11–12, 148–50
'theory-practice' gap 148–9
educational psychology 7, 11, 27, 148
experimental psychology 7–8
first laboratories 8
general texts on 13
of individual differences 9
phenomenological 10
and philosophy 3, 7, 9
psychodynamic approach 8–9
scientific method and 2, 5, 10, 11, 13
psychophysics 7–8

racism 12
reality television 73
reasoning 10, 15
Reber, Arthur S. 1, 2, 33
reproductive behaviour 9
Ristelä, Pasi 76–7
Robber's Cave experiment 73
Rogers, Bill 64–5, 80
Rogers, Carl 10, 139

Roland, Erling and Auestad, Gaute 125
Russell, Bertrand 2–3, 6, 7
Rutter, Michael 102

Satir, Virginia 74
science 2, 5–6, 28
scientific method 2, 5, 10, 11, 13
self, the 20, 28, 31–2, 44
 and society 31–2
self-actualisation 32
self-concept 32, 33, 37, 38
self-descriptions 37–8
self-esteem 12, 20, 28, 31, 33–46, 143, 149
 aspects of 35–6
 definitions of 33, 44
 developmental aspects of 31, 37–40
 and early school-leaving 43
 and educational attainment 31, 41–2, 45,
  46, 54, 61
 existential-analytic model of 35–6
 and expectancy effects 40–1, 45
 family and peer influences on 31, 39–40,
  41, 45
 and parenting 39, 41, 42, 45
 and peer popularity 39
 and physical appearance 40
 and teachers 36, 40, 41, 42, 45–6
 working model of 33–6
self-esteem enhancement 12, 36–7, 39, 2–4,
  148, 149
 programme-planning 34, 35, 36–7, 43
 whole-school approach 31, 43
 work in schools and classroom 31, 34, 35,
  36–7, 42–3, 44
self-fulfilling prophecy 40
selfhood, 31–2, 35, 37–8
 developmental aspects of 37–8
 existential-analytic model of 34–5
 psychological models of 32, 34–5
self-image 33–4, 41
Selye, Hans 135, 136, 138, 143, 146
sex 20, 21, 29
 biologically-determined 21, 29
Sherif, Muzafer 73

skepticism 5
Skinner, B.F. 9
Social and Emotional Aspects of Learning
  130
social groups, understanding 64, 69–74, 79
 anti-social groups 70–2
 child and adolescent groups 64, 73–4
  functions of 73–4
 individual versus group behaviour 69
social responsibility 119–20
 diffusion of 119
 'social loafing' 120
social psychology 70
socioemotional development 14, 15, 20–5,
  28
sociology 69–70
Sophie Lancaster Foundation 128, 130, 131
special educational needs 12, 15, 18, 81–97,
  149
 challenging oneself 81–2, 95
 critical view of research into 81, 95, 96
 and inclusion 96
 and legislature 86
 resources for teachers 97
 and terminology 96
 thinking about 81–97
 and working memory 18
Stanford Prison experiment 71
stress 12, 28, 132–47, 149
 conceptual content, understanding 135
 coping with 132, 139–41, 146
  physically 141, 146
  rational emotive behaviour therapy
   139–41, 146
  relaxation methods 141
 cognitive/psychophyiological model 138,
  144
 General Adaption Syndrome 135, 138, 143
 and learned helplessness 136–8
 physical effects of 135, 136, 143
 physiology of 132–3
 primary and secondary appraisal 136
 psychology of 132, 133–9
Social Readjustment Rating Scale 136, 147

stress management 12, 132, 144, 149
  teaching to students 144, 147
  and the teaching profession 132, 142–4, 147
Supporting LGBT Lives project 125–6
systemic family theory 74

teamwork 76–8
  critical views 76–7
  potential benefits 78
thought 10
transgendered people 29
Travelling Community 121
Turing, Alan 10

Vander Zanden, James 73–4, 122
VISTA project (Violence in Schools Training Action) 27, 30
Vygotsky, Lev 9, 14, 17, 29

Watson, John 9
whole-school approach 31, 43–4
  and self-esteem 31, 43–4
women's movement 21
Wundt, Wilhelm 8

Zimbardo, Philip 70, 71

DEVELOPMENTAL PSYCHOLOGY AND EARLY CHILDHOOD EDUCATION

A Guide for Students and Practitioners

David Whitebread *Cambridge University*

'David Whitebread introduces us to a rich array of recent research into early child development, showing how children master the ability to regulate their own learning when adults respect and value their play. His writing models the balance of emotional warmth and cognitive challenge which best supports self regulated learning' *-Rod Parker-Rees, Associate Professor in Early Childhood Studies, University of Plymouth*

The importance of high quality early childhood education is now universally recognised, and this quality crucially depends upon the practitioners who work with our young children, and their deep understanding of how children develop and learn. This book makes a vital contribution to this understanding, providing authoritative reviews of key areas of research in developmental psychology, and demonstrating how these can inform practice in early years educational settings.

The book's major theme is the fundamental importance of young children developing as independent, self-regulating learners. It illustrates how good practice is based on four key principles which support and encourage this central aspect of development:

- secure attachment and emotional warmth
- feelings of control and agency
- cognitive challenge, adults supporting learning and learning from one another
- articulation about learning, and opportunities for self-expression.

This book provides an invaluable resource for early years students and practitioners, by summarizing new research findings and demonstrating how they can be translated into excellent early years practice.

CONTENTS

Introduction: Developmental Psychology and Early Years Education \ Emotional Development \ Social Development \ Play, Development and Learning \ Memory and Understanding \ Learning and Language \ Self-regulation

December 2011 • 182 pages
Cloth (978-1-4129-4712-1) • £60.00
Paper (978-1-4129-4713-8) • £19.99

ALSO AVAILABLE FROM SAGE

WORKING MEMORY AND LEARNING

A Practical Guide for Teachers

Susan E Gathercole *University of York* and
Tracy Packiam Alloway *University of North Florida*

'The topic of working memory nowadays tends to dominate discussions with teachers and parents, and both groups can helpfully be directed to this easy-to-read but serious text ... (it) is likely to prove a turning-point in the management and facilitation of hard-to-teach children. In a situation muddied by ever-multiplying syndromes and disorders, this book delivers a clarifying and reassuring isolation of the major cognitive characteristic that cuts across all the boundaries and leaves the class teacher and SENCO empowered. I think very highly of the book and shall be recommending it steadily' *-Martin Turner, Child Center for Evaluation and Teaching, Kuwait*

A good working memory is crucial to becoming a successful learner, yet there is very little material available in an easy-to-use format that explains the concept and offers practitioners ways to support children with poor working memory in the classroom.

This book provides a coherent overview of the role played by working memory in learning during the school years, and uses theory to inform good practice.

Topics covered include:

- the link between working memory skills and key areas of learning (such as literacy & numeracy)
- the relationship between working memory and children with developmental disorders
- assessment of children for working memory deficits
- strategies for supporting working memory in under-performing children

This accessible guide will help SENCOs, teachers, teaching assistants, speech and language therapists and educational psychologists to understand and address working memory in their setting.

CONTENTS

An introduction to working memory \ Working memory in childhood. \ Working memory and learning \ Children with poor working memory \Classroom support for children with working memory\ Putting the intervention into practice

January 2008 • 144 pages
Cloth (978-1-4129-3612-5) • £69.00
Paper (978-1-4129-3613-2) • £22.99
Electronic (978-1-4462-0038-4) • £22.99

ALSO AVAILABLE FROM SAGE